Decolonising the African Mind

In this sequel to *The West And The Rest Of Us*, Chinweizu examines the colonial mentality, in its various manifestations, and how it has obstructed African economic development and cultural renaissance since political decolonisation was achieved.

Chinweizu is an occidentalist, poet and cultural critic. He was born in Nigeria and educated there and in the USA. Since writing his first book, *The West and the Rest of Us*, he has made a vocation of raising Pan-Africanist consciousness through books, newspaper and magazine articles, and public lectures in Africa, North America and Europe.

He has served as an Associate Editor of the African literary journal *Okike* since 1973; he served as the Economy and Business Editor of *The Guardian* (Lagos) from 1983 to 1985; his popular column, "The Chinweizu Observatory", appears in the *Sunday Vanguard* (Lagos). His second book of poems, *Invocations and Admonitions*, won the ANA (Association of Nigerian Authors) Poetry Prize for 1985.

He brings to his cultural work his training in various disciplines: Mathematics and Philosophy (M.I.T.), American Studies and History (S.U.N.Y. at Buffalo), and post-doctoral research in Economics (M.I.T.). His recreations are dancing and mathematics.

Books by Chinweizu

The West and the Rest of Us (1975: History)*
Energy Crisis and Other Poems (1978): Poetry)
Toward the Decolonization of African Literature
 (1980: Literary Criticism) – with Onwuchekwa
 Jemie and Ihechukwu Madubuike
Invocations and Admonitions (1986: Poetry)*
Decolonising the African Mind (1987: Cultural
 Criticism)*

* Available (outside Nigeria) from

SUNDOOR
BCM Box 4658
London WC1N 3XX
England

Decolonising the African Mind

Chinweizu

PERO PRESS

Pero Press
P.O. Box 988
Festac Town
Lagos, Nigeria

© Chinweizu 1987

All rights reserved. No part of this publication may be reproduced or transmitted, in any form by any means, without the prior permission of the publisher

ISBN 978 2651 02 8 (paperback)
ISBN 978 2651 03 6 (hardback)

Printed in Great Britain

Dedication

To the memory of the following thinkers and crusaders for the liberation of the Black World from European domination:

W. E. B. Du Bois (1868-1963)
Marcus Garvey (1887-1940)
Cheikh Anta Diop (1923-1986)
Amilcar Cabral (1924-1973)
Frantz Fanon (1925-1961)

and

To the liberation of all Africans whose hearts and minds are still controlled by anti-African interests.

Acknowledgements

Grateful acknowledgement is hereby made to the following magazines and newspapers in which some of these essays previously appeared:

Africa Journal (London); *The Guardian* (Lagos); *Monthly Review* (New York); *South* Magazine (London); *The Times Literary Supplement* (London); and The *Vanguard* (Lagos).

Preface

A quarter century after Africa's political independence from European colonial powers, the colonial mentality still lies like a fog on the African consciousness. It befuddles African perception, confuses African thinking, messes up African feelings, and disorganises African action. As a result, African efforts at nation building and development have yielded little. I believe that only when the fog of colonial mentality is burned off will Africa successfully grapple with its absurd and desperate realities.

The strategic aim of decolonising the African mind is the overthrow of the authority which alien traditions—Arab and European in particular—exercise over Africans. Until that is done, Africans will not regain the autonomous cultural initiative (destroyed in the course of 13 centuries by Arab and European invaders) needed for a renaissance of African civilisation in industrial mode.

These 21 essays are an exercise in cultural head-clearing. They examine the implications of mental decolonisation for African economic thought; for African strategies of economic development; for African history and historiography; for African literature and scholarship; for African relations with the Arab world; for Pan-Africanism, the Organisation of African Unity (OAU) and organisations of the Black World; for African attitudes towards the Nobel Prize, the Olympics, Christianity, Islam, Marxism, Arabism and Zionism.

Where, the reader might ask, do these essays stand in the tradition of Pan-African thought on decolonisation? As shown by the numerous epigraphs, nearly every essay is an application to some post-independence question of some idea or principle raised earlier by thinkers and crusaders for the liberation of the Black World from white domination. I came across most of these epigraphic passages just before the collection was ready to go to press; and I was delighted with this evidence that I was merely continuing an existing tradition in Pan-African thought.

I should like to hope that others would extend the discussion, till every facet of African life and culture has been scrutinised and decolonised, so that the long-stalled renaissance of African civilisation in an industrial mode can be accomplished.

Some of these essays were written from a Third World perspective rather than a purely African or Black World perspective. Nevertheless, I have not altered them for inclusion here. First of all, what they have to say about the Third World, or about North-South relations, applies with full force to Africa and the Black World, which are subregions of what now goes by the names Third World or South. Secondly, as they were responses to events, or interventions in controversies of the day, I consider it preferable that they should here retain the flavour of the times that provoked them.

Lagos, January 1987

Contents

Preface	*vii*
Introduction: Calibans vs. Ariels	1
Part One: Economics	
Cargo Cult maldevelopment	13
The Third World's trap into peonage	31
Averting debt trap peonage	40
Of suffering and development	57
For new directions in economic thought	62
Part Two: History	
Decolonising African history	71
The scramble for Africa: old and new	97
Partisan historiographies of Africa	104
Seasons of white invaders	109
Part Three: Politics	
Zionists, Arabists and Pan-Africanists	139
Gaddafi: Arab expansionist	149
Let us stop fooling ourselves	154
For a Black World League of Nations	159
Part Four: Cultural control systems	
Pan-Africanism and the Nobel Prize	175
What the Nobel is not	184
The Olympic Games and the Black World	201
Part Five: Literature	
Literature and nation building in Africa	211
Deriding the Derridians	231
African literature and Marxist criticism	242
Responsibilities of African literary scholars and critics	255
Index	286

Africa must re-examine herself critically. She must discover her true self, and rid herself of 'apemanship'. For only then can she begin to develop a culture of her own. Africa must redefine all cultural terms according to her own interests. As she has broken the political bondage of colonialism, she must continue the economic and cultural revolution until she refuses to be led by the nose by foreigners. We must also reject the erroneous attempts of foreign students to interpret and present her. We must interpret and present Africa in our own way, in our own interests.

—Okot p' Bitek

Introduction

Calibans vs. Ariels

The school teacher considered himself white. In Europe or North America this school teacher would be seen as a black person. When I laughed at him for considering himself white, he was shocked.... I said: "How can you consider yourself white when you are black?" He was angry and said he was brought up that way. His complexion would make the late Egyptian President Anwar Sadat look like a blue-eyed blond.

—Munyama Ngangura, Zimbabwean traveller reporting from Southern Algeria on the B.B.C., in 1986

The experience of colonial domination shows that in the effort to perpetuate exploitation, the colonizer not only creates a system to repress the cultural life of the colonized people; he also provokes and develops the cultural alienation of a part of the population ... As a result ... a considerable part of the population ... assimilates the colonizer's mentality ... A reconversion of minds—of mental set—is thus indispensable to the true integration of people into the liberation movement. Such reconversion—re-Africanization, in our case—may take place before the struggle, but it is completed only during the course of the struggle ...

—Amilcar Cabral

I*

In *The Tempest*, Shakespeare's parable on colonialism, when Prospero, the ruler of the island, sailed back to his own country, he handed power over his colony to Ariel, his obedient native auxiliary, but not to Caliban who had fought against his rule. In each Third World country, the colonial administrator's mission, like Prospero's, was to conquer, pacify and rule, and to extract as much wealth as possible for the West. The native auxiliaries of colonialism, the Ariels, were trained to assist this mission wholeheartedly.

The anti-colonial nationalists—the Calibans of their world—aimed to expel the conquerors, revitalise the nation, and develop its resources for its people. With independence, the Ariels have had to adopt at least parts of the Calibans' programme in order to stay in power. But can minds conditioned for the first purpose accomplish the second without re-education? Can Ariel carry out Caliban's mission, especially when it requires him to battle his mentor, Prospero?

There was once a stuntman who would stand his partner against a board and throw a knife at him, always missing him by a hair's breadth, until his partner's shape was outlined in knifepoints upon the board. One day the two quarrelled; the stuntman resolved to kill his partner during their next performance. But no matter how he tried, he could not hit him: he kept missing his partner's body by the habitual hair's breadth. His purpose had changed, but the habits of his eye and muscles had not.

Even if Ariel were to overcome his ingrained awe and turn on his creator, his conditioning would likewise conspire to defeat his new purpose.

For as long as Ariel leads in the Third World, Prospero's old world order—whether economic, cultural, political or informational—will be safe. For the present Third World

---

* This part was published in *South* (London) January 1983

struggle to succeed, Caliban must press on with his old battle until he routs Prospero's agent, Ariel.

Ariel and Caliban symbolise two factions in the Third World; indeed two rival tendencies in each Third World mind. Ariel's rout would mean the eradication of the colonial mentality. The decolonisation of the mind required to accomplish this is a necessary step toward a new world order which will be more than a refurbished version of the old.

II

In decolonising the African mind, as distinct from the Third World mind, certain particulars of African history need to be taken into account. The most important is that, for the past thirteen centuries, Africa has been invaded, conquered and colonised by Arabs and Europeans. Their cultural assimilation programmes, which continue till this day, have burdened Africa with Arabised and Europeanised Ariels.

Severed from his ancestral traditions and alienated from his natural African identity, the Arabised African strives to be even more Arab than his Arab master; and the Europeanised African strives to be even more European than his European master. Like Uthman Biri ibn Idris, a 14th century King of Borno, the Arabised African declares himself an Arab on the basis of his Arabised culture, or of a fictitious genealogy linking himself to some Arab ancestor, preferably to some alleged member of the Prophet Mohammed's tribe of the Quraish. The Europeanised African, like the late Kofi Busia, one-time Prime Minister of Ghana, declares himself a European because of his European education and culture. Fanon's famous phrase "Black Skin, White Mask" applies to both kinds of African Ariel. Both believe in the intrinsic superiority of the white invaders of Africa; each proselytises for the culture of his Prospero, is hostile to decolonisation, and is contemptuous of any re-Africanisation of African culture.

Believing that Arabs are Allah's chosen people, the Arabised African does not find it anomalous that there are so many "Arab Republics" on African soil. He is not moved to ask: How did they come into existence? What does their presence mean? Why are their numbers increasing? If anything, he views them as a matter for rejoicing. Obviously, he can't well resist Arab imperialism if he believes that Arabs are god's chosen mediators between man and god; or that Arabic, one of the major colonial languages in Africa, is the language of god himself. Any invitation to de-Arabise his culture would be viewed as sacrilegious; as an invitation to opt to spend eternity in hell.

The Europeanised African, for his part, is overwhelmed by the fantastic achievements of industrial civilisation. But having accepted the European propaganda that industrial civilisation is the genetic property of its European pioneers, he fails to distinguish industrial civilisation as a type from modern European civilisation as an instance of the type. His desire for the former is therefore perverted into a wish to assimilate himself into the latter. He overlooks the fact, which the Japanese and the Chinese have demonstrated, that industrial civilisation can be replicated by non-Europeans, and so cannot be regarded as somehow intrinsically European. And he is usually ignorant of the fact that Europeans were latecomers to scientific culture, and that their pioneering of the industrial revolution was based on the scientific heritage they borrowed from others— including the ancient Egyptian and Mesopotamian civilisations. Obviously, he can't resist European imperialism if he believes that Europeans are the sole owners of the paradise of industrial civilisation; or that European languages, which are colonial languages in Africa, are indispensable for participation in industrial civilisation. Any invitation to de-Europeanise his culture would be viewed as an invitation away from the industrial paradise and back to some pre-industrial hell.

Such veneration of alien cultures leaves the African Ariel susceptible to foreign domination. It makes him eager for approval and acclaim by Arab and European imperialists. He wants to write and read literature approved by these imperialists. He wants to contest in those sports that these imperialists organise and dominate. He wants to embark on the subservient economic development which these imperialists promote. He wants to accept the identity which these imperialists fashion for him. He is eager to abandon his ancestral religions for those concocted and dispensed by these imperialists. He wants to hear only the version of his history which these imperialists peddle. He is eager to join the "commonwealths" which these imperialists sponsor. If the African Ariel has his way, African countries would join or perpetually remain in the Arab commonwealth known as the Organisation of the Islamic Conference (OIC), the British Commonwealth, the French Community, and the COMECON of the Russians. Yet these are only thinly disguised continuations today of the old Arab, British, French and Russian empires.

The historic mission of present-day Africans is to effect a renaissance of African civilisation in an industrial mode so that Africa can henceforth defend itself against all invaders. In this connection, the African Ariel's commitment to alien religions has curious consequences for his defence of Africa. It was recently proclaimed that the Nigerian Army recognised only two religions: Christianity and Islam. This means that religions which were founded by Jews and Arabs, and which were imported into Nigeria, are the only ones recognised in the army of the leading nation of the Black World. Their shrines in Mecca, Rome and Jerusalem are sacred to the Nigerian state, which helps fund pilgrimages to them; but shrines at Ife, Benin, Calabar, etc., which belong to religions founded by the ancestors of Nigerians, are given no place in the rites of the Nigerian state. Thus, if Nigeria ever went to war against invading Jews or Arabs (as might well happen, given Nigerian passions over the Arab-Israeli conflict), patriotic Nigerians would march out, praying to Jehovah of the Jews and Allah of the Arabs to help them vanquish these invaders. But what god would desert his chosen people and side with outsiders against them? A sorry fix Nigerians would then find themselves in for relying on the gods of others.

As that example shows, our historic mission demands a re-Africanisation of the African even in such matters as his religion. But at the core of its demands is a restoration of the African cultural personality in a version consistent with an industrial economy. Doing that requires that Africans exercise an independent cultural initiative. Decolonising the African mind, freeing it from alien control, is a necessary condition for such initiative.

The reason is simple. The colonised mind, like a well-conditioned slave, is incapable of initiative independent of its master. Initiative in pursuit of the slave's own interest would be tantamount to revolt. Given his conditioning, all his master need do to end his revolt is to speak in tones that trigger his deeply ingrained habit of obedience. Ending his habit of submission to his master's voice, destroying his master's authority over him, become necessary if that slave is to do things in his own interest. A renaissance of African civilisation in an industrial mode is not in the interest of Africa's Arab and European enemies. So long as they have any authority over what Africans do, they will assuredly use it to sabotage such a renaissance.

The central objective in decolonising the African mind is to overthrow the authority which alien traditions exercise over the African. This demands the dismantling of white supremacist beliefs, and the structures which uphold them, in every area of African life. It must be stressed, however, that decolonisation does not mean ignorance of foreign traditions; it simply means denial of their authority and withdrawal of allegiance from them. Foreign traditions are part of the harvest of human experience. One should certainly know about them, if only because one must know one's environment, and especially one's enemy. One should certainly use items from other traditions provided they are consistent with African cultural independence and serve African objectives; but one should neither ape nor revere them, let alone sacrifice the African interest to them.

The strategic importance of overthrowing the authority of alien traditions lies in this. A renaissance of African civilisation in an industrial mode implies a far-reaching renovation of African cultures. Renovation calls for selectivity guided by the new objectives. Like a plank, brick or tile being used to renovate a house, every cultural item for use in renovating African civilisation has to be critically appraised to see if it meets the specifications demanded by the new objectives. Elements from African tradition, no less than elements from non-African traditions, have to be thus appraised. But such appraisal would be impaired, if not entirely prevented, if a tradition exercises an intimidating authority over Africans—as is now, alas, the case with the Arab and European traditions.

Overthrowing the authority of alien traditions will allow for the questioning of their contents, for selection of what is useful, for adapting to African conditions and needs whatever is selected as useful. It will prevent the unexamined importation of the harmful, as well as the unexamined importation of that for which equivalent, or even superior, African counterparts exist. If a foreign technique or principle (in law, medicine, politics, economics, architecture, etc.) has its analogue in the African tradition, there is no reason not to keep the African item, provided both are of equal benefit. And even if they are not, the foreign item would be selectable only if the African item cannot be adapted to do the job. Otherwise, we will clutter our culture with unnecessary borrowings.

It ought to be stressed that Europeanisation and Arabisation are, at best, superfluous to the creation of an industrial version of African civilisation. We need to remind ourselves that the Japanese and Chinese have not repudiated their civilisations, and did not abandon their identities when they set out to industrialise. The notion that industrialisation of a society demands Europeanisation of its culture (whether in the American, Russian or other version) is a piece of imperialist propaganda. The cultures of the industrial societies differ profoundly from one another. What each has done is to take its pre-industrial culture and place it on an industrial foundation. In the process, each has had to extensively renovate its culture to install the scientific ethos, and to satisfy conditions necessary for industrialism. Africa's pre-industrial cultures can equally expect to be profoundly altered by the demands of an industrial foundation. Such changes should not be confused with Europeanisation, just because they were first manifested during the industrialisation of Europe.

If a case cannot even be made for Africa to Europeanise its culture; if Europeanisation is, at best, a pointless distortion; Arabisation would be pure retrogression, a flight into an archaic feudalism with an anti-industrial mentality. We must soberly ask ourselves: Has Arabic culture enabled the Arabs to achieve an industrial society? Have they been able to defeat the industrialised Israelis whom they outnumber some 75 to 1? If they have not, why would any sane African want to copy their impotent culture? Of course, the Arabs could claim to hold the keys to the Arab heaven. Africans should then emulate the moribund Arab culture if death, with entry into an Arab controlled hereafter, is their aim, rather than survival and prosperity in the here and now.

According to Fanon, with the withdrawal of the colonial masters, "the country finds itself in the hands of new managers; but the fact is that everything needs to be reformed and everything thought out anew."* The Ariels cannot see

* *The Wretched of the Earth*, Harmondsworth, Penguin, 1967, p.79.

beyond merely managing their colonial inheritance; indeed, they see it as against their interest to do anything else. But the Calibans know, with Fanon, that the task is not to manage the colonial inheritance, but to reform everything, to think everything out anew. The task is to define our own objectives, set our own standards, and pick our own heroes from among those who outstandingly serve our own interests.

Clearly, those Ariels who are Arabising or Europeanising Africa must be defeated if Africa is to be free to concentrate on its historic tasks. A battle must be waged against them by the African Calibans, the inheritors of the movement for political decolonisation. The battle is against Ariels among our artists and critics who pine for Prospero's praise. It is against Ariels who parrot Prospero's version of our history. It is against economic and political Ariels who would keep us subservient to Prospero's economic and political systems. These are today's equivalents of the old slaving elites who destroyed Africa while hunting slaves for sale to Arabs and Europeans.

Decolonising the African mind may alternatively be seen as a battle between the Caliban and Ariel tendencies within each African, for bits of Ariel and Caliban exist within each of us. No African living in the 20th century has escaped the taint of the colonial experience. None has freed himself from the colonial mentality in every department, or from the structures which maintain and reproduce that mentality. The decolonisation of the African mind must therefore be seen as a collective enterprise, as a communal exorcism through an intellectual bath in which we need one another's help to scrub those nooks of our minds which we cannot scour by ourselves.

Part One: Economics

All development takes place by means of self-movement, not organisation or direction by external forces. It is within the organisation itself, that is, within the society, that there must be realised new motives, new possibilities. The citizen is alive when he feels that he himself in his own national community is overcoming difficulties.

—C. L. R. James

Cargo Cult maldevelopment*

> The concrete problem we find ourselves up against is not that of a choice, cost what it may, between socialism and capitalism as they have been defined by men of other continents and of other ages.
>
> —Frantz Fanon

> Africa's misfortune has been that our secret enemies, in defending their values, have made us despise our own. And so we now go around shouting slogans from their ideologies which we are naive enough to believe in.... Let us look at them. Take just the two greatest, who fascinate us like serpents. Look at them. They are North Americans and Russians before they are capitalists or communists. And they are right. They use their theories to develop their nations and increase their strength. They are right.
>
> —Leopold Sedar Senghor

Following the collapse at Cancún of North-South negotiations, South-South Cooperation is replacing it as a panacea for Third World underdevelopment. It aims to build a Third World economic system by creating regional economic unions, free trade areas, financial and monetary linkages, as well as by promoting scientific, technical and cultural exchanges among Third World countries. But how reasonable is it to expect that merely by inserting existing national development programmes into Third World counterparts of the EEC, COMECON, World Bank, IMF, GATT, etc., devel-

* *South* (London) May 1983

opment would be achieved? Would it also be necessary to dismantle, as dependency theory implies, the plundering linkages which bind the Third World to the West? And whether or not that is necessary, what else must the Third World do? Unless these questions are correctly answered, South-South Cooperation could become yet another in the series of ineffectual panaceas offered to the Third World since World War II.

Three panaceas have been offered by the principal schools of development experts. First, the liberalogues, who purport to derive theirs from the history of the capitalist transformation in the western bloc of the North; they recommend that Third World countries should persevere in the capitalist approach to development which had been introduced under colonialism. Second, the Marxists, who presumably derive theirs from the history of the socialist transformation in the eastern bloc of the North; they urge the Third World to reject the capitalist road altogether, to expropriate the capitalists and build socialism instead. And third, the dependency theorists; they say that the structure of the existing economic order—with its international division of labour, its terms of trade, its system for inequitably setting the prices of raw materials and finished products—is responsible for chronic underdevelopment in the Third World, and they recommend that Third World countries, capitalist roaders and socialist roaders alike, should together press for a New International Economic Order whose structures would be in their favour.

Most Third World countries are now well into the third decade of their post-colonial development effort, but they have little to show for it, in spite of the campaign for a New International Economic Order, and regardless of whether they have followed the capitalist or socialist recipes. Yet, in industrialised countries like the USA, the USSR and Japan, the fundamental transformation from feudal or agrarian capitalist society into an industrial nation state, whether capitalist or socialist, was demonstrably accomplished in approximately 30 years. In the USA this was done between 1865, when the American Civil War ended, and 1898, when the Spanish-American War took place. In the USSR it was done between 1917, when the socialist revolution took place, and 1939, when World War II began. And in Japan, it was done between 1868, the year of the Meiji Restoration, and 1904, when the Russo-Japanese War began.

For development to have succeeded in the North by capitalist and socialist recipes alike, and for it to have failed in the Third World, by both recipes, suggest that factors not in contention between capitalism and socialism could be obstructing Third World development. Similarly, the inability of the Third World to negotiate reforms in the world economic system suggests that dependency theory, for all its advance on liberalogue and Marxist explanations, has not touched the heart of the matter.

A fresh look at the nature and failings of Third World development efforts is needed. A similar examination of the development histories of leading industrial nations, both capitalist and socialist, may help uncover some crucial secrets of development, and thus pinpoint what else Third World countries must do.

Cargo Cult consumerism

In order to appreciate the nature of existing Third World approaches to development, it is useful to begin, seemingly far afield, by looking at the Cargo Cults which arose in Melanesia in the days of European colonial rule.

The Cargo Cults believed that the gods and their spirit agents were packing manufactured goods into crates, labelling them with Melanesian names and addresses, and loading them into the holds of ships and planes. When the cargo of rice, preserved meats, clothing, guns, lamps, tobacco, etc., arrived, cult members would be freed from the need ever again to work or pay taxes. To induce those spirit agents to bring the cargo, cult members had to perform rituals involving military parades, flag raising and lowering, and meticulous observation of the rules of club organisation. And in preparation for the expected cargo, airstrips, wharves, and immense warehouses were built. Thereafter, cult members would wait, and wait, and wait. Eventually, the failure of the cargo to arrive would be blamed on the malice of Europeans who, it was held, had intercepted the shipments, altered the addresses, and diverted the cargo elsewhere.

These Cargo Cults arose among peoples who had a magico-religious world outlook, who had marginal contact with industrial civilisation, who saw how the few European colonisers in their midst obtained manufactured goods, but who were unable to see, let alone understand, the nature of the manufacturing and commerce which created and brought these goods to their shores. Fixing upon some aspects of the behaviour of the Europeans, they interpreted them as rituals for obtaining material goods from the gods. By re-enacting them, they fully expected to be rewarded, just like the Europeans.

The elites of the Third World may laugh at the naivety of the Cargo Cult votaries. But what have so far passed for development efforts in the Third World bear much resemblance to Cargo Cult ritualism. True, Third World elites are far more knowledgeable about industrial civilisation. Having heard of, or seen, or worked in factories, they are able to connect industrial production with the manufactured goods they crave. But they still show confusion about the fundamentals of industrial culture, and about how to organise an industrial economy. Their greater contact with industrial society notwithstanding, they have invented a cult of development whose rituals they enact with much the same devotion and futility as Melanesian Cargo Cult members devote to theirs.

In present day counterparts of Cargo Cults, the great and

expected cargo ship—the bringer of consumer goods—is a mysterious process called development; the industrial countries of the North are the gods and spirit agents; the magico-religious rites are those of development planning, infrastructure building, and foreign investment. Third World governments have, accordingly, drawn up development plans, and devoted considerable effort to building such physical infrastructures as highways, airports, telecommunications systems, warehouses, assembly plants, turnkey factories, and industrial parks. They have also assiduously embarked on building such institutional infrastructures as universities, think tanks, research agencies, and state-owned economic corporations. In countries where capitalism is favoured, men of business make much of company letterheads, business suits, briefcases, elaborate business cards, and boardroom titles. Similarly, the men of labour make much of trade unions, strikes and cooperatives. Where socialist revolution is favoured, much is made of popular mobilisation, popular organisation, cadres, people's committees, vanguards, collectivisation, and of other organisational forms and rites gleaned from the histories and practices of the industrial socialist countries of the North.

When the first spurt of national infrastructure building failed to produce the desired cargo of development, additional rituals were invented. A ritual of North-South dialogue was started to persuade the guardian spirits of development to bring aid, to transfer technology, and to grant better terms of trade. When this ritual also failed, Third World spokesmen resorted to blaming the West for holding up Third World development. Like the Melanesian Cargo Cult votaries, they accuse "selfish" Westerners of blocking aid to the Third World, of putting up protectionist barriers against Third World exports, and of avariciously refusing to negotiate away their trading advantages. They accuse the North of inhumanity, of lack of altruism; and they sourly turn to the building of more infrastructure—international infrastructure, this time—which they hope will solve the riddle of development. Hence the calls for South-South Cooperation to establish more economic groupings and agencies like the already existing ACP, ECOWAS, SADCC, OPEC and the ADB. But how much closer to development would many more of such organisations take the Third World?

The failures of Melanesian Cargo Cults and of Third World development result alike from a superficial understanding of industrial culture. They have grasped some of its forms, but not its essence. Rather predictably, superficial understanding has led to ineffectual recipes. But whereas the failure of the Cargo Cults is perfectly understandable, given their total lack of acquaintance with industrial production, the failure of Third World elites is not. After all, these include scientists, engineers, economists, bankers, merchants and other trained professionals who have had intimate access to the industrial societies of the North. If they have not grasped the essence of industrialism, what has prevented them?

A considerable part of their failure probably derives from the liberal and Marxist ideologues who have so far dominated Third World development theory, policy and practice. In their antagonism, these rival ideologues have concentrated attention on the differences between capitalist and socialist recipes. But what the Third World might more usefully focus upon could well be the practical similarities between East and West, and how these set Northern success apart from Third World failure. For, if the Third World must imitate the northern pioneers of development, it should imitate the efficacious parts of northern procedures. But what might these be?

The making of industrial culture

There once appeared a cartoon in the magazine *Vanity Fair*

showing John D. Rockefeller and Joseph Stalin together beaming on an industrial city, like rival artists admiring some fine work. But what art could the prince of the robber barons and the commander of the commissars—archetypes of capitalist man and socialist man—have in common?

The industrial revolutions in the USA and the USSR—which built them into the two superpowers of the 20th century—were led by robber barons and commissars respectively. Each group accomplished essentially the same historic task of changing a third rate semi-agrarian society into an industrial superpower within a lifetime. To do that, robber barons and commissars alike created a national culture of industrial productivity, with appropriate social values and economic discipline. This required them to eliminate, by whatever means they found necessary, sociocultural attitudes and modes of organisation which would have prevented the maturation of their fledgeling industrial culture. It also required them to cultivate new attitudes and organizational modes which were conducive to the new type of culture and society. The processes and their results, whether capitalist or socialist, share some fundamental characteristics:

1) An acceptance of the nation-state as the paramount focus of the loyalties of citizens, with all other loyalties, sub-national and supra-national, being made subordinate.

2) An ideological commitment to the desirability of national wealth and power, with a further commitment to their increase.

3) An ethos in which scarcity is treated as an inspiration to creativity and productivity, and not as an excuse for fatalistic sloth, prayer, idle hope and national beggardom.

4) A devotion to vigorous productivity, under the pressure of profit maximization as in the USA, and of Stakhanovite production targets as in the USSR.

5) A high value on efficiency that is harnessed to productivity through the cultivation of a work and performance ethic.

6) A constant nurturing of the habit of saving and productive investment, together with the elimination of customs and social expectations which hinder it.
7) The cultivation of a rationalist world outlook and a problem solving approach to life.
8) An industrial mode of organising production and distribution, with appropriate family and social structures to support and benefit from industrial organisation.
9) A system of effective state institutions to provide guidance, support, and arbitration services to economic organisations.

By endowing their pre-industrial cultures with such requisites, these countries were able to transform resources—their own as well as those imported from the Third World—into the industrial goods and services upon which their power and prosperity would depend. But since "there is no free lunch", what price did the USA and the USSR pay for their achievement?

In each country, fashioning an industrial culture required the mobilisation and re-socialising of millions of people. In the USA, individuals were motivated by a mixture of fear of hunger and destitution, hope for personal wealth, and the social and industrial discipline enforced through public opinion, education, the private police of the industrialists, and by the forces of the state. In the USSR, individuals were motivated by a combination of ideological and patriotic fervour, material incentives, and political terror organised by the state.

In the second half of the 19th century, when the industrial transformation of the USA took place, it suffered a brutal civil war which was followed by decades of social strife which pitted the industrialising capitalists against any faction of society which opposed them. For instance, the slaving agrarian South of the USA was brutally crushed by military might. Then the emerging robber barons, with the complicity of politicians, looted the land and the state's coffers.

Then the Progressive Movement—a small town and rural agitation in defence of petit bourgeois values and ideals, and against the big business and big city interests of the robber barons—was politically defeated. Similarly, all resistance by labour groups was ruthlessly, and often brutally, put down.

In the first half of the 20th century, when the industrial transformation of the USSR took place, the old feudal order was first defeated by revolution and civil war. Then followed a period of social strife between Stalin's Communist Party and all manner of political opponents and economic dissidents from its draconian programme of forced-march industrialisation. The small capitalists were crushed and the richer farmers (kulaks who owned a cow or two, or employed one or two farm help) were liquidated. Then the small peasants who resisted the collectivisation of agriculture were starved into submission. Then, those sections of the Communist Party itself which objected to the Stalinist road to an industrial socialist society were bloodily put down.

These civil wars, economic conflicts and political upheavals were the hard schools in which new values, outlooks and disciplines were developed and instilled into millions of people. They were the hot crucibles in which the new industrial cultures and societies were forged. Whenever the costs are reckoned, it becomes clear that the fruits of industrial development did not come cheap. In particular, industrial society was not realised without sacrificing aspects of the pre-industrial culture which many held dear. Furthermore, it required an indomitable will to development from the leaders of the transformation. The capitalist robber barons were motivated by avarice and by the power dream of America's "Manifest Destiny"; the communist commissars were motivated by fear of destruction by a hostile, capitalist West, and by dreams of a socialist paradise on earth. But, whichever way, the same creative will had to be sustained against a seemingly endless storm of social resistance.

Economic development: an ambiguous misnomer

The conventional term, economic development, is an ambiguous misnomer. It is used for two quite dissimilar processes: the indulgence in Cargo Cult consumerism, and the creation of industrial culture. Neither process is, strictly speaking, economic; each being cultural in the broadest functional sense of that term.

The ambiguity and the misnomer are harmful. The tragedy of the ambiguity is that Cargo Cult maldevelopment is carried on under the illusion that an industrial culture is being created. As for the misnomer, to the extent that it narrows attention to factors purely economic, it is like an incomplete recipe. No matter how long you boil water alone, you can't produce pepper soup. It is therefore useful to remove the ambiguity and to avoid the misnomer by speaking, not of economic development in general, but either of Cargo Cult maldevelopment or of the creation of industrial culture. We might, for short, speak of maldevelopment and development, so long as we know what each denotes.

Maldevelopment vs. development

The creation of a national industrial culture contrasts profoundly with Cargo Cult maldevelopment in objectives, priorities, approaches, as well as in the type of leadership they require. In developing countries (those which are genuinely creating a national industrial culture), production holds preeminence over consumption; the accumulation of capital for local productive investment is a national habit; and the development of consumerism is discouraged, or even suppressed, till after an industrial productive capacity has been properly installed. Even when such countries have finally given way to consumerism, they still make sure that they produce most of what they consume, and that imports of finished goods stay marginal to their economy.

In contrast, in maldeveloping countries (those which practice Cargo Cult maldevelopment), most of what is consumed is imported. In fact, Cargo Cult maldevelopment is characterised by the development of consumerism without the prior development of the industrial culture which could produce consumer goods. By putting the cart of consumerism before the horse of productivity, Cargo Cult maldevelopment becomes antagonistic to the accumulation of capital (whether by private or state organisations) for local productive investment. Therefore, no matter how intensively or for how long maldevelopment is pursued, it cannot create a national industrial culture. After all, no matter how long a turkey is nurtured, it cannot become an elephant. Which is why, in both its capitalist and socialist versions, Cargo Cult maldevelopment has failed, and shall continue to fail, to create industrial culture and society.

Examples from countries where it was accomplished show that development proceeds from a self-reliant understanding of the nation's history and circumstances, and interprets for local practice whatever general economic and political theories the leadership of the nation chooses to be guided by. Maldevelopment, in contrast, proceeds from a happy ignorance or misunderstanding of the nation's history and condition. And the leadership often dragoons the nation into a religious worship of whatever economic and political theory it subscribes to, instead of adapting such theory to serve the nation. Theory becomes theology, by being applied dogmatically instead of scientifically.

Development requires a leadership cadre or class which is clearsightedly dedicated to the transformation of its society; which is willing, and has the confidence, to face the challenges of that social adventure; and which is undaunted by the price that must be paid. In contrast, leaders of maldevelopment usually either mistake it for development, or are unwilling to face the challenges and risks of development, or are scared off by the price it exacts. They demand the fruits of development but insist on avoiding its costs in social and personal discipline, deferred consumption, investment, talent, effort, and the dislocation or abandonment of some old ways and cherished values. It is as if, as the saying goes, they want to go to paradise but do not want to die.

Another contrast between the two types of leadership is in their attitude to their predecessors in development. In their day as developing nations, the USA, USSR and Japan regarded their European predecessors as models to be surpassed at their own game. Third World maldevelopers, however, see the advanced industrial countries, not as pace setters whose challenge must be sportingly met, but as fairy godfathers from whom cargoes of industrial products are to be begged or demanded; godfathers who are to be damned as demons should they fail to hand over the goods.

The maldeveloping world

The practice of referring to Third World countries as developing countries, though entrenched, is misleading. There are very few developing countries in the Third World; most are actually maldeveloping. In fact, developing countries are so few among them that it would be more correct to refer to the Third World as the maldeveloping world.

An example of the few developing countries of the Third World is China. During the first 30 years of the People's Republic, it concentrated upon a total social transformation which placed great emphasis on the development of a national industrial culture anchored on agriculture and heavy industries. To make this possible, the rate of national savings and investment was kept high; and only in the last few years has investment emphasis begun to shift towards consumer industries.

In stark contrast to China is Nigeria, an excellent example of the maldeveloping majority. In its years of independence, Nigeria has concentrated on developing its consumer appetite for imports, and has used its vast oil revenues to feed this habit. It has little stomach for saving and investment, and no inclination towards building a productive economy. It has only now begun to establish a steel industry that may, some day, provide essential inputs for a heavy industry. Any need for some fundamental social transformation to prepare its citizens for a national industrial culture has gone unrecognised.

But why has maldevelopment been so popular in the Third World? What is the paramount desire of Third World elites, and how does Cargo Cult maldevelopment satisfy it?

Contrary to popular belief the paramount desire of Third World elites is not development, but the perpetuation of their rule, with minimum disruption to their enjoyment of its perquisites. However, to legitimise their rule in the minds of populations hungry for material prosperity, these elites have found it necessary to proclaim development as the principal enterprise of the state. But believing that those they rule would not submit to the rigours of genuine development, and being themselves thoroughly disinclined to embark upon a process which might put at risk their enjoyment of power, they have sought some strategy of pseudo-development—one which would give the appearance of development by providing some of its fruits, yet save them the rigours of genuine development. For this purpose, Cargo Cult maldevelopment has, so far, proved adequate.

All it requires of them is to secure funds to pay for sufficient imports to satisfy the population's hunger for consumer goods. Hence the enormous appetite of Third World regimes for foreign exchange. This is preferably to be obtained from foreign aid, foreign loans and from payments for exports of raw materials—sources which would not require them to tinker with the colonial economy, let alone undertake fundamental social reorganisation. Consequently, Third World "development strategies" have tended to concentrate on how to obtain such funds for importing cargoes of Western consumer goods, and on building the infrastructures for distributing and using them. This sort of "development" naturally suits a West which is interested in markets for its manufactures, in sources of raw materials, but not in the emergence of competing productive capacity or the proliferation of industrial powers. Such a dovetailing of interests has produced an alliance between the industrial and financial corporations of the West, the aid agencies of Western governments, and Third World leaders—an alliance for the racket of promoting Cargo Cult maldevelopment in the Third World.

The crisis of maldevelopment

But circumstances have arisen which threaten the Cargo Cult maldevelopment racket. With growing populations and rising consumer expectations in their countries, Third World elites have needed to import more and more, and have come to need enormous amounts of foreign exchange. They have therefore sought more aid, more loans, and higher prices for their exports in order to raise more cash. This has pitted them against their allies in the West who do not want to pay more for raw materials, or to give more aid, or to grant more loans to risky customers whose debts are already enormous.

The International Monetary Fund (IMF), as guardian of the Western financial system, is averse to giving good credit ratings to Third World regimes unless they obey IMF dictates on how to run their economies. But to comply with IMF conditions would mean a drastic reduction in the consumption of imports, and this could de-legitimise Third World regimes. So, rather than go along with a racket which now threatens to undermine the consumerist basis of their political legitimacy, these regimes demand that the terms of the racket be revised to their advantage and for their salvation. Hence their clamour for a New International Economic Order.

Their campaign has been supported by a section of the Western leadership which fears that, without reforms, the whole racket could collapse, with grievous losses to both partners. It has therefore lobbied the hardline majority in the West for more aid, for softer loans, and for schemes to stabilise prices for Third World products. It has also been lobbying Third World regimes for a "basic needs" approach to development which would spread imports and services to the large majority beyond elite circles. This section of the Western leadership would like the Western hardliners to accept that, with a "basic needs" approach, aid and soft loans would not only finance short term exports from the West, but would also spread the habit for Western consumer products to many more people in the Third World. This would lay the groundwork for even more exports in the longer run. Besides, a "basic needs" approach would concentrate Third World efforts away from the building of those heavy industries without which they could never rival the advanced industrial nations. In other words, that a "basic needs" approach would reinforce pressures for Cargo Cult consumerism in the Third World.

But none of this lobbying and mediating has moved the North-South negotiations forward. The West adamantly refuses to give up advantages and profitable interests which took it centuries to accumulate, and would gladly have the negotiations ended. The Third World, in growing desperation, tries to keep alive these elegant, well publicised, but futile begging sessions which masquerade as negotiations. Why? They supply the stage for a morality play which allows Third World leaders to offload on to the North the blame for chronic Third World poverty! The general intransigence of the North, its refusal to redistribute resources to the South, its curtailment of aid, its refusal to be guilt-tripped into public admissions of past exploitation—all this is dramatised for the Third World public by the highly publicised "negotiations" of which Cancún is a symbol. The message which the morality play is meant to convey to the people of the Third World is this: "Third World leaders are fighting hard for the welfare of their people. But it is the wicked, greedy and shameless West which denies them the means to development."

But the true causes of chronic Third World poverty are rather different from what this Cargo Cult morality play would have us believe. The prime obstacles to development are the Third World elites' lack of that autonomous will to industrial development which motivated the capitalist pioneers of the West, and their lack of that dread of Western invasion which drove the Soviets to their draconian strategy of socialist industrialisation. What Third World elites want is to reap as much as they can of the consumerist benefits of Northern industry—for that, they would like to preserve their dependency ties to the West. Therefore, when they have criticised dependency, it has not been in order to abolish it, but to reform it for their greater consumerism and local power.

Towards development

But that may be changing now. The failure of North-South negotiations to save the maldevelopment racket, together with the general crisis of the world economy, appears to be finally driving Third World elites to consider such hitherto unappealing measures as South-South cooperation. Should they also ever realise that the crisis of maldevelopment is indeed terminal, and that only genuine national development will, in future, supply those material goods without which they would lose legitimacy, then these elites might find it in their interest to abandon maldevelopment altogether and go in for development. In that event, South-South cooperation would be conducted in the spirit of development, and as an adjunct to, and facilitator of, national development. Only then would the cooperation be between energetic, developing economies, rather than between moribund, maldeveloped ones.

But for all that to happen, Third World elites must accept that domestic industrial productivity is the only sure fount of national prosperity and power. Therefore, any country which desires development must mobilise itself for the social transformation—with all its inevitable upheavals—whereby an industrial culture is fashioned. It must accept that the enterprise of development is one of imaginative and inventive hard work, not of waiting for miracles of heavenly cargoes, or for the miracles of foreign aid, technology transfers and capital imports.

This is where the failures of the Third World intelligentsia could be a severe handicap. All of them, of whatever stripe, need to appreciate that monographs on the conflicts between traditionalism and modernity, myths about the stages of take off, marvellous descriptions of internal class contradictions and of external dependency relations, are of little practical value until two things are understood: that the plunder of the Third World by the West is only part of the set of factors responsible for Third World poverty and Western prosperity; and that attention must focus on how the industrial wealth of nations, East as well as West, was first created, and is maintained by their national cultures and organisations.

To the extent that dependency relations contribute to Third World poverty, the mechanisms elaborated, and the powers accumulated by the West for maintaining such relations, have to be dismantled. It is foolish to expect them to be dismantled by negotiation, or by the manipulation of whatever strands of guilt some Westerners feel about their history, or by self-righteously denouncing Western self interest. After all, the Third World elite's campaign for a New International Economic Order is based on its own self interest, is it not? The Third World intelligentsia needs to make it clear that development will depend on the will to development, and on strategies which reckon on Northern resistance and hostility, rather than its benevolence and charity. The North cannot be expected to voluntarily sacrifice its interests for the benefit of the South.

Should any Third World country become sufficiently motivated to undertake development, it should recognize the following as among the crucial tasks to which it should address itself:

1) It must sufficiently disengage, or even secede, from the Western economic system in order to avoid being further plundered of resources it would need for its own development. This implication of dependency theory cannot be avoided.

2) It must help, through South-South cooperation, to build a Third World economic system, one from whose systemic linkages it would stand to benefit. For no country is sufficiently large and endowed to be able to dispense with the advantages of international trade between some suitable group of nations.

3) It must uncompromisingly abandon Cargo Cult maldevelopment, and just as uncompromisingly embark upon the social adventure of creating a national industrial culture. Those countries which have chosen the socialist road should do what it takes to succeed; and those which have chosen the capitalist road, should also do what it takes to succeed.

If a country should do all three, it may not matter much (as the examples of Northern successes demonstrate) which ideological model of society it adopts—capitalist, socialist, or others, according to taste—so long as it adopts one and sticks with it until it accomplishes its own transformation into an industrial culture and society.

The Third World's trap into peonage[*]

> I am frightened by the so-called friends who are flocking to Africa. Negro Americans trying to make money from your toil, white Americans who seek by investment and high interest to bind you in serfdom to business as the Near East is bound and as South America is struggling with. For this America is tempting your leaders, bribing your young scholars, and arming your soldiers.
>
> —W. E. B. Du Bois

The financial difficulties which Nigeria, in spite of its oil boom, is now entering are no different in their fundamental causes from those which Nkrumah's Ghana entered upon in spite of its initially large foreign reserves derived from cocoa. Both experiences are rooted in the philosophy of development which orthodox economics prescribes, and they are consequences of trying to develop under plans devised and supervised by the International Monetary Fund (IMF). However much money a Third World country may have, it is the hidden purpose of IMF strategy to fleece and bankrupt it, and hand it over to Western creditors for debt trap peonage.

Since they gained independence, the elites of most Third World countries, in response to the welfare and nationalist expectations of their populations, have sought to develop the economies of their countries. The imperial powers of the

---

[*] *Africa* (London) July 1978; the *Daily Times* (Lagos) October 20 & 21, 1978; *The Guardian* (Lagos) October 9, 1983.

West also have, for their own purposes, sought to promote a limited development of Third World economies so as to make them more serviceable to Western interests. Between these seemingly identical goals of development there is, however, a basic conflict. This conflict, between nationalist development and neo-colonial maldevelopment, can be highlighted by the question: development for whom? For the people of the country or for foreign imperial interests? Specifically, should a country's resources and efforts be expended primarily for the well being of its people or for foreign beneficiaries?

As they relinquished direct political control over their colonies, the imperialist powers of the West tackled the problem of how to retain control over the definition, purposes and execution of whatever development took place in Third World countries after independence. The answer they devised was debt trap peonage. They would impose peonage upon Third World countries, and the orthodox modernisation recipe which they offered to the Third World was the very programme devised for leading them from colonialism into debt trap peonage. An assortment of tricks, and the institutions for playing them, was put together; and to the venerable IMF, with its mask of technical objectivity and sacrosanct impartiality in giving advice, fell the task of supervising the programme at its highest levels.

There are four important questions to be considered. What is debt trap peonage? How are Third World countries manoeuvred into it? What in the modernisation recipe is indispensable for this manoeuvre? And how is a country held in debt trap peonage against its efforts?

A succinct description of debt trap peonage is supplied by Cheryl Payer in the following passage from her book *The Debt Trap* (1974):

> The system can be compared point by point with peonage on an individual scale. In the peonage,

or debt slavery, system the worker is unable to use his nominal freedom to leave the service of his employer, because the latter supplies him with credit (for overpriced goods in the company store) necessary to supplement his meagre wages. The aim of the employer/creditor/merchant is neither to collect the debt once and for all, nor to starve the employee to death, but rather to keep the labourer permanently indentured through his debt to the employer. The worker cannot run away, for other employers and the state recognize the legality of his debt; nor has he any hope of earning his freedom with his low wages, which do not keep pace with what he consumes, let alone the true value of what he produces for his master.

Precisely the same system operates on the international level. Nominally independent countries find that their debts, and their constant inability to finance current needs out of imports, keep them tied by a tight leash to their creditors. The IMF orders them, in effect, to continue labouring on the plantation, while it refuses to finance their efforts to set up in business for themselves. It is debt slavery on an international scale. If they remain within the system, the debtor countries are doomed to perpetual underdevelopment, or rather to development of their exports at the service of multinational enterprises, at the expense of development for the needs of their own citizens.

How is a country manoeuvred into it? Excellent and enlightening case studies of the process can be found, for the Philippines, Brazil, Indonesia, Indochina and India in Cheryl Payer's *The Debt Trap*. A book length study of Ghana's experience of it can be found in *Development and the Debt Trap*, by Andrzej Krassowski. But the basic strategy may be summed up as follows: The orthodox strategy for developing a country calls for massive infusion, by purchase and import from abroad, of industrial and agricultural technologies and equipment; of processed and semi-processed materials for assembly; of plans, planners, advisers, technicians, and other experts. Thus, practically everything said to be required for development, it is recommended, must be imported—formulas, nuts, bolts and brains. All these must be bought on the international market of the Western economic system. By the rules of that market, however, they must be paid for in foreign exchange, something which most underdeveloped countries are short of. Barter between countries is discouraged. The payment rules of this international market, the orthodox strategy of buying development and carting it home, and the low earnings of Third World commodities relative to the prices of what they must import, together guarantee that any such country, should it embark upon an infusionist development plan, shall spend its way into a chronic foreign exchange crisis. Corruption of public office merely hastens what the strategy would bring about, even without corruption. This foreign exchange crisis can then be temporarily relieved by entering into a huge foreign debt which, in turn, cannot be obtained without considerable economic and political concessions being exacted by creditors.

Thus, the orthodox strategists guide you to opt for *buying*, rather than *working up* your way into development, developing your different muscles and organs as you need them. You are taught to hurry and buy up everything all at once, instead of building up at a sure and steady pace. But you are poor and chronically short of the only kind of payment which the seller of these items will accept. So you go to your only available money lender, who happens to be your adviser, as well as the maker and merchant of the goods he has persuaded you to buy in one spree. But no matter. He smilingly offers you both money and goods, but on condition that you pledge to work off the money debt on the farm which he has, through dependency relations, made out of what you still consider your ancestral homestead. Once you agree to these terms (and he has excellent ways to manipulate your weaknesses and your laziness and your greed until you agree), you become an indentured sharecropper, or peon, on what you are still permitted to regard as your land. And the massiveness of what you must buy from him, at prices which he dictates, is such that you cannot really ever work off your ever-increasing burden of debt.

What elements in the orthodox modernisation recipe guarantee that those who adopt it will be manoeuvred into debt trap peonage? For an answer, we need to examine both the explicit and implicit operational assumptions of orthodox development plans. The explicit assumption is that a mixed economy with comprehensive central planning is the appropriate mode for Third World development. The trouble with this assumption, from the Third World position, is that a genuinely comprehensive central plan is largely ineffectual for a mixed economy if its crucial sectors are under foreign control, and especially antagonistic foreign control. Under that condition, what appears to be comprehensive central planning is not so, but rather partial planning with considerable wrecking powers left in a private sector that is under powerful external control. The foreign dominated private sector is thus free to respond to any items in the plan which serve its foreign interests; free to ignore whatever it wishes to ignore, no matter how vital to the overall development effort; free to thwart developments in the public sector which it feels are incompatible with its alien interests; and free to resist state control over its activities.

There have been efforts during the Second UN Development Decade to limit or control the activities of the foreign private sector, by compelling it to go into partnership with indigenous private investors, and even with the state itself. But it is not easy to see which side curbs and controls the other in such partnerships between unequal powers. Majority stockholding by the citizens and state of a Third World country does not guarantee them operational control.

As has happened even in the West, under what John Kenneth Galbraith calls the New Industrial State, operational control of industry has shifted from stockholders to managers and the financial institutions which the managers must please. In the case of Third World stockholding, this shift in the locus of industrial power is compounded by the fact that Third World states and citizens are, in effect, junior partners to giant multinational corporations, no matter how much stock they may actually hold in what are local subsidiaries of those multinationals. The interest of the multinational corporation in its local subsidiary is still backed up, ultimately, by the enormous financial, political, diplomatic and military power of its parent state. And among the watchdog financial agencies whose job is to protect the interests of the multinational corporations, is the venerable, impartial IMF. So, in the end, it does not really matter how much a Third World state goes into joint ventures with foreign companies, what percentage of local subsidiary stock it holds, so long as the state's economic thinking and activity are conducted under the guidance of the IMF, that prestigious guardian of the interests of the club of multinational corporations.

Given this power background to the public picture of indigenisation by partnership, it would appear that such partnerships are far less an instrument for local control over foreign investment than for deepening foreign control and supervision over both the public and private sectors of a Third World economy. Thus, autonomous nationalist enterprises which might have developed without the encumbrance of foreign embrace, are placed in a position to be supervised, smothered and absorbed by more powerful foreign interests which are backed, ultimately, by vast armies and nuclear arsenals.

The implicit, but fundamental, assumption in orthodox development planning is that a Third World economy is, and must be kept, a satellised member of the Western economic system. The explicit assumption requiring it to have a mixed economy with foreign participation serves this hidden purpose; IMF guidelines to the state sector also serve this purpose. Thus, foreign investment and official IMF tutelage to the state sector, are the grand loopholes through which a weak Third World economy is manoeuvred to serve the interests of its satellisers.

Some might wish to object by asking: what about OPEC countries and the members of other raw materials cartels? Do their high incomes not put them in a position to escape satellisation? Can't they now surge forward to genuine and autonomous development? The correct answer would be no. Such an objection reflects the conventional, but erroneous belief that the principal barrier to Third World development is low income and lack of capital. Against that carefully fostered mistake, it should be pointed out that *the average Third World country is a net exporter of capital to the West*. The main hindrance to autonomous Third World development is rather in the structural arrangements, domestic and international, which prevent a proper domestic investment of surplus, and instead promote its flight abroad. These facts are, of course, contrary to the fashionable illusion fostered by a West which seeks to control the disposition of the surplus generated by Third World countries. It prefers to suck such surplus into its own hands, through trade and unequal exchange, and then reintroduce some of it, entirely under its own control, through aid and foreign investment.

This is not the essay in which to present the motives behind the income transfer to OPEC countries which was plotted by the United States in its economic rivalry with Europe and Japan. Suffice it to say that OPEC money by itself, however large, provides no detour around the debt trap. How large an income a country earns abroad is not as crucial to its development as how it employs at home whatever income it has. The signs are becoming clearer now that such OPEC countries as Iran and Nigeria, which were encouraged to embark on massive infusionist development planning, are well on their way to repeat, with their vaster oil income, the debt trap experience which Ghana, under Nkrumah, went through with its cocoa income. The OPEC countries will just be bigger catches in the same trap.

In fact, right after OPEC incomes began to soar, the recycling of petrodollars, as it was called, became a major enterprise in the United States. The debt trap setters rushed out to encourage in the OPEC countries the illusion that development can simply be bought abroad, imported and installed, like any consumer item. And they have been waiting in glee for the day when, with their petrodollars completely recycled back into Western hands, and with their oil reserves completely exhausted, these OPEC tycoons will have to come begging to the Western money market for funds with which to carry on their misguided development strategy. Back in 1976 one gleeful report declared that "there is recognition that oil-rich Nigeria will be coming to the world money market to borrow for specific projects as early as next year." Now that this has happened and the Western money lenders have their hands on Nigeria's oil revenues, you can except them to run it down with interest and other charges, till a bankrupt Nigeria will have to do whatever its foreign creditors say it must do.

If the OPEC countries, with their oil billions, are using a recipe designed to plunge even them into insolvency, and so guide them into the waiting debt trap, what hope then is there for the non-OPEC countries of the Third World?

Finally, how are Third World countries held in debt trap peonage once they are in it? Simple. By the normal workings of Western management of their economies. This management is imposed on acquiescent countries by IMF prescriptions and supervision, and is backed by threats of sundry economic punishments if IMF "recommendations" are disregarded; it is imposed on rebellious countries by the threat of political destabilisation and, if necessary, by actual coups or invasions. When a Third World country refuses to obey the IMF, and boldly embarks upon a path that could lead it to autonomous prosperity, the West, deploying its enormous economic powers and its considerable leverage within the private and public sectors of the "offending" economy, destabilises its government, installs another, and shoves the economy back into the debt trap and IMF supervision.

The West's ready resort to destabilisation is a common feature of contemporary history, as the list of their attempts, with varying degrees of success and failure, shows. For there is something very much in common between the destruction of Sukarno's Indonesia, Nkrumah's Ghana and Allende's Chile, and that something is the West's determination to remove those regimes and drag their countries back into debt trap peonage.

Averting debt trap peonage[*]

> Here comes the con man
> Coming with his con plan
> We won't take no bribes
> We've got to stay alive
> We gonna chase those crazy bald heads
> Out of our town.
>
> —Bob Marley

> Here then, my brothers, you face your great decision: will you for temporary advantage—for automobiles, refrigerators and Paris gowns—spend your income in paying interest on borrowed funds, or will you sacrifice present comfort and the chance to shine before your neighbors in order to educate your children, develop such industry as best serves the great mass of people and makes your country strong in ability, self-support and self-defense? Such union of effort for strength calls for sacrifice and self-denial, while the capital offered you at high price by the colonial powers like France, Britain, Holland, Belgium, and the United States, will prolong fatal colonial imperialism, from which you have suffered slavery, serfdom and colonialism.
>
> —W. E. B. Du Bois

For a country such as Nigeria, which is on the verge of being caught, the problem of averting debt trap peonage breaks

[*] Presented in March 1984 at the conference on "Foreign Debt and Economic Development", sponsored by the United Bank for Africa, held at the National Institute of International Affairs, Lagos. First published in *The Guardian* (Lagos) April-May 1984; reprinted in *Monthly Review* (New York) November 1985.

down into two tasks: retreating up the path it has travelled, and resisting all future temptations to get back on it.

In order to find solutions to these two tasks, I am going to look at five questions:
1) What is Nigeria's debt situation today, and how was it brought about?
2) What makes it a case of debt trap peonage?
3) Why is it necessary to avert debt trap peonage?
4) How could that be done?
5) What stops Nigeria from taking the steps necessary for averting it?

Today, six years after we were lured into unnecessary borrowing by lenders eager to recycle the petro-dollars, Nigeria's foreign debt is officially said to be ₦11.08 billion ($16.6 billion). Debt servicing charges are expected to consume ₦3.272 billion ($4.9 billion), some 38.47 per cent of our 1984 export revenue ₦8.5 billion ($12.75 billion). And that is before service charges are included for the $5.5 billion trade debts which we are anxious to convert into long term debt. As if all that mountain of debt were not burden enough for our shoulders, we are seeking an IMF loan of about $2 billion for "structural adjustments", so we can get even more loans from international bankers.

As our oil revenue declines, we seem to be turning into a loan addict. Our urge is to grab loans and even more loans, like a drug addict who must have more and yet more of his heroin to keep going. And like the heroin addict, we are craving these loans, not for sound purposes, but simply to finance our spendthrift consumer habits and our ambitious maldevelopment programmes.

In classic peonage, a worker, though nominally and legally free, is held in servitude by the terms of his indenture to his master. Because his wages are set too low to buy all his necessities, his master grants him credit, but restricts him to buying overpriced goods from the master's store. As a result, the peon gets deeper and deeper into debt. For as long as the arrangement lasts, the peon cannot pay off his mounting debt and leave, so he must keep on working for his master. Which suits his master perfectly. For the master's aim is neither to starve the peon nor to see him free from the chain of debt, but rather to keep him working until he dies. The peon can't run away either. The law recognises his debt, and will enforce his master's claims. Besides, no other employer will take him on so long as he owes his old master. So, if the peon runs off, but doesn't get clean away, he is either captured and brought back, or starves in hiding.

Third World countries which today are accumulating debts are in an analogous situation. Their earnings from the export of their mineral and agricultural products are not enough to pay for the overpriced manufactures they import from the West. The West, through international banks and government aid, lends them the difference. Each year they need more loans to make up these deficits, and so their foreign debt mounts. Unable to pay off their debts, and powerless to survive the dire consequences of repudiating them, these countries are obliged to continue in permanent underdevelopment, supplying low priced raw materials to their industrial creditors, and unable to concentrate their own attention and resources on developing their economies in their own interest.

Such is precisely the situation into which Nigeria has put herself. And I must stress that Nigeria was not captured and forced into this situation, but volunteered herself into it. In 1978, when she agreed to contract the first billion of these debts, Nigeria had more income from oil than she could sensibly spend. Though she didn't need the debt, she allowed herself to be persuaded to sample the pleasures of debtorship. In that, she is more like the man who was persuaded to take his first shot of heroin, got to like the thrill it gave him, took more and more of it until he became an addict. Indeed, Nigeria got to enjoy the thrills of being a spendthrift, and soon became a loan addict. In effect, Nigeria has become, not just a debt trap peon, but a squander-addicted debt trap peon.

Nigeria indeed shares three crucial characteristics with a heroin-addicted debt trap peon. First, both debts are unsecured consumer debts, made up of expenses for subsistence and for a spending spree, and with future income as the only collateral. Second, both loans are pure peonage loans, that is, loans made not because of the potential of the project the loan is to be used for, but simply in order to secure a legal control on the economic and political behaviour of the debtor. Thirdly, the only way made available for "getting out" of both debts is by getting into more debt.

But what is wrong with the situation? Why is it necessary to escape it? Those of us who look forward to a day (which we may not ourselves live to see) when Nigeria will be an industrial world power, and those who wish to contribute to the early arrival of that day, cannot feel happy about our getting into a debt trap peonage which removes our economic sovereignty, and hands the piloting of our economy over to our creditors. Today that means turning Nigeria into a financial protectorate of the IMF. We can already see what that means. IMF teams come to inspect our books; we take our economic programmes to them for approval and they dictate what kinds of social and economic restructuring we can pursue. It is just as if we were back in the old colonial days, when the Colonial Office had to approve our budget and economic programmes, subject, of course, to these being serviceable to the larger imperial aims of our masters.

If we had any sense of national honour, we ought really to cringe in shame. Here we are, an allegedly sovereign nation, being treated, twenty-four years after independence, like some delinquent schoolboy or some bankrupt incapable of managing his finances. But the reasons for escaping debt trap peonage go far beyond the sentimental matter of national honour, and beyond the (perhaps, to most people) abstract matter of our economic and political sovereignty. Debt trap peonage is injurious to any country's development prospect; and the squander-addicted peonage, which Nigeria is getting more deeply into, is doubly injurious. Besides making us peons, it ruins our social fabric and disorients us. Let us see what injury has already been done, first to our finances, then to our national psychology.

For today's $16.6 billion debt (i.e. 2 years' export revenue) we must now pay some $5 billion a year in debt charges. For us, that doesn't make sense! But you can see why the banks came after us to borrow, and still want us to borrow more, provided the IMF can guarantee policies which will enable them to keep pumping similar billions out of us each year. And what do you think is their weapon for keeping us hooked on loans? Our habit of profligacy, that's what! We are addicted to loans because we are addicted to profligacy!

At first, to justify a relatively minor loan of $1 billion to be added to our huge oil revenue, we were encouraged to go on a spending spree. We were even helped to put together a lavish purchasing catalogue which we mistook for a development plan. As our profligacy became a habit, the doubling of our oil income didn't matter: we still needed a bit more to pay for our even more rapidly enlarging desires, and so we still wanted loans. This habit of spending beyond our means is at the root of our condition. If we learned to feel fine with our expenses well below our income, we would psychologically be in a good condition from which to start plotting our escape from debt trap peonage. But curbing profligacy, like getting off heroin, is not easy, especially if it involves a drop in what we imagine our living standards to be.

Regarding our development prospects, debt trap peonage forces us to place our economy under IMF supervision. Given the fundamental antagonism between the interests of the peon and the master (in this case, between Nigeria and the West), we can fully expect that policies will be insisted upon by the IMF which will divert us from our national goal of developing into a powerful, prosperous, modern, industrial nation. Anyone who thinks that the IMF will approve programmes or sponsor policies which will develop Nigeria in such a way as to threaten the economic hegemony of the Western powers, needs to go and think again. The IMF's job, as overseer of the global economic arrangements of the West, is precisely the opposite.

The other reason for getting out of debt trap peonage is that, under it, policies will be imposed which will bring social chaos upon us. If we think that things are bad now in Nigeria, we should look down the road a few years ahead and see what peonage will visit on us. For that, all we need do is look at the cases of countries which have allowed the IMF to tell them how to manage their economies. If you like, study the recent history of Brazil. In brief, this is the Brazilian story.

In the 1970s, Brazil went on a borrowing spree. Today, its debt is almost $100 billion. Its debt trap agonies fill the headlines these days. Since its exports cannot pay the debt service charges, Brazil is in the treadmill of seeking the rescheduling of its debts. But before banks agree to roll over its loans, Brazil has to agree to the austerity measures decreed by the IMF. These measures, however, call for severe hardships to be imposed on the population. As a result, Brazil has been plunged into semi-permanent social unrest. Strikes, riots, and factory closures have become the disorders of the day. Hunger roams the streets and countryside. Last August and September, numerous supermarkets were looted by hungry city dwellers. Starving rural folk who fled to the cities were reduced to cannibalism. Indeed, where in the 1970s Brazil went a-borrowing, in the 1980s it has gone a-sorrowing.

Caught in an endless round of debt rescheduling, and endlessly screaming for fresh loans to pay off the old debts, Brazil has been subjected to the insolence of powerful nations. When, last October, the US Treasury Secretary Donald Regan, while on a visit to Rio, voiced "fear" for the future of Brazil, a Brazilian senator cried out that the remarks were "insolent, inadmissible and intolerable." And there were demands to have Brazil's honour defended. And there is no end still in sight to Brazil's debts, social unrest and international humiliation.

But then, some might say, the IMF insists on inculcating financial discipline, and that can only be for the good of any financially indisciplined nation like Nigeria. My answer to that is, not necessarily. It all depends. Though the IMF has come to be used by Third World governments as a bogeyman who forces them to impose the hardships of financial discipline on their countries, we must ask: Is it really necessary to use the IMF as a bogeyman? And is the kind of discipline it imposes the kind we need?

Citizens have been known to make great sacrifices when they believe in the cause for which sacrifices are demanded. So, to use the IMF as bogeyman simply suggests that a government has not bothered to earn the confidence of its people in its ability to lead them on the hard and risky journey to development. As for the kind of discipline which the IMF likes to impose, it is the wrong kind for the wrong aims. What we need is the discipline of the farmer who plants his seeds, tends his fields, harvests his crops, and guards his granary from thieves and rodents alike. What we don't need is the pseudo-discipline of the robot who, once programmed, assists robbers in looting his own house.

If, for the above reasons, debt trap peonage is not good for us, how do we get out of it, and stay out of it? Let me begin by disposing of one alleged solution which, in fact, is not a solution at all, but the very problem itself. The conventional unwisdom says that the solution to our mounting debt is to reschedule it. But seriously, isn't that just what the peon is obliged to do by his master? For so long as his earnings are not enough to meet his needs and pay off his growing debt, rolling it over is no cure at all, but a prolongation of the disease. For Nigeria, switching from short term debt to me-

AVERTING THE DEBT TRAP

dium term loan, or from either to long term loan, is like switching from heroin to methadone. It is merely a substitution of one addiction for another, whereas what is needed is the ending of the addiction. Of course, the addicted peon, if driven too hard, could commit suicide; but that would be cutting his own throat to spite his enslaver's or dealer's pocket. The only remedy for his condition is to give up his craving for heroin, and then, either repudiate the debt (by running far beyond the reach of his master's power and the power of the law), or see to it that the terms of any rescheduling permit him to work off the debt within his lifetime. For only then could he walk out free, with his master powerless to use the law to stop him. Let us consider these options.

A peon's chances of running away from his debt are pretty slim. But can't a sovereign state do that? Well, that becomes a matter of power, doesn't it? And it boils down to the question: Does the debtor state have the power to defy the armed might of the nations to which its creditors belong? If you examine the history of the Caribbean, you'll find that, earlier in this century, debts owed to European and American interests served as occasions for the takeover of countries by the US marines, and for the takeover of their finances for the purpose of collecting payments. One remarkable example was that of the Dominican Republic. In 1905, the USA took over its finances, and used the proceeds from its customs to pay off foreign debts. This exercise lasted till 1924, when the American military finally left.

You may say that the world has changed considerably since then. But has it? And in the appropriate respects? The Western countries may not be able to enforce their will by armed might wherever they wish, as the recent examples of Iran, Vietnam and the Lebanon show. But they have other ways available to them. Perhaps their most fearsome weapon today is economic warfare. The USA was unable to get its hostages back from Iran through an Entebbe style raid; but when it embarked upon economic war against

Iran, by seizing Iranian assets all over the world, Iran had to yield. If the Western powers waged economic war on Nigeria; if they cut off all trade, all credit, all food supplies, seized our assets around the world, and blockaded our ports and air space, wouldn't Nigeria collapse under the economic pressure? That is because Nigeria (or any Third World country for that matter) hasn't the consumption habits and production capacity to withstand concerted economic war from the West. Cuba has survived American economic pressures for 25 years, but Europe did not go along with the American blockade, and the Soviet Union served as Cuba's umbilical cord and defender. Who would do the same for Nigeria if all our Western creditors ganged up on us?

Such considerations probably explain why all that Latin American talk of forming a debtors' cartel remains just talk. The most they were able to propose at the Quito debtors' summit last January (where 27 Latin American and Caribbean countries met on how to get out from their $350 billion debt burden) was to seek three things from their creditors: a drastic reduction in interest rates on past and future loans; an extended repayment schedule; and the limiting of loan repayments to manageable percentages of national export earnings. The implication of the Quito summit is that, if we lack the power to walk away from our debt, then the best we could hope for is to work it off. Thus, we must take on no new loans, and we must pay off our existing debt. For Nigeria, this cure would require us to end our squandermania, reduce drastically our spending on imports, and apply most of our export earnings to paying off our debts. But, most importantly, we would have to avoid any new debt.

Of course, there is room for variation in the severity of the programme of cure. On current projections, $16.6 billion is roughly two years' export revenue for Nigeria. We could, in the most extreme version of the regimen, shut out all imports for two years, and use all the earnings to retire our debt. This would probably be the best cure; but would a spoilt and pampered population stand for such a short sharp shock? You could hear them muttering: What? Go without my daily Chivas or Remy? Drive a dented Benz? And for all of two years? The psychological wrench of this variant of the cure may be just too much. So we might have to plan to take four or five years to retire a debt that could be inconveniently paid off in two.

But how would such a total freeze on imports and new debts differ from the unacceptable IMF medicine? In at least two ways. First, the IMF "medicine" is futile. In as much as it does not require us to stop getting into new debts, it does not aim to cure. It is simply an alleged cure which puts us through the hardships of hospitalisation and medication, but also keeps giving us fresh infections of the debt disease it pretends to be curing. If the aim is to regain health and freedom, then, from the point of view of a victim economy, the IMF hardship is pointless hardship. In contrast, the self-administered cure is both appropriate to the disease, and drastic enough to kill it off in the shortest possible time, and get us out of hospital to enjoy our freedom.

Secondly, in development terms, the self-imposed programme of cure has irreplaceable advantages. To get cured of the squandermania and import mania which make us into loan addicts, we need a therapeutic shock to our system. Like Chu Teh, the Chinese general who got rid of his opium addiction, we need to put ourselves into isolation on a boat without a scrap of our "heroin" (imports and debts) on board, and sail off for the years it would take to overcome our withdrawal pains and be cured. For that, we must collectively have the discipline and determination which come from a conviction that a difficult course of action is in our best interest. Such resolve, being voluntary, would mobilise our spirit of sacrifice for national salvation, and organise us for the long hard march to development. The IMF programme of hardship, on the contrary, being imposed by an outside overseer, and being clearly contrary to our interest, cannot gain our free consent. To impose it would call for such repression as would pit government and people against each other, and tear Nigeria apart.

If we frankly want to get out of debt trap peonage, we should have nothing to do with the IMF and its type of "cure". All this preoccupation with debt rescheduling, with scampering about for new loans; all this flitting about from here to Washington and London and Paris and Bonn and Riyadh is a dramatic waste of time, a monumental misdirection of effort. Dr Soleye, the Finance Minister, would make better use of his time by staying here, working out the details of a regimen of total withdrawal, and writing to tell the international bankers and the IMF to expect a full repayment in two or four years time.

But if we shun such a cure, why might that be? This question goes to the psychological heart of the matter of averting debt trap peonage. For what keeps us from the cure is not unrelated to what caused us to be lured into debt trap peonage in the first place, and might lure us back into it if we get out this time.

I am told that the ultimate basis of the banking business is confidence or trust; which is why many banks in the USA go by the name of Trust Companies. Confidence and trust are matters of psychology. Alas, however, they can be abused. In fact, the confidence man (con man), with his confidence tricks (con plans), cannot operate if he hasn't obtained the confidence of his intended victim. And getting people to fall into debt trap peonage is done by conning them.

But why do some people fall for con tricks while others don't? After all, they say that it takes two to tangle; and the con man can come with his con plan, but it is up to you to fall or not to fall for it. This is a crucial point to understand, if we wish to avoid getting conned into debt trap peonage. So, let us probe that part of the conning process which we ourselves could control.

When you analyse how people (who, after all, have not

been captured in battle and dragged off to a slave farm) are lured into a debt trap and kept in peonage there, you soon discover that the operation's success depends on the victim having a psychology which makes him susceptible to confidence tricks and crackpot ideas. Let me illustrate this from how Nigeria was lured, back in 1978, onto the path that led to the debt trap, and from how Nigeria is now allowing herself to be conned into getting even deeper into debt. When we see the crackpot ideas we have been accepting from those who want to con us, we can more easily appreciate why we fall for them.

One of the key arguments used on us in 1978 was that, if we borrowed money we didn't need, the experienced lenders would be in a position to supervise and guide our development efforts, since they would then have a financial stake in our development. It was a foolish argument, and some of us said so at the time. It still is a foolish argument, and all that our falling for it did was to enable the international loan sharks to get their teeth into the succulent belly of our future earnings! But why did we fall for it?

As is usual with confidence tricks, the con man presented to us only a part of the picture, and relied on our own stupid expectations to make us go along. And we did. We fell in with his plans by thinking that, if he took such a deep interest in furthering our development, we might get the development we wanted without any strenuous effort or risks on our part. We would let him take the wheel and do the driving and instructing while we would half listen, and nod or giggle occasionally, while cosily taking in the lovely view as we got driven to our destination. So we eagerly let him get into the driver's seat, and have been taken for a ride. But the petrol being consumed has been ours, and the wear and tear has been on our car; however, the destination hasn't been the one we thought we were being driven to (the paradise at the end of the road of development), but the peonage farm the driver had intended all along to take us to.

The basic illusion underlying our behaviour in the matter is the notion that development is some sort of turnkey project, or some trophy on a wall which we could just buy without going through the rigours and dangers of a hunt. But development happens to be none of that. You can't buy it and fly it in and install it. True, the foreign financiers may have all the expertise in the world on development. But the point about *our* development is not the supervisory transfer to us of *their* expertise, but our development of our own. And the way to develop Nigerian expertise is by giving ourselves the opportunity to try, fail, learn and succeed. Development, like a child's learning to walk, involves shaky steps, falls, bruises, pain and cries as well as steady stands and, finally, firm footsteps. And just as nobody else can learn to walk (or drive, or eat, or talk) for another, likewise nobody else can do our developing for us. We must do it ourselves, taking responsibility and risks, and being quite prepared for failures, since some are inevitable.

In contrast to what we did (or rather allowed others to do *to* us while thinking that they were doing *for* us), development requires us to take full control of our economy, and to tackle for ourselves the problems of building it up. That is how every developed country did it. That is the secret of how Russia and Japan and the USA did it. That is how Britain and France did it. That is how China has been doing it. None of them did it by handing over the directing and problem solving involved to another nation or group of nations. Even the Chinese had to kick our their "big brother" Russians in 1959, and take complete charge of their own development.

When, back in 1978, Western con men sold us the crackpot notion of the value of creditor supervision, they did so by playing on our lazy greed for the fruits of development and our lack of inclination for the process itself. Now, in 1984, in order to hold us in peonage, we are being sold two notions by con men. And alas, some of our own high officials have fallen for them!

AVERTING THE DEBT TRAP

One of these notions concerns the alleged need to create confidence in Nigeria among the international banking community. According to a report in the *Broad Street Journal* of December 1983, the permanent secretary in the Ministry of Finance, Mr. Abubakar Alhaji, tried late last year to gain the support of the Nigerian Labour Congress for the government's efforts to get an IMF loan. He explained to them that the most crucial benefit Nigeria needed from the IMF loan was the restoring of international confidence in Nigeria, a confidence which would enable Nigeria to secure additional loans from the international capital market.

Now, let us appreciate what all that means. Mr Alhaji was, in effect, saying that a loan from the IMF, which would give Nigeria access to more of the very loans that would get us deeper into debt trap peonage, was a good thing for Nigeria! Well, as far as I can see, the only thing that would restore confidence in a man who is determined to hang you, is evidence of your stupid docility, of your resignation to his power, of your unwillingness to holler or even make a fuss, of your not trying to escape or hang him instead. So, instead of worrying about restoring that kind of injurious confidence abroad, we should concentrate on creating confidence among Nigerians in the development potential of our economy, and in our ability to realise that potential through our own efforts.

Another crackpot notion which Western con men have been trying to sell us is that of our being "underborrowed". They appear to be making headway. Even the minister of finance in the last administration, Adamu Ciroma, began to bandy it about. And our present government officials are getting into the habit of reminding us all that we are "underborrowed". They seem to believe that there is some minimum debt which a nation ought to enter into, and below which it should eagerly borrow more.

However attractive this notion may be to eager lenders, it

is hardly in the interest of debtors. The debt-maximising mentality, which the notion of "underborrowed" encourages, promotes a tendency to acquire debt for debt's sake. For this reason, this hare-brained notion may well prove the greatest danger to our national independence and development. If Nigeria accepts it, and borrows to its debt servicing limit, it could increase its debt to over $100 billion. At that point, Nigeria's exports would be barely able to meet the interest payments on its debts. Nigeria would then be exactly where Brazil now is—"fully borrowed". Whereupon the IMF and foreign lender banks would be able to dictate the politics and economics of Nigeria.

Well, it seems to me utterly foolish to accept that we are "underborrowed" even as we have to use nearly 40 per cent of our export earnings to pay charges on a mountain of spendthrift debt. As far as I am concerned, Nigeria became *overborrowed* that day in 1978 when we allowed ourselves to borrow one kobo that we didn't absolutely need. By that I mean one kobo we didn't have the absorptive capacity to invest prudently. And what did we use our $16.6 billion loan for? Most, if not all, of it was squandered. If you consider that, according to Mr Oladele Olashore of the International Bank for West Africa (IBWA), Nigeria did not get more than 25 per cent value for all our imports, you can see that no less than $12 billion of that mountain of unnecessary debt was wasted. In other words, our injudicious imports merely helped the Western countries to recycle into their pockets most of the money they were loaning us or paying us for our oil.

What disposes Nigerians to accept such crackpot notions? What keeps them from taking the cure for their condition? What are they trying to evade by relying on foreign debt to finance their development? Without foreign financing (through oil and loans), Nigeria would have to undergo internal capital accumulation, and endure the rigours of internal capital mobilisation for productive enterprise. As the economic history of every developed country (whether capitalist or socialist) shows, internal capital accumulation and mobilisation is not an easy process. It is accompanied by great hardships and risks. But basically, Nigerians do not want the rigours and risks of development. All they want are its fruits. So they think they can beg (aid), borrow (loans), sell (oil) and buy (imports) their way to development.

Obviously, Nigeria falls for these con tricks and crackpot notions because, deep down, Nigerians (or at least the elite from which all our leaders come) have the psychology of the sucker. A sucker is greedy but lazy, and wants the easiest way to his overblown ambitions. A sucker believes that there is such a thing as a free lunch, and that he is smart enough to snatch it from a hungry lion's table. A sucker wants to go to paradise but doesn't want to die. A sucker believes in perpetual motion machines. His lazy greed blinds him from the elementary knowledge that, in the real world, as opposed to that of fantasy, what you get is what you paid for, no more, and quite often less!

You are, of course, quite free to want an easy way to the paradise of development. But is there one? Economic history shows that development happens to be one of those journeys (much like climbing Mt Everest) for which there are no easy paths, only more or less difficult approaches. So, if you think you have found a broad and easy road, you can be sure (if Christ is to be believed) that it doesn't lead to paradise. If Nigerians are at all serious about development, and therefore serious about averting their debt trap peonage, then they need to sack their sucker psychology and fantasies. They need to alter their expectations to conform to the truth that the price of development must be paid; not in money alone, but in effort above all; and not by others but by ourselves.

In that regard, let me tell you what a lawyer friend of mine, a Nigerian, once told me. He said that any man who goes to the police and complains that he has been swindled by a money doubler, should himself be locked up. I think that is a position we, as a nation, should adopt. So, instead of self-righteously complaining about the wickedness of those who conned us into the debt trap (usually done against the West); or against those who refuse to give us all the aid we crave (usually done against the Eastern Bloc countries), we should speedily end our foolish spending spree, retire our debts, and free ourselves from the strangulating strings of foreign aid and loans. Then we could use our resources to develop ourselves. Should we ever need to get into some international lending and borrowing after that, our watchword ought to be: Never lend more than you can afford to write off; and never borrow more than you can invest and repay without strain.

In conclusion, let me say this: Ultimately, there is no magic formula for averting debt trap peonage. Like corporate or military strategy, the task calls for intelligent analysis of concrete situations, clear formulation of goals and objectives, meticulous application of principles derived from experience, some practical inventiveness, and a dogged watchfulness against con men and crackpot ideas. In the light of our current experience, we should, above all, rein in our sucker's psychology, beware of Greeks bearing gifts, and practise that eternal vigilance which is the price, not only of political, but also of economic liberty. In short, we should get into the habit of using our heads in our national interest. But unfortunately, as one Lagos taxi driver once told me, "Nigerians think the head is a spare part." May I suggest that we attach it at once, and put it to work immediately?

Of suffering and development[*]

> A modern State is not built for the pleasure of building it. It is not an end in itself. We must keep ourselves from the love of power which makes a god of the State, crushing man under it.
>
> —Leopold Sedar Senghor

Contrary to what many appear to believe, suffering is not an economic concept; nor is sin. Neither has a place in the drama, or the analysis, of economic development. However, they belong comfortably in the theological drama of sin, fall from grace, redemption through suffering, and a final ushering into some eternal domain of spiritual bliss.

For all that is made of it, suffering never made corn grow on barren soil, or even on fertile soil. What makes corn grow are water and manure and, of course, sunshine, air and the farmer's care. Suffering did not produce the train or aeroplane or computer, or any other modern machine. Rather, these were invented to relieve toil, and were the products of knowledge and ingenuity.

Yet one gets the unmistakeable impression that if African leaders had their way, they would throw cornseeds on desert sands, and expect that, by having their people suffer scorching heat by day and freezing cold by night, while eating nothing in a long season of vigil, somehow the magnitude of all that suffering would turn the seeds into a bumper harvest of corn.

[*] First published in *The Guardian* (Lagos) August 4, 1985.

Of course, any modern mind would dismiss such antics as pathetic and unscientific; as a delusion due to a magical conception of the world. Like any other piece of superstition, the notion of development through suffering is intellectually silly, and in the unfortunate event of its being put into practice, it inevitably reveals its bankruptcy by producing even more suffering. This may be aptly illustrated by the example of Guinea.

Sekou Toure, a reputed socialist, made suffering one of the cornerstones of his strategy for developing Guinea. As one of his slogans proclaimed, "To Suffer is to Succeed." For a socialist, and presumed believer in the labour theory of value, a more appropriate slogan might have been "To labour is to succeed"; unless, of course, from the Utopian point of view of the lotus eaters, merely to labour is to suffer. But no matter; Sekou Toure's programme of suffering had little to do with strenuous labour. In any case, its bankruptcy is evident in the results. Despite a fine beginning, despite an enormous mobilisation of popular will and enthusiasm for a brave adventure to independence and prosperity, Guinea got nowhere. In 26 years of suffering, success never bothered to come their way. But why?

Sekou Toure, who was called the Clairvoyant Guide, set out first and foremost to abolish crime, corruption, prostitution, street begging, and other social vices; he believed development could be better tackled later on. And the means to achieve his objective? Repression first; discipline first; networks of spies and informers first. Being a socialist, he made sure he had a programme of equality in poverty. He held prices rigidly down for whatever little there was; the cost of living was thus officially low for those lucky enough to have wages and salaries, but impossibly hard for those who didn't. Such mundane things as roads, farms, markets, well-stocked shops—all had to wait till virtue had been stamped into the Guinean populace.

To that supreme end, he turned his country into a virtual

prison school where the citizens were harangued with the gospel of economic virtues. He sealed the country's borders against escape by the citizen inmates; he confiscated their money; he reduced the press to a presidential mouth organ; he created an efficient spy network for detecting deviations and dissent from that programme of rigorous righteousness which, he seemed to believe, the mysterious dialectic of the universe would reward with development.

While he fed them a diet of exhortations, only 12% of the land was cultivated; per capita income declined in real terms; only a few hundred miles of roads were paved. But despite restrictions on movement inside and out of the country, two million of Guinea's six million citizens fled into exile by the end of Toure's era. Of those who were restrained from thus voting with their feet, 2,000 detainees perished in his prisons. Nevertheless, 26 long years of suffering did not deliver prosperity to the Guineans. Which was quite predictable, since economic development is not a drama of moral redemption.

In the late afternoon of his long rule, Sekou Toure summed up what he had been up to in these words: "For the first twenty years, we in Guinea have concentrated on developing the mentality of our people. Now we are ready to move on to other business." Presumably, after twenty years on a diet of rhetoric, virtue, ideology, theology and harangues, they could be shown a path to a few crumbs and to some drops of water.

But just how well did Sekou Toure succeed, even in the mentality aspect of his programme? Did the diet he fed his people discipline and organise them? Did it stamp out tribalism, instil nationalism, put an end to greed and self-interest, and thereby lay foundations for national advance? Far from it! If tribalism was not evident in Guinea while he lived, it wasn't because he had developed the people's mentality to so high a level as to have overcome it; it simply was that Toure's repression was so overwhelming that nothing could thrive there, not even tribalism, with all its legendary resilience. However, no sooner was his political machine tossed out than tribalism popped out of its dormancy, as is evident in its role in the anti-Conte coup led by Diara Traore, a mere year after Sekou Toure departed from the scene.

As for greed, self-interest and all that, evidence revealed after Toure's death indicates that they were alive and well within Toure's ruling circle. Thus, in 26 years of his programme, the Guineans got neither material prosperity, nor moral regeneration, nor the developed mentality which he set about to instill; all they got were loads and loads of suffering.

While the Guineans endured all the suffering he prescribed, the man enjoyed their drama of national pilgrimage to paradise—a drama which he wrote, and in which he starred. His was the role of priest-magician; one who was invincible, a many-lived cat who survived the machinations of the powerful and ubiquitous enemies his programme generated. And with each reported escape from plotters and assassins, his aura of magical invincibility was enhanced, so much so that, when he finally died, some of his foes would not believe the news. One of them treated the news as one more of the man's tricks!

Leaders like Sekou Toure, who approach development as if it was a redemptive passage through purgatory, are operating from a feudal, theological, paternalistic and magical world outlook; whatever their delusions, they are not addressing their people's economic problems, but rather some problems, probably psychological, of their own. As we all know, priests who recommend sacrifice usually do not include themselves among what should be sacrificed; for they usually have their eyes on the carcasses left at the altar. As for the sheep that are to be sacrificed, they usually do not have a say in selecting the rites. Were the Guinean population given a say in their development strategy, I doubt that they would have opted for it through endless sacrifices and suffering. But, of course, the responsibility for the choice, which was, no doubt, heavy, was mercifully lifted from their shoulders, and carried by the Clairvoyant Guide! Well, may Africa be saved from any more such guides!

For new directions in economic thought[*]

> I feel like an awful fool
> with the theories that they season
> to the taste of their needs.
>
> —Léon Damas

> In dealing with this subject [colonisation and civilisation], the commonest curse is to be the dupe in good faith of a collective hypocrisy that cleverly misrepresents problems, the better to legitimize the hateful solutions provided for them.
>
> —Aimé Césaire

> Everything needs to be reformed and everything thought out anew.
>
> —Frantz Fanon

In the current search for a New International Economic Order, neo-Keynesian doctrines and neo-Marxist theories of dependency dominate the approaches. They have narrowed the range of the search to the terms of foreign aid, foreign investment and technology transfers from the rich to the poor countries, and to the social and economic ends to which these might be deployed. Before this, the search for means for national development in the Third World had degenerated into a confrontation (between neo-classical economists and Marxists) over the free market vs state planning, capi-

[*]*South* (London) November 1983.

talism vs socialism, social reform vs revolution, growth vs development. Thus, Northern schools of thought have consistently set the framework within which Third World economic policies have been devised.

Commenting on the African case, the Secretary of the Economic Commission for Africa, Adebayo Adedeji, noted that

> the very strategies of development the African governments have been pursuing since independence have come from outside, derived as they were from theories of economic development that were developed during the colonial and neo-colonial periods to rationalise the colonial pattern of production in Africa. Not unexpectedly, these foreign theories of development and economic growth reinforce the economic dependence of Africa.

Thus, behind Africa's failure at development lies a poverty of economic thinking created, at least in part, by inappropriate theories imported from the North—and as in Africa, so in the other parts of the so-called developing world.

The damage from the fact of their Northern provenance has been compounded by a failure to transform or abandon them in the light of Third World experience. If anything, rather than supply empirical foundations for alternative theories that could assist their development, the experiences of Third World countries have served as grist for the debating mills of rival Northern theories. Consequently, there has been little of that fruitful interplay between local historical experience and speculative theorising which makes for the scientific solving of local problems.

The Third World obviously needs to develop its own tradition of economic thought, based on its history and its philosophies of life and society. This means that it needs its equivalents of Quesnay, Adam Smith, Ricardo, Karl Marx—

pioneering economic philosophers who will analyse Third World experiences and supply theories which can provide answers to practical economic problems.

Among other things, this development will require detailed study of whatever body of Third World economic thought there already may be. In addition, the superficial unities upon which the Third World negotiating coalition has been based, will need to be deemphasised. For, despite their common condition of underdevelopment, and their basic dependency relationship to the international capitalist system, Third World countries differ considerably in their economic characteristics and potentials.

A preliminary classification would recognise these groups:
a) large nations, with diverse resources, which could develop with minimal linkages to other economies; such as China and India;
b) medium-sized and small states which are optimising their advantages and becoming specialised units within the international capitalist and socialist systems. These include the OPEC nations, and such Newly Industrialising Countries (NICs) as Taiwan, Singapore and the two Koreas;
c) Least Developed Countries (LDCs) which lack most of the endowments necessary for economic viability, and constitute the basket cases which have been referred to as a Fourth World;
d) the other nations which, though not as advantaged as the NICs or the OPEC states, are not as desperate as the LDCs. With a bit of luck and astute management, some could imitate the NICs or the OPEC states; and with a bit of ill luck and mismanagement others would follow the LDCs into the Fourth World.

Given such different groups, differences are inevitable in the development aims and strategies open to various Third World countries. If development studies are to provide fruitful strategies for specific countries, various other changes in economic thinking would be necessary. First, we would have to shunt aside the tired issues, ineffectual assumptions, jaded themes and unproductive habits of thought which have been taken over from intra-Northern debates. For instance, the ideological debate between free marketers and state planners would have to be fruitfully transformed into the practical question of what, in a given culture and economy, would be best left to the market to regulate, and what best planned by bureaucrats. Similarly, the tired issue of economics vs political economy would have to be replaced by the far more useful view that economies are aspects of socio-cultural totalities, and that economic development is only part of overall socio-cultural evolution, and should be approached accordingly.

Second, we would have to be constantly on the alert for false panaceas peddled to us by Northern interests. Theories, frames of reference, and even detailed recommendations like that for technology transfers would have to be subjected to tests of appropriateness. The hidden agendas of Northern recommendations, such as the Green Revolution, would have to be routinely probed.

Third, we would need to understand the various economies of the world and their historical evolution. We would need to discover not only how and why some have succeeded at development, but also how and why other have failed. And the more cases we know thoroughly, the better our understanding of development processes and strategies. For instance, the determination of a national leadership, and its ability to manipulate its internal and external environment, could make all the difference between successful development and failure.

Fourth, we must look for fresh concepts of development, and for strategies for implementing them in the context of a given country's endowments, aims and opportunities. In this quest, it would be invaluable to build upon groundwork already done by such theorists and pioneers of self-reliance as Gandhi, Mao and Nyerere.

It is particularly important to emphasise the existence of such work, for it means that, in opting to liberate themselves from Northern traditions of economic thought, the Third World would not be abandoning light, however inadequate, to stumble and forage in total darkness. Such existing points of departure should make it easier to develop an alternative tradition.

Despite the increasing frequency with which Third World leaders and economists now invoke self-reliance, it remains a slogan from the sidelines of affairs. Economic thought and policies continue to be formulated under the hegemony of Northern theories and ground rules which have little to say on self-reliance. This is partly because of the globalist and internationalist bias of the theories (a bias now inculcated in most of the Third World elites), and partly because self-reliance, though a catchy slogan, has yet to be made part of a theory from which economic policies are readily derivable. But the urgency for developing a theory of self-reliant development should become clear from the following prospect.

If the negotiations for a New International Economic Order should fail to produce development in the Third World, what then? Or if the international capitalist system should disintegrate, or contract and abandon all the countries it has no further use for, what would the discarded nations do?

Left to their own devices, discarded countries would have no choice but to embark upon self-reliant development if they want any development at all. They would then have to redefine their problems of development, not in terms of global systems or world market relations, but in local and regional terms. Gandhi's concept of *swadeshi* ("that spirit in us which restricts us to the use of our immediate surroundings to the exclusion of the more remote"), and Mao's stress on *tzu li kong sheng* ("regeneration through our own efforts") would then become inescapable.

In preparing for that time, a theory of economic self-reliance must raise and answer some vital questions. For instance: What are the systemic conditions for economic self-reliance? Is there, perhaps, some minimum size without which an economic unit cannot develop self-reliantly? Are there conditions of ecology, culture and resource endowment which must be met? What structures are necessary for weaving the requisite endowments into a self-reliant system? What kinds of leadership are most conducive to self-reliant development? What would it require to initiate a self-reliant economic dynamic when the necessary conditions are satisfied?

If Third World leaders and economists tackle such questions, the principal intellectual barriers to the decolonisation of the Third World economy would be breached. The adventure of breaching the barriers ought to be exhilarating, and should attract the most able minds in the Third World.

Part Two: History

The history of Black Africa will remain suspended in air and cannot be written correctly until African historians dare to connect it with the history of Egypt.... The ancient Egyptians were Negroes. The moral fruit of their civilization is to be counted among the assets of the Black world. Instead of presenting itself to history as an insolvent debtor, that Black world is the very initiator of the "western" civilization flaunted before our eyes today.

—Cheikh Anta Diop

Decolonising African history[*]

A visitor to Thebes in the Valley of the Kings can view the Moslem inferno in detail (in the tomb of Seti I, of the Nineteenth Dynasty), 1700 years before the Koran. Osiris at the tribunal of the dead is indeed the "lord" of revealed religions, sitting enthroned on Judgement Day, and we know that certain Biblical passages are practically copies of Egyptian moral texts.... To his great surprise and satisfaction, [the incredulous Black African] will discover that most of the ideas used today to domesticate, atrophy, dissolve, or steal his "soul", were conceived by his own ancestors. To become conscious of that fact is perhaps the first step toward a genuine retrieval of himself.

—Cheikh Anta Diop

... But fear
Has been known to make people
Do things more strange than
African belief in Jehovah or Allah

—Keorapetse Kgositsile

History can play the same role as the psychoanalyst. To understand one's past is to be freed of it.

—Joseph Ki-Zerbo

---

[*] First presented at the Conference on "Third World: Development or Crisis?", held at Penang, Malaysia, in November 1984, and organised by the Consumers' Association of Penang. First published in *The Guardian* (Lagos) December 1984.

Africa is in a deep crisis. Its symptoms include a heavy debt burden, declining agricultural output, failure at industrialisation, drought, famine, increasing dependence on foreign aid, and the deterioration of economic and social services. These are well documented in newspapers and research reports. But what are their causes?

It has become fashionable to see as the crux of the crisis the unequal nature of the relationships between the West and Africa; an inequality which was created and is maintained by the West. But I don't see that as the entire explanation for the crisis. The relationship between the West and Africa involves two sides, and we ought not to pretend to ourselves that it is maintained by the villainous will and might of the West alone. In honesty we must ask: Are all the causes of our condition exogenous? Must we simply bewail the fetter of colonialism, neo-colonialism and imperialism without finding out what we ought to do to free ourselves from our lamented condition?

If we truly wish to bring Western domination of Africa to an end, we must take control of our history, and steer it away from where the West would like to maroon it. But that calls, not for absolving ourselves from all responsibility for our fate, nor for the lamentations and tantrums of the campaign for a New International Economic Order (NIEO), nor for elegant begging sessions like Cancún, but for cultural and historical initiative on our part.

As I see it, whatever may be the causes of our condition, it is entirely our responsibility to end it. At the heart of our inability to do so is a failure of conscious historical initiative by societies suffering from complexes and disorientations they acquired under colonisation by European conquerors. But how do we get rid of those complexes and disorientations? This is where I see the importance of history as cultural therapy.

The complexes I speak of have been partly fostered by a certain kind of history created by imperialism to beat the sense of autonomous initiative out of us. And the task for African historians who care to contribute to Africa's development is to decolonise the history of Africa by developing a more accurate and truthful history, free from colonialist distortions. Such a history might be able to show us that we are not, contrary to the claims of colonialist history, congenitally devoid of historical initiative; that we have an obligation to clearsightedly resume that initiative; and that the onus is on us to chart our own path out of maldevelopment to development, and to vigorously break up the structures of Western domination—cooly, methodically, without wallowing in self-pity, or contenting ourselves with the tantrums of frustrated dependents.

While, of course, the managers of the affairs of African countries will be understandably preoccupied with the day-to-day difficulties and crises brought on by the present structures of international relations, it is up to the African intelligentsia to take a longer range view of the matter and (a) supply an analytical history of the development and management of the unwanted system of relations—an analytical history which makes clear what we ourselves contribute to our plight; (b) prospect for weak points in the present system and discover how to turn them to Africa's advantage; (c) seek out and articulate potentialities for new and advantageous linkages—cultural, political and economic—between the countries of Africa, and work out how such potentialities may be harnessed for African development; (d) re-educate Africans for the task of liberating themselves from the hegemonic arrangements which have produced the African crisis.

Before we attempt to do all that, we need to shift intellectual gear from what Europe has done to us (How Europe Underdeveloped Africa), to what we are doing to ourselves (How Africans Maldevelop Africa), and to what we must do for ourselves in order to get out of our condition (How Africans Can Develop Africa). Not to learn to shift gears back and forth between these positions would be the depth of irresponsibility on our part. For we would then be unable to bring to bear on the solution to our problem knowledge of its key aspects. But before we can put ourselves in the proper frame of mind for such shifting of gears, we must submit to the therapy of a decolonised history.

History as cultural therapy

The possibility of history providing cultural therapy for development has been remarked upon by Joseph Ki-Zerbo, an African historian from Burkina Faso, who is one of the editors of the *UNESCO General History of Africa*. In an unpublished 1982 interview, he said:

> History can play the same role as the psychoanalyst. As long as we don't know how to explain certain events, certain behaviour which exists today in the individual and collective planes, we will remain prisoners of our past because we don't understand it. But if one doesn't understand his history, even his own private history, he can cultivate complexes, believing, for example, that one is damned. History allows us to understand who we are. If one doesn't know who one is, one can't know what one wants or what one will become. I think that the almost exclusive role of history is to lay down this fundamental base of development. Very often today Africans centre around the means of development without asking two basic questions: "where are we going? And what do we have to do to get there?" As long as these questions are unanswered, and we rush into development, we're bound to fail.

Following the line of thought expressed above by Ki-Zerbo, I have come to believe that our past, by the tasks it implicitly sets for us, is a compass to our future; that a map of our past is the pathfinder to our destiny. Thus, if we misread the map of our past, or consult an incorrect map, we will misdirect our efforts in shaping our future.

Indeed, history, as a recapitulation and interpretation of our past, has the power to release our energies and direct our initiatives. Recognising this, numerous African societies used the praise poem as a device to motivate socially valuable behaviour. These poems would remind their subject of his famed attributes and deeds, of the characteristics of his lineage, and so put him in a frame of mind to emulate the recapitulated virtues, and to strive to surpass the praised deeds. In the case of songs of abuse, the derogatory recapitulation can fetter undesirable initiatives. Thus, incidentally, the combined use, in many African societies, of praise poems and songs of abuse to motivate and confine behaviour within socially useful directions.

On the other hand, if its particulars are false, or its interpretation misleading, a mischievous recapitulation of history can quite easily confuse our aims and our sense of direction, and plunge us into an impotent, self-destructive rut. I believe that colonialist history was aimed at blocking African initiatives by supplying us with an incorrect and distorted map of the African past. In short, the colonialist history of Africa was composed and used as a song of disorientation. The false image of Africa it concocted was a paralysing bullet for our souls. If we are to rouse ourselves from the induced paralysis, we have to counter that image, change that song, draw up a correct map.

But how exactly did colonialist historiography give Africa a false history? And what should a decolonised African historiography do to supply an accurate one?

The colonialist version of African history

> The countries and peoples of Africa are always presented as people who never progressed, who

> were fixed at one stage of development and stayed there for hundreds and thousands of years. This isn't true.
> —Joseph Ki-Zerbo
> (unpublished interview, 1982)

Under the colonial dispensation, the most virulent attack on the cultural and historical initiative of non-Europeans was reserved for the black race, the aborigines of Africa. The view was assiduously propagated that, before the coming of Europeans, Africa had been a dark continent of dark skinned savages living in primitive jungles with other wild animals. Africans were said to be without industry, religion, history, and even without the capacity to reason. This image of Africans was part of a racist fiction which modern Europeans, during their emergence to world dominion, chose to live by because it shored up their self-esteem and facilitated their enterprise of enslavement, conquest and colonisation.

As corollaries to this fiction, the European mind propounded three dogmas: (1) that Africans have contributed nothing to civilisation in Africa; (2) that Africans have contributed nothing to non-African civilisations; and (3) that anything found in Africa which was worthy of European respect had to have been put there by white invaders of some earlier period. This last is the "external influence" or infusionist dogma.

A notorious version of the infusionist dogma was the Hamitic Hypothesis promulgated by C. G. Seligman in 1930. He declared:

> Indeed it would not be very wide of the mark to say that the history of Africa south of the Sahara is no more than the story of the permeation through the ages, in different degrees and at various times, of the [indigenous Negroes and Bushmen] by Hamitic blood and culture. The Hamites were, in fact, the great civilizing force of black

Africa from a relatively early period.... The Hamites ... are "Europeans", i.e. belong to the same great branch of mankind as the whites...[1]

According to J. D. Fage, doyen of the neo-colonial British school of African historiography, up till the 1950s:

It was still a commonplace among professional university teachers that "Africa had no history before the coming of Europeans", or that "the civilizations of Africa are the civilizations of immigrant peoples; its history the record of these peoples and of their interaction with the indigenous stocks" (to quote or to adapt two notorious phrases).[2]

But why were these views promulgated? According to Fage:

Most of those who, during the colonial period, sought to reconstruct the earliest history of Africa, were themselves outsiders, members of the colonising nations of western Europe. They came from a society which technologically and materially was vastly more powerful than was late nineteenth-century Africa, and which was therefore able to conquer, rule, dominate and change Negro African societies in a most dramatic fashion. When these men began to discover the evidence for the earliest West African civilisations, they were therefore predisposed to think that these could not have been created by the Negro peoples they themselves had so easily conquered and come to rule. They believed, therefore, that they must have resulted from earlier invasions by alien conquerors comparable

---

1) C. G. Seliman, *Races of Africa*, London: OUP, 1966 (4th edn.) pp 8, 61.
2) "Continuity and change in the writing of West African History", *African Affairs*, July 1971, p. 237.

to themselves. The wished-for conquerors could be found near at hand in the non-Negro inhabitants of north-east and north Africa, who had indeed long been impinging on the Negroes of the Sudan.

There is no really satisfactory collective name for the non-Negro peoples of north and north-east Africa such as the Berbers and the ancient Egyptians. They are commonly called Hamites, but the terms 'Hamite' and 'Hamitic' can properly be applied not to the peoples, but only to the languages they speak (or which they spoke before the Arab and Muslim conquest)... The Hamitic-speaking peoples, ... are often quite dark-skinned. But in features and in physical type they are fairly easily distinguishable from the Negroes, and the European historians and anthropologists of the colonial period came to think of them as 'whites' like themselves....

There thus developed an overall scheme for the interpretation of African history which may be termed 'the Hamitic hypothesis'. This assumed that the African 'Hamites' were 'whites' akin to the Europeans, and that they and their culture were inherently superior to the Negroes and their culture, so that wherever an apparently Negro people had made a striking advance, the explanation must be sought in 'Hamitic' influence or infiltration....

Seligman in fact leaves a general impression of wave after wave of incoming Hamitic pastoralists, 'better armed as well as quicker witted than the dark agricultural Negroes', imposing themselves on the Negroes, mixing with them, and galvanising them into political and economic advancement.[3]

---

3) *A History of West Africa*, Cambridge University Press, 1969, pp 6-7.

But after thus exposing the racism and imperialist wishful thinking which created the infusionist doctrine of African historiography, Fage goes on:

> Nevertheless, in at least two aspects, the Hamitic hypothesis was not altogether as absurd an interpretation of the African past as we may now be inclined to think. Agriculture was first developed in Africa in the lower Nile valley, and its people, the ancient Egyptians, spoke a 'Hamitic' language. On the basis of their agriculture, they went on, by about 3000 B.C., to develop one of the first great civilisations in world history. Among the major features of this civilisation was the concept of their king as supra-human, a god who could only marry his equally godly sister, and who was the absolute arbiter over the land and all human activities on it, especially perhaps of the times of sowing and harvesting. In these and in many other details, many Negro African kingdoms seem to have had so similar a type of kingship—usually referred to as 'divine kingship'—that it is tempting to conclude, as many good historians still do, that it must have spread throughout Africa from this Egyptian and 'Hamitic' source.[4]

To see through this game of imperialist and racist historiography, please observe that "Negro" means black or dark-skinned, and that, even on Fage's own disingenuous account, these 'white' Hamites "are often quite dark-skinned". Which means that these so-called 'white' Hamites, being dark-skinned, are not non-Negro at all, but Negroes, just like the rest of the aboriginal Africans. Consequently, talk of Hamitic influence upon Negroes means no more than

---

4) *Ibid.*, p.8.

the influence of some blacks/negroes upon other blacks/negroes—an admission which, in light of the undisputably great cultural creativity of the ancient Egyptian, would make nonsense of the white supremacist effort to present blacks/negroes as incapable of creating civilisation or sustaining historical initiative.

Furthermore, it exposes the notion of 'white' Hamites for what it is—a way of turning some blacks into 'honorary whites' so as to expropriate their great achievements for the white race.

Clearly, such versions of African history are simply scholarly versions of vulgar white-skin-chauvinism. Their message was quite simple: Africans have contributed nothing to civilization; all historical advances have been made by Europeans and other branches of the white race. But though that message is demonstrably false, the impact of such propaganda on Africans was far reaching. For those who came to accept it, it bred complexes of racial inadequacy, a sense of fated inferiority, a belief in the congenital superiority of whites, and a sense of the pointlessness of African initiative. All of which would foster a paralysis of the will when contemplating the daunting task of developing Africa from its present backwardness to a point where it could achieve parity with the advanced world of today. For, as it were, how could any people, if they believe they have never invented anything, ever catch up with the creators of the multifarious inventions of the modern industrial world?

Professor Ki-Zerbo, in his 1982 interview, reports and reacts to an encounter with an African who was apparently a victim of that colonialist propaganda.

> I remember being at a conference in Kinshasa some 6 years ago, and I was struck by one of the questions asked by a Zairean student: "Professor, why are we at the stage where we are today? Why are we behind others? Are we damned?" It is a very serious question. Someone who really knows

the history of Africa wouldn't ask such a question because he rationally sees that that can't be—because there is a logic in historical development. These are things which can be explained rationally, naturally. There is no need to have recourse to curses or fatalism. Men, being equals in all parts of the planet, have the same initial stock and initial capital in terms of intelligence, and from the point of view of will; and although man has had different developments, it is because there have been causes, conditions, different historical circumstances. That is what we need to succeed in making clear in works of history, and as long as we don't do this we are prisoners.

Fortunately, even as that Zairean student was asking whether Africans were damned, results were emerging from the efforts of various pan-African scholars to challenge that colonialist version of African history upon which his question was predicated. Had he been aware of those results, or known even the outline of the image of Africans which these results provide, not only would he not have asked that question, but the very doubts about African capabilities out of which his question grew would not have arisen at all.

Instead, seeing the present backwardness of Africa, and knowing the heights of achievement which Africans attained in previous eras, he might have reacted by exhorting contemporary Africans to arise and fulfil their natural potential. Like the hunter (in the Zulu tale retold by J. K. Aggrey and Melvin Tolson) who found an eagle eating dung along with a flock of chicken in a barnyard, and generally conducting itself as if it was a chicken, he would have cried: "Aquila fly! You are not a chicken but an eagle."

The beginnings of the decolonising of African history

Against the psychologically damaging historiography of

Africa sponsored by colonialist racism, Pan-African historians have, in the past three decades, advanced along two main lines.

The first has set out to fully recover ancient Egypt for Africa and the black race. This has been done by unearthing the abundant evidence that it was blacks who founded the Egypt of the Pharaohs, and kept its civilisation going for 3,000 years before it was finally overrun by white invaders from western Asia and Europe. Furthermore, basing itself on comparative studies of African languages, arts and artefacts, technologies, social organisation, political systems, beliefs, cosmologies and other culture forms, this line of research has also shown that Pharaonic Egypt was no aberration from the African pattern of culture; it was simply the astonishing peak of the Nile Valley variant of a basic pattern of culture which all Africa shared, and still shares. Thus, the glories of ancient Egypt belong to the Black World; and whatever impact the Nile Valley civilisations have had on the rest of Africa does not amount to an infusion of civilisation into the Black World by non-black outsiders.

The leading force in this line of historical research has been the Senegalese Egyptologist, Cheikh Anta Diop. His principal work on the matter is *Antériorité des Civilisations Nègres: Mythe ou Vérité Historique?* [1967] It has been published in English as *The African Origin of Civilization; Myth or Reality?*[5]

The other line of attack has consisted in documenting the process which reduced the black civilisations to the deplorable conditions they were in by the 19th century when Europe so easily overran them. The leading account, to date, of this decline and fall of black civilisations is in *The Destruction of Black Civilization*[6] by Chancellor Williams, an Afro-American historian.

---

5) Translated by Mercer Cook, published by Lawrence Hill and Company, Westport, Connecticut, 1974.
6) Chicago: Third World Press, 1974.

Two subsidiary lines of Pan-African historical inquiry have exploded the dogma which holds that Africans have given nothing to other civilisations. The first reveals Africa's great contributions to European civilisation. Works such as *Stolen Legacy*[7] by George G. M. James, another Afro-American, have actually reversed the picture of indebtedness by showing the black Egyptian contribution to the emergence of white Europe from barbarism to civilisation. When the scattered fragments of this line of inquiry are brought together, it emerges that Africa and Asia, between them, taught Europe civilisation. Egypt and the Mesopotamian civilisations, through their empires in the eastern Mediterranean, taught the Phoenicians, Hebrews and Greeks, who then supplied Europe with the cultural beliefs, techniques and scientific knowledge out of which it has built its present world-dominating civilisation.

It is not, of course, that the African origins of European civilisation have never been known. It is simply that modern Europe, out of white-skin-chauvinism, sought to distort and suppress the evidence. In setting up white Greece as the autogenous progenitor of European civilisation, it went even against evidence contained in the writings of the ancient Greeks themselves. Herodotus, "father of history" among the Greeks, not only acknowledged the antiquity of Egyptian civilisation, and its having served as the civiliser of the Greeks; he also gave his eye-witness testimony that the ancient Egyptians were black skinned and wooly haired. Aristotle, though in an insulting vein, supports Herodotus on the race of the Egyptians when he remarked that the Egyptians and Ethiopians were cowards because of their "excessively black colour".[8] All of which, would make the Egyptians blacks/negroes.

The testimony of the full historical record is quite clear.

---

7) San Francisco: Julian Richardson Associates, 1976.
8) *Aristotle: Minor Works*, translated by W.S. Hett, in Loeb Classical Library, Harvard University Press, 1956, p.127.

Europe, and especially western Europe, is a Johnny-come-lately to civilisation. During the over 3,000 years before Julius Caesar's Roman legions brought civilisation to the tribes of Gaul, Celtic Britain and Druidic Germany in the first century B.C., the black African civilisations of the Nile Valley—Pharaonic Egypt, Nubia, Cush and Ethiopia—had literate cultures; had taught the art of alphabet writing to the Phoenicians, Hebrews and Greeks; had given them their religions and gods; and schooled them in mathematics, astronomy, architecture, medicine, philosophy, engineering, and other arts and sciences.

In his *Egypt of the Pharaohs*, Sir Alan Gardiner, one of the 20th century's most distinguished Egyptologists, makes clear that Egyptian hieroglyphic writing is the progenitor, through the Phoenician, Hebrew and Greek scripts, of the modern Western or Roman alphabet.[9] And according to Herodotus, among the things Greece acquired directly from Egypt were astronomy, astrology, geometry, the correct calendar, "almost all the names of the gods", and the practice of "solemn assemblies, processions and litanies to the gods."[10]

The list of Greeks who, thirsty for knowledge, journeyed to Egypt to acquire the learning with which white-skin-chauvinist history now credits them as originators, is a who's who of the "fathers" of Greek intellectual culture: Thales, Solon, Hecataeus, Pythagoras, Democritus, Herodotus, Plato, Eudoxus are only a few. Pythagoras, for instance, spent 22 years there, studying astronomy, geometry, medicine, philosophy and the religious mysteries from various Egyptian priests. He returned to Greece to teach what he had learned.

What these Greeks went to acquire was learning which the Egyptians had developed over the preceding 2,500 years, and had used to build, among other things, pyramids,

---

9) Alan Gardiner, *Egypt of the Pharaohs*, OUP, 1964 [1961] pp. 25-26.
10) *Herodotus: The Histories*, translated by G. Rawlinson, in Great Books of the Western World, Encyclopedia Britannica, Chicago, 1952, pp. 49, 50, 60-65, 69, 70.

irrigation systems and the calendar. According to George Sarton, "it is childish to assume that science began in Greece. The 'Greek miracle' was prepared by millennia of work in Egypt, Mesopotamia and possibly other regions. Greek science was less an invention than a revival."[11]

However, the white-skin-chauvinism of modern Europe would not accept the African share in the origin of its civilisation, lest it be thereby forced to acknowledge that blacks were capable of civilisation. In accounting for its own civilisation, modern Europe therefore stole the legacy of ancient Egypt by attributing to white Greece a cultural originality which actually belonged to Egypt and Mesopotamia. And when it came to matters of African history, modern Europe tried to annex the ancient Egyptians for the white race through the bogus notion of a 'white' but dark-skinned race of Hamites.

In the other subsidiary line of advance, Pan-African scholars, led by the Afro-Caribbean Ivan Van Sertima, have assembled evidence of pre-Columbian connections between Africa and the Americas. They have uncovered two main cases: first, between Nile Valley Africans (Egyptians and Nubians) and the Olmecs of the Gulf of Mexico, a contact which took place in the first millennium B.C.; and, second, between the Mande speaking West Africans of the upper Niger Valley and Central American Indians in what are now the Caribbean, Mexico, Columbia, Panama, Ecuador, and Peru, a contact which took place in the millennium before Columbus. These contacts left a trail of major cultural exports from Africa to the Americas, including pyramid tombs and temples, scripts and alphabets, calendar systems, and sculptures. The findings of this line of research may be followed in Van Sertima's book, *They Came Before Columbus: The African Presence in Ancient America*;[12] and in the *Journal of African Civilizations* which he edits.

11) *A History of Science*, Harvard University Press, 1959, p ix.
12) New York: Random House, 1977.

The image of Africans which begins to emerge from these pan-African investigations is quite the opposite of that projected by colonialist history. Africans turn out to be, not stuck in primitivism from the dawn of time, not passive recipients of civilising influences from outside, but rather cultural innovators of the highest order, and disseminators of civilisation to various continents. A realisation of the astounding cultural initiatives of Africans throughout history creates space and credibility for the kind of African history which is now being attempted under the aegis of UNESCO.

The aim, in this kind of African historiography, is to produce a scientific history in which emphasis is placed on internal developments in Africa, on African cultural initiatives and social evolution, and not on the doings of invaders from outside. The scope of that history extends from the emergence of the human species in Africa over 3 million years ago; through the development at diverse African locations of tools, agriculture, iron works, ancient carbon-steel making, writing scripts, astronomical observational structures and calendar systems; through the rise of the world's first high civilization in the Nile Valley; through the pre-16th century A.D. empires of Africa, some with advanced arts and metallurgical crafts which produced instruments refined enough to perform eye-cataract surgery in the 13th century; on to the decline of these African civilisations under blows from successive white invasions, and from the holocaust of the European and Arab slave trades. It then moves on to the trauma of European conquest and colonisation, and to the faltering new beginnings in this post-colonial era.

This kind of historiography, of necessity, uses a wide variety of sourses, including art forms, oral traditions, archeological findings, linguistic analysis as well as written documents.

The ingredients of this new history explode the image of Africans as people "who invented nothing, explored nothing". Nobody schooled in it would ask the sort of question which that Zairean student asked Professor Ki-Zerbo. For it would be clear that the African condition of the past few centuries is an aberration from the ancient pattern; that it has its causes; and that given the intelligence and will with which Africans, like any other people, are endowed, and which Africans abundantly demonstrated over the millennia, the present condition is not permanent, is not a prison, and does not signify that Africans are damned.

All of which should provoke an activist and confident attitude to the challenges of contemporary development. For if our ancestors did great things before, we can do them once again. The result of such an acknowledgement is that confidence replaces the inhibiting complexes implanted by colonialist history and racist propaganda. And once we emerge from the colonialist intimidation of our spirit, a task that seemed futile would be seen as accomplishable. And to believe that you can do a thing is already half way to doing it.

Some tasks for the new African historiography

Notwithstanding the far-reaching consequences of the research results I have described above, the decolonisation of African historiography is still in its infancy. It is therefore pertinent to ask: What remains to be done? And what are the nature and scope of the project?

The history we write has to meet the needs of our times. Frantz Fanon has taught us that "each generation must, out of relative obscurity, discover its mission, fulfil it, or betray it." As I see it, our mission is not to transfer Western technology and transplant Western culture onto African soil; it is, rather, to prepare the grounds for a new flowering of African civilisation. The projects which will therefore occupy us, well into the 21st century, are two: the social reorganisation and economic development which will undo the damage done to Africa by the five century holocaust of slaving, conquest and colonisation; and the preparation of the grounds for the next phase of African civilisation. For this great task of African reconstruction, we need a new post-colonial psychology, a fresh sense of identity, an energising consciousness, and therefore a vitalising perception of our history. Our explorations of our past for the purpose of drawing a useful map of it must therefore be guided by fresh themes supplied by our project; while the results of scientific investigations will supply the details which will flesh out the story.

In this connection, there are two mental attitudes, derived from our colonial experience, which our new history should help us to break out of.

Because the West has played a dominant part in shaping our recent past, we all too often allow ourselves to see the key to our affairs as lying in Europe or North America where the dynamo of history is supposedly lodged. To cure us of this tendency, it is necessary, in decolonising African history, to reconnect us fruitfully with our entire pre-colonial past and so reduce the European intervention to its proper minitude. That would help to restore our sense of where the moving centre of our history is—in Africa. After all, however profound its short run impact, what are five centuries of destabilising contact, including one century of intense colonisation, within a recorded history of over 50 centuries?

To appreciate the short duration of the European intervention (that of the Arabs has lasted nearly three times as long!) is to alter our perception of the central themes, not just in all of African history, but even in the history of the intervention. The theme of the era of European intervention ceases to be, as colonialist historiography would have it, the civilising of Africa by the Europeans; it, rather, becomes the reactions and adaptations to European influence by the societies and cultures of Africa.

This change of theme, though apparently subtle, is quite

monumental. The West shifts from being seen as overlord, dominator, and prime mover; it is seen instead as a temporary catalyst in a far longer and more dynamic process. Its intervention becomes an interruption in a historical journey of many millennia. To recognise that is to see that the management of the journey is in our hands; that we should again take conscious charge of the reins; that the path is still ours to chart.

In all this, I am reminded of that period, lasting a couple of centuries in the 3,000 years history of Pharaonic Egypt, when the kingdom was dominated by white Asiatics, known to us as Hyksos. But eventually, the native Africans rallied their energies, expelled the aliens, and resumed the march of their own history. We too need to do likewise.

There is also a certain touch of embattled, back-to-the-wall despair noticeable in African attitudes today. It was not so even 30 years ago during the anti-colonial struggle, with its mood of exhilaration and exuberant expectations of post-colonial wonders. I believe our chances of carrying off the project of African reconstruction would be greatly improved by a shift in attitude. Instead of a desperate hopelessness, what we need is a sense of adventure, a realisation that African reconstruction can be accomplished only in a mood of adventurous experimentation. What we need to appreciate is the value of the psychological counterpart of the military dictum that attack is the best form of defence. A sense of adventure, in which we eagerly look out for, and then explore and exploit new possibilities, would serve us far better than a siege mentality which leads us to fear exploration, and to dig ourselves into unviable trenches.

This means that the new African historiography must seek out and highlight the adventurous and highly creative periods in African history so we can draw inspiration from them. Periods such as the late pre-dynastic times in the lower Nile Valley and the first four dynasties of Pharaonic Egypt (c. 3500 B.C. to c. 2500 B.C.) when Egypt was founded by uniting two preexisting lands; when phenomenal advances were made in social organisation as well as in the arts and sciences; and when architecture and engineering advanced rapidly and culminated in such monumental works as the pyramids and the diversion of the Nile to create a site for the capital of the kingdom.

Other inspirational periods which deserve to be highlighted would be the development of agriculture in the upper Niger Valley *c.* 4000 B.C.; the origination period, in the region of present-day Mauritania, of the precursor societies to the empire of Ghana, whose heritage was continued, down to the 16th century A.D., by the successor empires of Mali and Songhai. Yet another period for highlighting would be the creative period of the Nok culture complex in the lower Niger Basin, c. 2,000 years ago. Of course, this list is not exhaustive.

On the technical, as distinct from the thematic side, the decolonisation of African historiography requires at least four major things:
1) the expansion of the horizon of African history to include its full temporal span, from the emergence of the human species on the African continent, down till today;
2) the recovery and correct interpreting of long available materials which were suppressed, misrepresented or sidelined by the objectives of colonial historiography;
3) vigorous research efforts to expand our knowledge and fill gaps in our inventory of events in African history;
4) a jettisoning of the colonialist habit of imposing on African history schemes of periodisation derived from those of European history. It is, unfortunately, still the practice for African historians to describe as "medieval African kingdoms and empires" those whose dates happen to lie within that period in European history that is referred to as medieval. But these so-called middle ages are in the middle between two specific ages of European history—the Graeco-Roman Era and the Italian Renaissance—and not two ages

in African history.

In contrast to this practice, there is a need to discover the internal stages of African historical evolution, and to base the periodisation of African history upon such internal markers. We need to adopt the natural historical approach. The developmental stages of the termite, the butterfly or the elephant have to be discovered by study of its developmental process; and you don't fit the development stages of the elephant into the schema derived from the natural history of the termite.

The decolonisation of Third World history

Africa has had historical contacts with other regions besides the European world. Like our awareness of ourselves, our awareness of such contacts has been mediated by the colonial experience. Decolonising African history would therefore require that the history of African relations with the non-European or Third World be amended to rectify whatever Eurocentrism may have been injected by colonialism. Let me approach the matter by raising a few questions.

What exactly is the Third World? What makes it possible to consider as one unit or species of polities these countries that are spread out over Asia, Africa and Latin America?

A shared historical experience of various brands of European colonisation and semi-colonisation would appear to be one of the defining characteristics. Others include post-independence efforts like the Bandung Conference of Afro-Asian leaders; the Non-Aligned Movement; the Group of 77; the discovery of shared economic misfortunes and the campaigns, within and outside the UN, to negotiate away such misfortunes—all these experiences have helped to create a consciousness of the Third World as a distinct economic, political and historical bloc of nations which need to build more linkages among themselves.

However, it seems to me that our historical sense of the

Third World bloc needs deepening. How much do we know of each other's history and circumstances? Has a Third World history that presents us together as one historical group been attempted? Have we no other points of cohesion besides a common struggle against the hegemony of the advanced industrial countries? And unless we get to know ourselves well, how can the Third World expect to win its struggles? Didn't some Chinese sage advise: "Know yourself; know your enemy; a thousand battles, a thousand victories"?

Lest we overlook it, one advantage the West has in its dealings with the rest of us is a coherent self-image which holds its various peoples together. And its version of the history of Western civilisation (which it daily repeats in books, in the media, from pulpits, through *Time* magazine and Hollywood films, etc.) is one of the means whereby it sustains this cohesive image of itself as a world apart. I submit that until a coherent and cohesive Third World history is internalised, the Third World may remain a grand tactical alliance; it will still lack that measure of self-awareness without which it would not prove a match for its Western adversary.

The strategy for decolonising Third World history, is to remove the West from the central place it occupies in our image of the world and its history. This would require giving the West as well as the Third World their proper places in world history.

The struggle against Western imperialism (in its two stages: the political anti-colonial struggle, and the economic anti-imperialist struggle of today) has determined our sense of the dynamics of our history. Unfortunately, that has left us preoccupied with our relationship with our former colonisers. It is as if, without the difficulties we are experiencing in our ties with them, we wouldn't have any reason for gathering together as a bloc. But is it indeed true that the destinies of the non-European world must be decisively determined by their connections with the West? Did our destinies depend on the West before 1500 A.D.? Why must we then proceed as if, for ever after, our destinies must be tied to the West and its activities? What if the West, for whatever reasons, were tomorrow to retreat into its pre-15th century isolation, and cut off its ties with us? Would a Third World bloc then lose all reason for being?

What about the pre-Columbian, pre-Da Gama, pre-Magellan and pre-Marco Polo connections between parts of what we now call the Third World? Faint as their legacies may be today, can they not be seen, not as fossils, but as prototypes of future possibilities? In other words, if international linkages between the different regions of the Third World are essential for generating the momentum for Third World development, then perhaps we ought to break away from the Eurocentrism of our perceptions of world history. Our roads to each other ought not to pass through the West.

And this is where I find a historical awareness of the contacts between the regions of the Third World—long before the West joined them up in its own fashion—full of potential for Third World liberation from Western hegemony. They are a mine for themes for a comprehensive Third World history that would provide historical bases for the linkages and solidarities we may need in the coming centuries.

I am thinking of such themes as the pre-Columbian contacts between the Nile Valley and the Americas; between West Africa and Central America. I find it somehow inspiring to learn that there was fruitful cultural exchange between Africans and Americans long before the coming of Europeans to both places, and I think we should all know more about that.

I am also thinking of the pre-Western contacts between Africa, India and South-west Asia, contacts which, I understand, go as far back as the times of Pharaonic Egypt, Ancient Mesopotamia and the flowering of the Indus Valley civilisation. These contacts evolved over the millennia and, by the pre-Da Gama era, had turned the Indian Ocean into a busy commercial and cultural highway. On the east coast of Africa, these contacts led to the ripening of Kiswahili culture from a cross-fertilisation of an African flower with cultural pollen from the Persian Gulf and India. I think we all should know more about all that.

And I am also thinking of the pre-Marco Polo contacts between India, China and South-east Asia. What were they? How were they organised? What did they lead to? I think we should all know more about that.

And I am also thinking of the pre-Western contacts between east Asia and east Africa; of the China-East Africa voyages which ended in the 14th century; and of that movement of peoples from distant parts of tropical Asia to the African island of Madagascar. I certainly would like to know more about all that.

Besides emphasising the historical initiatives and past connections between Third World peoples, another important part of the strategy for ending the Eurocentrism of the Third World is to rewrite world history and accurately reduce Europe to its proper place within it. This would require us, in particular, to allow the facts to restructure our understanding of the Mediterranean, Atlantic and Indian Ocean civilisations, and their evolutionary inter-relations.

Consider the following dates and facts. Recorded history in the Nile Valley goes back at least to 3200 B.C., i.e. over 5,000 years ago. Recorded history in the Tigris-Euphrates valley goes back about as long. Recorded history in the Indus Valley goes back to 2500 B.C., i.e. 4,500 years ago. Recorded history for the earliest civilisation on continental Europe, i.e. Greece, goes back to about 1000 B.C., i.e. only 3,000 years ago, if we assume that Homer flourished in the 10th century B.C., and that the events he wrote about are historical and not mythical.

For recorded history on the Atlantic front of Europe, we must wait till the first century B.C., when Julius Caesar pushed Roman power and civilisation into the then backwoods of Gaul, Germany and Britain. Thus, it was not until 2,000 years ago that the peoples of the swaggering modern West appeared in recorded history. But even then, they remained in the backwaters of world affairs, and only rose to prominence within the last 500 years. And in doing so, they built upon the accumulated legacies of the earlier civilisations, including gunpowder from far away China.

Within the context of such facts, the rise of Western Europe to world prominence is not as awe inspiring as imperialist purposes and racist historiography would make it. Our sense of ourselves and our capabilities ought therefore not to be unduly humbled by the undoubtedly far-reaching impact of the West upon our lives. And we should treat the truculence and the tense outlook of the West as no more than the brash crowings of an upstart younger brother, one full of himself from the heady experience of finally coming of age. When the novelty of his new status wears off, he too will mellow down. In the meantime, we would do well not to get preoccupied with his struttings and muscle-flexings, lest we lose our sense of balance.

Rewriting world history to put Europe in its proper place would help us to turn our attention more fully on ourselves. And the more we learn of the pre-Western relations between the diverse parts of the Third World, the better for our efforts at building new linkages for our economic liberation and development. The more we know of such things, our mutual respect for our various peoples would increase, and the easier it would be, I think, to dissolve the dividing walls of ignorance, and the subtle barriers to cooperation posed by our internalisation, under colonialism, of the hierarchies of peoples concocted by white, Western racism.

But over and above all that, there is one crucial benefit I believe would result from decolonising Third World history by ending its Eurocentrism. The more we find out about the histories of the non-Western world, the more we would discover of the diverse characters of the high cultures the human species has produced. That may well get us to accept that development should not be considered synonymous with Westernisation. Which, I believe, would enlarge our sense of the possible aims of social development, and perhaps free our imaginations to explore other options which might prove healthier for the species than the Western model which we still seem so determined to strive after.

In this regard, let us recall that, according to the physicists, it will still take billions of years for the sun to burn itself out, and for entropy to render our solar system dead. So, despite the 5,000 years of recorded human history, human history could, in principle, still go on for billions of years, provided our social systems remain compatible with the earthly environment and with the solar system. So it is vital that we explore alternatives to the Western system which has so quickly brought us all to the brink of nuclear armageddon and environmental collapse.

To help us gain perspective and courage for that exploration, the Nigerian novelist, Chinua Achebe, has eloquently reminded us that the West has not put the final touches to creation, and that it is morning yet on creation day.

The scramble for Africa: old and new[*]

For Africans familiar with their history, the year 1884 signifies the partition of Africa which put its history on a new trajectory and profoundly altered African life and culture. No sooner was the 1884 Berlin conference of European powers over than European soldiers set out to conquer Africa for their respective countries. By 1914, the result of that scramble was a quiltwork of colonial boundaries upon which present day African states are still attempting to build modern nation-states.

For the first 60 years after Berlin, African political initiative was submerged; many African polities were either destroyed or sent into a slumber from which they did not stir until the Second World War. When Africans finally recovered their political initiative, they sought political independence, not for their precolonial polities, but for the protonations marked out by the colonial boundaries.

Furthermore, they sought independence on terms dictated by European cultural forms—like democracy, nation-state, industrial development—together with one major import from the aspirations of the black diaspora in the Americas, namely pan-Africanism. Pan-Africanism sought the solidarity of black peoples and aimed to anchor that solidarity on the political independence and unity of the black homeland, Africa.

Among the enduring legacies of 1884, the most far-reaching are the transformation, through colonisation, of African life and culture from endogenous and Afrocentric to exo-

[*] *South* (London) December 1984.

genous and Eurocentric; and the two kinds of unification movements which partition triggered off—the national integration of the peoples within each colonial boundary, and the political unification of Africa.

In the vocabulary of Kwame Nkrumah and his pan-Africanist wing of the African independence movement, the European partition of Africa was a balkanisation—that is, a division of large states into small and antagonistic states. But was Africa really balkanised?

In reality, only a few of the 19th-century African polities (like the Sokoto Caliphate and Somalia) were territorially split up by colonial boundaries. On the contrary, almost every colony brought together within its boundaries several pre-existing polities and culture groups. As a result, the colonies (40-odd) were far less numerous than pre-conquest polities (more than 1,000). And if anything, it was the small and antagonistic pre-1884 polities which were forced to mute or inhibit their antagonisms by the power of the European conquerors. In Nigeria, for example, pax Britannica neutralised the old conflict between the expanding Sokoto Caliphate of the Fulani and the disintegrating Yoruba empire of old Oyo.

In fact, although the African continent was partitioned, its constituent polities were amalgamated: and the real impact of partition was to lay the foundations for the larger polities of today.

With independence in the 1960s, the African inheritors of the colonial administrative apparatus set out to transform each ex-colony into a modern nation-state. Those inheritors who were inspired by the pan-Africanist dream also set out to unify Africa.

A quarter-century later, neither project has been completed. While the OAU has fallen far short of the aim of turning the ex-colonies into the United States of Africa, each ex-colony is still deep in the throes of transforming itself into a nation-state. A major reason for this failure appears to be the lack of any national identity or programme with sufficient appeal to wean their citizens from their ancient allegiances to ethnic polities. Having produced no equivalents of the US constitution and the American dream, African states have resorted to attempting national integration through dominance by one group or another, as with the ethnic Arabs in Sudan, the Kikuyu in Kenya, the Shona in Zimbabwe, or the Fulani in Nigeria. This strategy has understandably provoked resistance from other groups, revived antagonisms dormant under the colonial blanket, and even led to ferocious wars.

In their strategy, most African states have not had the option of the USA. There, a culturally homogeneous Anglo-Saxon group of 13 colonies founded a nation-state, and for two centuries has recruited immigrants and absorbed them through a cultural assimilation which used the enormous appeal of the US Constitution to indoctrinate them with a new national identity, and used the American dream of prosperity to materially bind them to their new nation.

The lack of such appeal partly accounts for the difficulty African states have in containing separatist and re-unification movements which appeal to strong pre-colonial identities. Ethiopia and Kenya, for example, continue to be threatened by Somalia's campaign to excise from its neighbours those parts inhabited by ethnic Somalis.

Still, Africa's colonial century has continued the political work, albeit on non-indigenous foundations, which indigenous unification movements began in the 19th century, before the colonial conquest interrupted them. For as long as the colonial boundaries hold, it could be said that Lugard, Rhodes, and the others who carved out the European colonies are the 20th-century counterparts of Menelik II, Chaka and Dan Fodio, who in the 19th century enlarged or created the polities of Ethiopia, Zululand, and the Sokoto Caliphate respectively.

As for the cultural contents of colonisation, the activities launched inside the new boundaries by the Lugards and their successors have produced a profound cultural disruption which has, within a century, rendered African life and culture exogenous.

Partition without Europeanisation might not have changed Africa profoundly, for Europe might have been content to trade with or exact tribute from African rulers. However, the needs of the industrial economies of Europe for raw materials and markets made it necessary for the conquerors to embark upon a comprehensive Europeanisation of African life. The enormity of the change they induced might be judged by estimating how much a young African adult of 1984 would have in common with his great-great-grandfather, who was probably a young man in 1884. In their languages, dress, homes, modes of transport and distances they could travel; in their beliefs, social ideals, marriage rites, and even the foods they ate, the two would be very different.

In all likelihood, the young African of 1984 would have more in common with the European of 1884 than with his own great-great-grandfather.

One not-so-obvious area in which this century-long cultural shift is afflicting Africa in 1984 is its inability to feed its population. We may be reasonably sure that Africa did not import food in 1884 except perhaps a few luxuries for the palates of coastal princes. But today, a century later, Africa is plagued by hunger and appeals by African governments for more and more food aid have become routine.

Of course, desertification, drought and wars, which have driven millions off their lands and turned them into refugees, account for some of the need. But the cultural shift in progress since 1884 has contributed a great portion of it.

With European-style education and the enormous prestige and rewards of bureaucratic work, millions of Africans have drifted from farming to various kinds of clerking. This massive shift from production to administration has weakened the farm base of Africa.

Taste has shifted away from the traditional staples to new foods. For instance, rice has, within a generation, become the single most important food item in West Africa. The demand for it is still growing enormously. Yet, because local production is developing quite sluggishly, Africa must import ever-increasing quantities from Asia and the USA.

All this is also true of wheat (for bread) and barley (for beer). Bread has become a breakfast staple in African towns and cities, yet Africa doesn't grow much wheat. Africans now drink a lot of barley-based beer, while such traditional drinks as palm wine and millet beer are out of favour.

Such flights from traditional staples have led Africa to depend on foreign food growers, and the food import bill has contributed to the serious economic crises faced by African countries.

Of course, Africa's craving for imported industrial products is well known. One consequence is the attenuation of traditional crafts and the atrophy of the ancient iron, tin, copper and gold mining which supplied the practical and artistic crafts.

This detachment of African life from its traditional supports within its local physical environment has been accompanied by a detachment from endogenous cosmographies—as witness the decline of traditional African religions and the vast inroads made, in the colonial century, by European Christianity and Arab Islam. On the secular plane, one must note the appeal of the capitalist and socialist ideologies imported from western and eastern Europe.

All in all, where in 1884 the African lived within an endogenous culture firmly anchored on African soil, African crafts and African cosmographies, the African of 1984 looks to foreign soils, foreign factories, and foreign heavens for bodily and spiritual sustenance.

The political unification of Africa (a project which had no precolonial equivalent) has, for its part, been stymied by identity confusions, and by the antagonism of various external hegemonists.

The pan-African dream, in the original form expounded by W. E. B. Du Bois, Marcus Garvey, Ras Makonnen and others, was a dream of black unification and black power to wipe out the humiliations of the past five centuries. It proved highly energising for the movement for political independence.

However, Nkrumah, for tactical reasons connected with the anti-colonial movement, sponsored a variant of pan-Africanism which drained it of its inspirational energies. In his continentalist version, African unity meant the political unification of the African continent, as distinct from the African peoples. This meant uniting the Africans together with that fraction of the white Arab world which had invaded and expropriated the northern end of the black homeland, and which had actively enslaved Africans until the European conquest restrained them. One result of this bastardisation of pan-Africanism was that the unification of the black world—blacks of both the homeland and the diaspora—was lost to view.

Though energetically sponsored by no less a charismatic leader than Nkrumah, this bastard brand of pan-Africanism has failed to stir the emotions and fire the imagination of Africans.

The prospect of unifying with the Arab occupiers of the African homeland has been as unedifying to the African psyche as unification with white South Africans would be were it proposed. Which is one unheralded reason why the OAU, that vehicle for a bastard idea, flounders and has not caught on.

At a more overt level, pan-African unification has floundered because of political, economic, cultural and ideological hegemonies emanating from the West, the East and the Arab world.

On withdrawing from its occupation of Africa, the capitalist West changed its system of domination from direct political rule to that economic and cultural hegemony known as neocolonialism. The socialist East, led by the USSR, entered into competition with the West to win Africa for socialism, and the Soviet Bloc.

With the coming of OPEC billions, and the prestige that wealth bestowed on them, the Arabs promptly reactivated their ancient hegemonic advance into Africa. Hungry for Arab money, some African rulers hurriedly adopted Islamic (Arabic) names, while some countries, notably Somalia, transformed themselves into instant Arab republics. Furthermore, some Arab countries on African soil, notably Libya, began to annex and occupy parts of the territory of their African neighbours.

Thus the East, the West and the Arabs have become active in a new scramble for Africa. Each brand of hegemonism seems determined to displace the African identity from the moving centre of the African personality, and to replace it with the ideological or religious identity it is sponsoring.

The African identity is today in the sort of danger which African polities and cultures encountered first in 1884, when European colonies and cultures moved in to displace them.

It is quite likely that a political map of Africa for the year 2000 would look like a quiltwork of Islamic or Arab republics under Arab hegemony; socialist African republics under Soviet hegemony; and Christian and capitalist republics under the hegemony of the West. Unless, that is, pan-Africanism, in its original and potent form, revives, reasserts itself, and defeats the hegemonists.

Partisan historiographies of Africa[*]

Sir,—Readers unfamiliar with the controversies in African historiography are likely to miss the depth of partisanship which invalidates most of Roland Oliver's points in his review of *Africa under Colonial Domination 1880–1935*, Volume VII of the Unesco *General History of Africa* (August 9); so they may well be persuaded to dismiss a pathbreaking work. Professor Oliver savages a book which emanates from a rival scholarly camp, which undermines his own political and ideological interests; he does so without declaring his interest, and in tones which leave the unsuspecting reader with the impression that he is objective.

He takes issue with the use of African initiatives and resistance to colonial domination as the theme of almost one-third of the chapters of the book; he does so on the grounds that "resistance to conquest was not the only, or even the most important, feature of the early colonial scene". That choice of theme, he asserts, combines with "selective amnesia" to produce grave distortions and omissions which, by making short shrift of the good works done by the colonisers and their African collaborators, mistreat the image of the conquerors. He also wonders whether, in the period covered by the book, there was anything which could be called the colonial economy—a subject to which four chapters are devoted. He laments that, in the book, African nationalist rhetoric has seeped into a tradition of historiography which, presumably, has hitherto been insulated from political intentions. And he takes swipes at the styles and historio-

[*] Letter to the Editor, *The Times Literary Supplement*, 27 September 1985.

graphic credentials of some of the contributors to the volume. But do these charges stand up to examination?

Consider the matter of political rhetoric and bias which he raises in the first, and again in the last sentence of his review. African historiography has been bedevilled by accusations and counter-accusations of propaganda masquerading as history. The colonialist historiography to which the Unesco history is a reaction has long been notorious for its propagandistic aims. In keeping with colonialist ideology, it has insisted that the colonial enterprise was a civilising mission; that Africans had no history; and that the only history of Africa was the history of what foreign invaders did in Africa. When Oliver writes of educated Africans "mediating civilization to their still benighted countrymen", one catches echoes of the rhetoric of imperialist propaganda, *à la* Kipling's "lesser breeds without the law"—a political disparagement which colonialist historiography has attempted to dress up as historical fact. Thus, even as he deprecates political rhetoric in historiography, he deploys that brand of it for which his school is well known.

When he complains, for example, that the works of colonial administrators are not given as much attention as he would like, I am tempted to remind him that the title of the volume is *Africa under Colonial Domination*, and not "The History of Colonial Rulers in Africa". One therefore expects to read about what Africans did and what was done to them under colonial rule; one cannot legitimately complain if the bulk of the work is devoted to African resistance, to the rise of African nationalist opposition to colonial domination, to the plight of Africans under the economic reorganisation instituted by the colonisers, and to the consequences of colonial rule for African society, art, religion and demography. That only one chapter is overtly devoted to the methods and institutions of European domination is unsurprising; this is a history from the viewpoint of the vanquished. Those who think that only the victors should write history may object to this, but it ought to be clear that such an objection is partisan and political.

Oliver is probably at his worst when he attempts to deny the existence of the colonial economy. His argument fails on every score. That the economies of the colonies were administered to raise government revenue is no argument against their colonial character since they were complements subordinate to the economies of the European colonising powers. The conditions for the viability of the colonial administrations were of course, as Oliver asserts, taxes. But what was the nature of the economic reorganisation from which taxes were to be milked? Was it not a system of exports to Europe, and imports from Europe, organised by African outposts of companies controlled from Europe, outposts in whose employment Africans would earn money for taxes?

It is deliberately disingenuous to claim that the roads and railways in the colonies "were designed not in order that primary products could be evacuated cheaply to European markets, but in order that the inhabitants of the African colonies might have the wherewithal to pay taxes and so cover the costs of their own administration". Surely, if roads and railways were for the purpose that Oliver claims, one would expect a dense network reaching out to every administrative community that was taxed, and not spurs which invariably ran from the coast to mines and to areas where export crops were grown in the hinterland.

Oliver buttresses his claim that there was no colonial economy by asserting that "colonial governments were not greatly concerned to ensure that metropolitan trading companies or white settlers made maximum profits. They saw them as instruments for mobilizing African labour into tax-paying employment." In making that claim, he chooses to disregard clear statements, by the promoters of the imperial adventure, of their economic intentions, like that made by Lord Salisbury in 1895 about smoothing the path for British commerce, enterprise and capital by opening up the colonies —a statement which is quoted in *Africa under Colonial Domination 1880-1935*. Oliver further claims that colonial governments "were quite content that the job should be done and the profits made by Indians or Greeks or Lebanese". A leader's willingness for some of the job to be done and its profits made by camp followers in an expedition is no demonstration of his lack of interest in his own profits. Or does Oliver wish us to forget that UAC, De Beers, Union Minière and the other economic giants were interested in profits, indeed made huge profits, and were not owned by Indians or Levantines?

Oliver dismisses Wole Soyinka as unqualified to write the history of the arts in Africa during the period of colonial rule. One wonders if he can have read Soyinka's contribution, or if he merely wishes, by casting aspersions on Soyinka's credentials, to discredit his portrait of the combined assault by Christian and Islamic zealots on the traditional arts of Africa. One would have thought that the ultimate proof of qualification is the quality of the product. But, presumably, a man of letters who is also a professor of drama and a much-travelled observer and commentator on the visual and musical arts and aesthetics of Africa is not competent to write a history of his field, because he has not taken a degree in history. Presumably we should also disregard Winston Churchill on the Second World War and Trotsky on the Russian Revolution.

Oliver's review is the sort of attack which a jaded orthodoxy is liable to make on its supplanters as it is being pushed from the stage. Its quality, and the prejudices which it insists on perpetuating, demonstrate the great need for corrective works like the Unesco *General History of Africa*, which has never concealed what it set out to do and why and how. Indeed the volume that Oliver reviews opens with a preface and a description of the project and its justification. By not indicating this to the reader, he contrives to indict a work for failing to be a history of the colonial enterprise in

Africa—something it clearly set out not to be.

A comprehensive, magisterial history of Africa will not be possible until histories written from the various partisan interests become available. Until the principal sides in the events have had their say, a judicious and impartial summing up will not be possible. The Unesco project, by bringing out the African version of the African experience, is contributing to the foundations for the eventual writing of a comprehensive non-partisan history of Africa. If only for this reason, it deserves a fair hearing.

Seasons of white invaders[*]

> Present thought and action are all too often guided by old and discarded theories of race and heredity, by misleading emphasis and silence of former histories. These conceptions are passed on to younger generations of students by current textbooks, popular histories and even public discussion.
>
> —W. E. B. Du Bois

I

Once upon a time, a young man was called a bastard. Though mortally offended, he was sensible enough not to go to his father to ask the facts; he instead asked some elders to tell him his family history. It turned out that the man he was brought up to revere as father was no such thing, but instead a wandering preacher who killed his actual father, occupied his father's land, and sired siblings on his mother. After his initial shock, and after verifying what the sympathetic elders had revealed, the young man's purpose in life changed utterly. Throwing out the usurper and reclaiming his patrimony became his moving passion.

As Frantz Fanon said, "Out of relative obscurity, each generation must discover its mission, fulfil it, or betray it." As the above story shows, one of the important uses of history is to shape human purposes by helping to remove obscurities from situations. Another is to supply a wealth of

---

[*] A review of the *UNESCO General History of Africa* (Vol. I: *Methodology and African Prehistory*; Vol. II: *Ancient Civilizations of Africa*; Vol. IV: *Africa from the Twelfth to Sixteenth Century*; Vol VII: *Africa under Colonial Domination 1880-1935*. First published in the *Vanguard* (Lagos) October-November 1986.

experience to those who undertake to accomplish a mission; for what is history but experiences collected for reference? A celebrated example of that is the case studies method of teaching management. By analysing cases from the past, and by evaluating alternative solutions to the problems they pose, the future manager gathers vicarious experience for tackling the problems he will encounter later in his work.

With these two uses in mind, we can appreciate that Africa's future demands a great deal from African historians. They have an obligation to end our ignorance of our history, for a man ignorant of his people's history is a man without social memory, a man stripped of his essential inheritance, a zombie. They also have to ensure that the versions of our past they supply are authentic, and address our present circumstances and future needs.

One of our vital needs is to end all foreign rule, occupation and hegemony in Africa. This means that, in addition to ending the last vestiges of European imperialism, we must defeat the renewed Arab attempt to spread their hegemony over the whole of Africa. And just as we must expel the remnants of white European invaders from southern Africa, we must, at some future date, end Arab settlement in all of North Africa and send them packing back to their homeland in the Arabian peninsula. In order to address these tasks successfully, case studies of African experiences under previous white invaders would be vital.

These long range tasks apart, there are some pressing regional and national problems which contemporary Africans are facing, whose ancient roots must be understood if correct solutions are to be found. The conflicts in Chad, Sudan, Ethiopia and Somalia, for example, are contemporary irruptions of ancient Afro-Arab conflicts which undermined African sovereignty and cultural confidence in the millennium from the 7th to the 16th century A.D. Re-emerging within the boundaries of post-colonial nation states, they appear as civil wars, wars of secession, and territorial wars between states. If they are to be properly approached, the ancient historical passions fuelling them must be taken into account.

Those to whom it falls to tackle both sorts of problems (the long range, continental ones, and the pressing regional and national ones) need to appreciate their origins, their evolution, and the world historical context within which they must be analysed. It would be to their advantage to ask: How did Africans, in other periods, respond to the pressures and opportunities of their day, with what results, and why? How did they meet, or fail to meet, challenges from the same imperialists and hegemonists who are still menacing African autonomy today? And given such questions, what type of African history ought to be a standard part of every educated African's mental furniture?

The view has gained ground, and rightly too, that the version of African history concocted by colonialism is quite unsuitable for post-colonial Africa. It was a history designed to prop up foreign domination by sponsoring debilitating myths about Africans and their abilities. It portrayed an Africa of eternal savagery, and cultural backwardness. It claimed that Africa had no history other than the doings of foreign invaders, and it went to all lengths to appropriate for foreign invaders, real and imaginary, whatever Europeans found in Africa that they felt obliged to respect. By so doing, it sought to rob Africans of their historical memory, and to make them believe in the congenital incapacity of their race. This was all calculated to paralyse African initiative. Even the neo-colonial "Fake and Liar" school of African historiography, with headquarters in British universities, has not been much of an improvement. It has merely sought to cast in less absurd terms the myths and "hypotheses" which colonialism sponsored.

It is such colonialist versions of African history which the *Unesco General History of Africa (UGHA)* has set out to replace. Such a replacement is right and proper, for what use is a version of African history that is not only false, but is ill-suited to a people who must exercise autonomy and initiative to create a sovereign, prosperous and unhumiliating future for themselves?

The overall aim of the 8-volume *UGHA* (each of some 800 pages) may be said to be the Africanisation of African history. The preface and the project description in Volume I inform us that it is to be an Afro-centric history of the ideas, civilisation, societies and traditions of the peoples of the African continent. Using the findings and techniques of various relevant disciplines, it is to tell, from the African point of view, what happened in some 3 million years of human presence in Africa. If the *UGHA* should accomplish its aim, it would make decisive, and probably irreversible, the hitherto gradual break with the exocentrism that has persisted in African historiography into this post-colonial era.

Midway through any project is a good time to evaluate it. Now that four of the projected eight volumes have appeared, let us see how well the project is doing. Has it corrected the false image of Africans? Has it made Africans the prime actors in African history? Is it such a history as would serve this and future generations well?

II

Volume I of the *UGHA*, *Methodology and African Prehistory*, edited by J. Ki-Zerbo, details the case for using contributions from archeology, linguistics, geography, language maps, palaeontology, the oral tradition, etc., to supplement evidence from African and non-African written sources. Making the case was necessary because such disciplines lie outside the boundaries of conventional historical sources. The prehistory of the continent is then presented in seven different chapters specialising on East, South, North, West and Central Africa, the Sahara and the Nile Valley.

Volume II, *Ancient Civilisations of Africa*, edited by G.

Mokhtar, presents the prehistory and history of various parts of Africa from about the 8th millennium B.C. to the eve of the Arab invasion of North Africa in the 7th century A.D. Volume IV, *Africa from the 12th to the 16th Century*, edited by D. T. Niane, treats a period that is notable for Arab penetration and cultural destabilisation of the Sahelian belt of sub-Sahara Africa. Volume VII, *Africa under Colonial Domination, 1880-1935*, edited by A. Adu Boahen, presents the European conquest of Africa. These four volumes thus present the prehistoric foundations and first flowerings of indigenous African civilisation, plus three of the devastating seasons of white invasion and cultural destabilisation which have marked African experience for the last 2,500 years.

We are shown the hominisation process in Africa, wherein the species half-seriously known as *homo sapiens* emerged from the family of primates. His prehistoric cultural career as tool maker and culture maker is traced from the stone age on. We see him as hunter-gatherer, as domesticator of plants and animals, as cultivator and herder, as metal user, as developer of social systems, and as prehistoric artist enriching his surroundings with paintings, jewelry, pottery and sculpture. By this career the foundations were laid for African civilisation.

When African man first crossed the prehistoric threshold, he fashioned the Nile Valley civilisations of Egypt and Nubia. After a long and brilliant career spanning some 3,000 years, the Egypt of the Pharaohs was overwhelmed in the first season of white invasion. The invaders also overran the Berbers of supra-Sahara Africa, but were contained for 12 centuries by the Sahara Desert and by the Nubians who guarded the Nile corridor into the rest of Africa.

The second season of white invasion falls into two phases: the initial invasion, colonisation and Arabisation of North Africa; and the subsequent destabilising of Sahelian Africa, from the Atlantic coast right across to the Red Sea and

Indian Ocean coast. Each phase lasted some 500 years; and it is the second of these that Vol. IV deals with.

The third, or European, season of white invasion falls into three broad phases: the slaving holocaust, which softened up Africa for the European conquest; the conquest and colonisation itself; and the decolonisation era. Of these, it is the story of the conquest which is told in Vol. VII.

Such is the broad outline of the story as told in the four *UGHA* volumes which have appeared so far. Now to some of the important details.

III

The periods covered by Vols IV and VII, and the issues they raise, have been of traditional interest to post-colonial Africa. The European conquest of Africa, derisively termed the "scramble" for Africa, was seen as an utter humiliation. In contrast, the five centuries preceding the European expansion was the era when famous African kingdoms and empires flourished. Mali, Songhai, Kanem, Makuria, Alwa, Ethiopia and Mwenemutapa are among those kingdoms and empires whose existence made Africans proud of their ancestry. They gave the lie to the colonial propaganda that Africans were eternal primitives before Europe brought them the gift of civilisation.

African nationalists have hitherto used the glories of these kingdoms to salve the wounds of colonial conquest. On evidence from the two volumes, however, a contrast between a humiliating European conquest and that pre-colonial period of glorious autonomy turns out to be superficial. Both, it turns out, were times when sub-Sahara Africa was put on the defensive by white foreign invaders. Africans, it emerges, were not entirely without cause for respect from the quality of their resistance to the European invaders: weakened as Africa was by the slaving holocaust, it still took a 30-year war for Europe to conquer her. And under Arab expansionist pressure, Africans were obliged to compromise away significant parts of their cultural, if not their political, independence. The main difference turns out to be that whereas the European conquest was comparatively swift and near total, the Arab penetration was slow and only partial. Nevertheless, both did undermine African civilisation, culture and self-respect. In consequence, the fashionable African nationalist attitudes are not entirely warranted. Neither abject humiliation over the European conquest, nor vaunting pride over the independence of the 12th to 16th centuries is warranted. How do these volumes urge such a revision of views?

Volume VII deals with four main themes: African attitudes and preparedness on the eve of the European invasion; African resistance to conquest and occupation; what Europeans did to effect their rule; and subsequent African initiatives to temper and then eliminate that rule. In so doing, it departs from the colonialist historiography which prefers to dwell on the doings of Europeans in Africa while minimising almost out of existence the vigorous resistance which Africans put up against conquest and against the new order.

After the European powers partitioned Africa on paper at Berlin (1884-1885), they had to actually seize and divide it up on the ground. Whatever scramble took place between the rival invading forces, the conquest of the Africans required a slow, brutal and bloody thirty years war (1885-1914). Whatever their initial attitudes to the Europeans—whether friendly or hostile; and whatever the initial tactics of their response, African rulers, when they understood that the Europeans meant to deprive them of sovereignty, rallied their people and fielded armies to defend their polities and cultures. Menelik's celebrated resistance to the Italian invaders of Ethiopia was not an exception but the norm. This is demonstrated by the cases of Samori Toure of the Mandinka, Kabarega of Bunyoro, Prempeh of the

Asante, Mwanga of Buganda, Machemba of Yao, Behanzin of Dahomey, Cetshaweyo of the Zulu and countless others. The difference between Menelik and the other African rulers was that he defeated his invaders and chased them away, whereas the others yielded to superior arms.

It was not until 1919, at the end of World War I, that the victorious Europeans settled down to reap the fruit of their victory over the Africans. They organised administrations, introduced schools to teach supportive ideologies and skills, and undertook social and economic reorganisation to ensure profitable exploitation of Africa's human and ecological resources. Forced labour, land alienation, taxes, low prices for export products, high prices for European imports, racial discrimination and segregation—these were among the means the conquerors used to entrench their new order.

After its military phase, African resistance now sought to make life less oppressive, and to extract benefits for Africans from the new dispensation. This new campaign was conducted by different means: petitions, delegations, strikes, boycotts and riots against specific aspects of colonial rule. This mode of resistance was to prove the beginning of that political nationalism which, in the post World War II era, would lead to political independence for the countries brought into being by the European conquest.

An equally significant, but politically more consequential change in perception results from reading Vol. IV. Three main features of its period emerge. First, the triumph of Arabisation against prolonged resistance from African societies on the Sahelian and Indian Ocean frontiers. Second, the evolution of autochthonous African kingdoms of the forest and savanna zones, far from the Afro-Arab borderlands; some of these states would later blossom as intermediaries in the Euro-African slaving economy. Third, the existence of a continental trading system which linked Africa across the Sahara Desert and the Indian Ocean to a pre-modern world economic system that loosely integrated

Asia, Europe and Africa. The basis of African integration into that system was the production and export of gold, ivory, iron, hides, pearls, salt, kolanuts and slaves which were exchanged for porcelain, silk and brocade from China, and for glass, beads, books, cloth and Islam from the Arab world. This last feature explodes the colonialist myth that Africa was isolated from the world before the advent of Europeans on their voyages of discovery.

The volume pays commendable attention to the administrative structures of the kingdoms and empires of the period. They are shown to be based on control of trade routes, and on royal monopolies of the principal commodities of trade. Their rulers are shown immersed in their administrative labours, keeping order, dispensing justice, attending to the disruptive problems of succession. They are also shown at war with their neighbours over the usual questions of land, trade and religion.

But the main theme of the volume is African resistance to Arabisation. Some one-third of the volume tells the story of infiltration and settlement by Arab groups; the Islamisation of African trading communities and from there of African courts, and then of the ordinary people, with often dire consequences for the cultures and whatever religion (Christianity or African indigenous systems) the Arabisers met there. Arabisation caused the adoption or imposition of Arab dress, of the Arab language, of Arab names, of Arab administrative structures and titles, of Arab social norms, of the Arab religion of Islam. It imposed on princes and prominent families an obligation to construct fake genealogies claiming Arab ancestry for jet-black Africans. This long and slow cultural colonisation was primarily effected by Arabising African merchants, nomads, missionaries, soldiers and kings who saw it all as a purely religious matter of Islamisation. Their eventual victories, where they became victorious, came at the end of dogged fights with the defenders of African culture and civilisation.

Typical of such long battles was the Islamisation of the Songhai empire long after it was established. After the death of Sunni Ali Ber who, though a muslim, never gave up the practice of the African religion of the Songhai, a religious civil war broke out. And when his successor, Sunni Baare, refused to convert to Islam, he was overthrown by Askiya Muhammed Toure, who then established an Islamic dynasty in 1492.

Such pressures to Islamise the state religion and Arabise the culture were felt in kingdom after kingdom on the Afro-Arab frontier. We find a succession of Ethiopian kings fighting against muslim encirclement, the most celebrated of them being Amda Seyon (1314-1344). We also find Mansa Musa of Mali, a black African muslim, warding off pressure to compromise his sovereignty by bowing in obeisance to the Arab ruler of Egypt through whose land he was passing on pilgrimage to Mecca. We find the Sefuwa dynasty in Kanem obliged to Arabise its Berber ancestry, yet unable to save its members from abduction, export and trans-Sahara enslavement by Arabs. We also find the Christian Nubian resistance to Arabisation and Islam in what is today the thoroughly Arabised northern Sudan.

In north Africa under the Arab settlers, we find the expropriation of land from the Berber natives, the planting of Arab settlements and colonies, the enslavement of imported Africans from the sub-Sahara regions, the re-export of some to Europe, the indoctrination of both the native Berbers and the imported slaves with the Arab coloniser's religion of Islam, and the intensive Arabisation of their identity and culture. All in all, there emerges a picture of Arab colonialism every bit as effective as that of the Europeans later on. Indeed, present day European settlers in South Africa have nothing to teach the Arab settlers in Africa about the business of conquering, expropriating, enslaving and imposing cultural imperialism on Africans. That is the dominant picture which emerges from Vol. IV. It changes the

WHITE INVADERS

view, long entrenched and still being popularised, that Arabs are and have been a benign presence in Africa.

IV

Unlike the periods treated in Vols IV and VII, those treated in Vols I and II have not hitherto featured much in the consciousness of post-colonial Africans. In many minds, African history is a matter of roughly one thousand years: the old kingdoms of Ghana, Kanem, Great Zimbabwe and so on being the last outposts beyond which lie vague, mist-covered aeons, unexplored and presumed barren. These two volumes profoundly revise that view by extending the period of African history to some five thousand years, and by supplying some three million years of its prehistoric foundations. The five-fold expansion of our sense of the scope of African history is primarily done by restoring the Nile Valley to its seminal place in African civilisation. Thus, what the educated post-colonial African hitherto took for all of African history turns out to be but its narrow foreground.

Vol. II picks up where Vol. I leaves off the three million year story of prehistoric cultural developments in Africa, and brings it up to 700 A.D. It also tells two moving stories: the autogenous development of the spectacular Nile Valley civilisations, and the overwhelming of Egypt and Berber North Africa by a succession of white invaders.

An account is presented of Pharaonic Egypt, from its pre-dynastic beginnings, through the march of its dynasties, down to its conquest by Persia in 525 B.C. This conquest was the turning point in Egypt's long resistance to would-be conquerors. We are offered accounts of Egypt's origins, its racial composition, the nature of its society, its economy and culture, and its monumental legacy to subsequent civilisations. In the summary by the volume editor G. Mokhtar, we read:

> The ancient Egyptian civilisation, besides being old, original and rich in initiative, lasted for almost three thousand years. It resulted not only from favourable environment factors, but also from the efforts to control those factors and put them to beneficial use.... The ancient Egyptians, through the invention of writing in their predynastic period, made a considerable advance towards civilisation.... a great deal of scientific knowledge, art and literature emanated from [Egypt], and influenced Greece in particular. In the fields of mathematics (geometry, arithmetic, etc.), astronomy and the measurement of time (the calendar), medicine, architecture, music and literature (narrative, poetry, tragedy, etc.), Greece received, developed and transmitted to the West a great part of the Egyptian legacy. (pp. 732-733)

The story of Nubia, Egypt's southern neighbour and cultural sibling, is given, from before it was outstripped by Egypt, and during the two and half millennia when it straggled along in the shadow of Egypt. When Egyptian power began to wane, the Nubian kingdom of Kush, based first in Napata, and later in Meroe, rose to eminence, and even conquered and ruled Egypt for a time. The story of Napata-Meroe is told from 750 B.C. to its collapse in about 300 A.D. Thereafter, the story of Nubia becomes that of the various Christian kingdoms (Nobadae, Makuria and Alodia) which rose and merged in the middle Nile Valley and flourished until well beyond the Arab conquest of Egypt and North Africa. The story of their destabilisation and fall to the Arabs belongs in the second phase of the Arab invasion of Africa, and is told in Vol. IV.

The story of the overwhelming of supra-Sahara Africa in the first season of white invasion covers the period from 525 B.C. to the early part of the 7th century A.D. In those 12 centuries, supra-Sahara Africa, from its southern desert edge to its Atlantic, Mediterranean and Red Sea coasts, experienced successive invasions and colonisations by Phoenicians, Persians, Greeks, Romans, Vandals and Byzantines. The decisive phases of these invasions were the Greek in Egypt and the Roman in the Berber lands to the west of Egypt. Under its Greek conquerors, Egypt was Hellenised; and on being conquered by Rome, the land of the Berbers was Romanised. The Hellenisation of Egypt was carried out during a period of three centuries by a settler elite of Greeks led by the Ptolemies. Greek was made the official language of Egypt; Greek names were substituted for the original Egyptian names of towns, persons and gods. One terrible result of that is that the African character of Ancient Egypt still lies hidden from general view under a layer of Greek names, now further overlaid with Arabic names.

The Sahara and Nubia marked the southern limits of the first season of white invasion. One fascinating question is how Nubia, for some 2,000 years (6th c. B.C. to 15th c. A.D.) held off white pressure from the north. An attempted Persian invasion by Cambyses was beaten back by Kush. An expedition from Roman Egypt captured Napata in 23 B.C., but, following a peace treaty, the Romans withdrew and a boundary was established between the Roman empire and Meroe. When Meroe collapsed, the Christian kingdoms which took its place guarded Nubia's northern borders until they were undermined by steady and relentless Arab pressure, and were overrun in the first decade of the 16th century.

V

It is now time to evaluate the *UGHA* on the basis of three key questions: What image of Africa emerges when Africans are made the prime actors in their own history? How serviceable to the needs of post-colonial Africa is the

UGHA? And how thorough has been its expurgation of colonialist myths, and its adherence to Afrocentrism?

When the focus of African history shifts from the doings of foreigners in Africa to the doings of Africans, as it ought, an image begins to emerge of an Africa far different from what imperialist propaganda had proclaimed. Africa has not been an isolated and passive recipient of civilisation brought in by outsiders; it has been an active maker and defender of its own civilisation, and a seminal contributor to the civilisations of western Eurasia. It has also had to resist, compromise with, and assimilate influences as circumstances demanded or power realities allowed.

The fundamental pattern of its five-thousand year history is that of autogenous African societies and civilisations being undermined, then overwhelmed by white invaders, who then settle to rule them, to expropriate their land and achievements, and to dislocate their societies and plough their civilisation under. The Nile Valley and the supra-Sahara zone were the first parts of Africa to undergo this experience. It then befell the northern fringes of sub-Sahara Africa. In the western Sahel zone, a sequence of successor states in the upper Niger Valley (which built upon the autogenous foundations laid by ancient Ghana) was ended by the Moroccan destruction of Songhai in the last decade of the 16th century. To the east, the Nubian successor states to the ancient Nile Valley civilisations fell to Arab pressure from Egypt in the first decade of the same 16th century. Thus, the Arabs repeated below the Sahara what they, and other whites before them, had inflicted on supra-Sahara Africa.

This pattern was to be repeated at the hands of European invaders. The slaving states of the Atlantic coast of Africa; the kingdoms of central Africa and the Great Lakes; and the Zambezi basin kingdoms had all developed far from the zones appropriated by earlier invaders. Whichever of these did not decay under the pressures of slaving, were finally overwhelmed by the European invasion at the end of the 19th century. All in all, after some 3,000 years of spectacular and autogenous cultural achievement, Africa attracted a succession of white invaders who, 2,500 years later, finally overran the entire continent at the beginning of this 20th century A.D. The European conquest thus marks the nadir in the fortunes of African civilisation.

Whether the recent reassertion of African independence will reverse the long decline remains to be seen. Much will depend on whether this generation of Africans will recognize that it is their historic mission to lay sound foundations for an Africa that can roll back the invaders. If they fail in this mission, and if success attends the current effort by the Arabs to overrun the entire continent on their own, just as the Europeans had done before them, it could well mean the end of African civilisation, and possibly of the African race in its African homeland.

Such is the fundamental African history which this and future generations must know if they are to discover and carry out their historic mission. The rest are details which a new African historiography shall fill in. For supplying materials from which it could be gleaned, the *UGHA* must be commended.

The *UGHA* also allows insight into the ways and means by which the various white invaders succeeded. It contains materials for case studies of how African societies were destabilised, conquered, pacified and then Hellenised, Romanised, Arabised or Europeanised. An impressive and early example was the Romanisation of the Berbers of North Africa, between 146 B.C. and 212 A.D. For that reason, the excellent account thereof given in Vol. II, chp. 19 deserves close attention.

When Rome conquered Carthage in 146 B.C., the various Berber kingdoms in its hinterland came under the shadow of Roman power. One by one, after long resistance, the Maurusiani, Musulamii, Gaetulians, Garamantes, Numidians and

Mauretanians were conquered. By 40 A.D., all of North Africa, from what today is Libya to the Atlantic coast of Morocco, became the Roman provinces of Africa Minor. The Roman takeover of ancient Mauretania—a vast land stretching along the Mediterranean coast of what is today Algeria, all the way to the Atlantic coast of Morocco—is an instructive lesson in destabilisation. It was a long process effected by sustained interference in local affairs, and by the installation and removal of Romanised client rulers. Here is an account of its final phases:

> The kingdom of Mauretania ... had been bequeathed by King Bocchus the Younger to the Roman empire as far back as −33. Octavian, the future Augustus, accepted the legacy and availed himself of the opportunity to plant eleven colonies of veterans in the country, but in −25 he gave up the kingdom to Juba II, who was succeeded by his son Ptolemy in +23. The cautious Octavian probably thought that the country was not ripe for a Roman occupation and that it was necessary to prepare the way through the intervention of indigenous leaders. In +40 Caligula, judging that the time for direct administration had arrived, caused Ptolemy to be assassinated. Finally, Claudius decided, at the end of +42, to organise the two provinces of Mauretania: Caesariensis to the east and Tingitana to the west, separated by the Mulucha (Moulouya). Like Numidia, both Mauretanian provinces came directly under the authority of the emperor. (Vol. II, p. 471)

Thus, some 200 years after the defeat of Carthage, Rome swallowed up a Berber kingdom that had been one of its allies against Carthage and against other Berber kingdoms, and which it had patiently bitten to death.

Once they were overrun, the Berbers were subjected to

harsh expropriation. When some, like the Numidians, rebelled, they were brutally crushed. And once Roman power was secure, an assimilationist programme of Romanisation was unleashed on them. The fundamental ploy was to give a Roman style education to their elite; and thereafter to gradually extend the economic, social and political privileges of Roman citizenship to their leading citizens and upper classes. The culmination of the process was the granting of Roman citizenship, in 212 A.D., to all free inhabitants of the Roman empire who had not individually acquired it. Thus were the Berber elite and urbanites transformed into Romans, with some even taking seats in the Roman Senate itself.

Centuries later, Arabisation and Europeanisation followed a similar course all over Africa, after a similarly prolonged destabilisation. Writing about the Europeanisation, Amadou Hampate Ba noted that "the major preoccupation of the colonial power was, understandably, to clear away autochthonous traditions as far as possible and plant its own conceptions in their place. Schools, secular or religious, were the essential instruments of this undermining." (Vol. I, p. 202). This was no less true of Arabisation. Koranic schools proved to be vital centres of indoctrination and cooptation into Arab beliefs and pro-Arab sympathies. This was reinforced by breaking the transmission processes of African traditions by interdicting initiation rites as infidel. The traditions themselves were attacked as pagan; campaigns were mounted to replace African laws and customs with the Arab sharia; and resilient African traditions were recast to conform to the tenets of Arab Islam. These were among the issues which fuelled the prolonged clashes between Arabisers and the defenders of African culture in the Sahelian lands discussed in Vol. IV.

Those experiences are not without their counterparts in post-colonial Africa today. To appreciate the meaning and consequences of the events in Vol. IV is to have a mirror in which to see clearly the significance of certain developments of today. When news reaches us of the proclamation of yet another "Arab Republic" on African soil (Sudan, Somalia, Saharaoui); of annexations of African territory by Arab states (Chad's northern strip by Libya); of Arab nomadic encroachments and a scorched-earth war on African agriculturalists (Southern Sudan); of the imposition of sharia laws on non-muslim Africans (Sudan); of lavish campaigns to promote "Islamic identity" (Nigeria, Senegal, etc.); of the conversion of African rulers to Islam (Omar Bongo of Gabon); of attempts to kidnap non-muslim countries into the Organisation of the Islamic Conference—OIC—(Nigeria); of the Arabisation of educational programmes (Somalia); of wars of secession and dismemberment directed against African countries and financed by Arab money (Eritrean secessionists from Ethiopia, and Somali attempts to slice the Ogaden from Ethiopia), it should be clear that we are witnessing yet another season of Arab expansionist destabilisation of African societies. It is then up to us to take up or evade the mission spelt out for us by that understanding of the situation.

These ancient campaigns of destabilisation, takeover and de-Africanisation show that Africans have to contend with foes who persevere for centuries to accomplish their purpose. They will take advantage of whatever developments favour them, however seemingly inconsequential. The little gains eventually add up, and when the decisive conflict erupts, they are strong enough to carry the day. If African civilisation is to reverse its long decline, nothing short of a long-term strategy will be required. And it must be a strategy geared to a permanent and uncompromising historical objective, namely, African political independence and cultural autonomy. It is thus that, if properly presented, the materials in the *UGHA* could provide serviceable case studies on how to meet, and not to meet, present and future challenges to Africa.

Now to the third question. As part of its scholarly and Afrocentric objectives, the *UGHA* aims to expurgate various myths and prejudices about Africans and their history. In that aim it has been largely successful. Surely, no reader of these four volumes could continue to honestly maintain that Africans have no history, or have not been originators of distinguished cultures. After seeing what contributions they have made to the *UGHA*, none can now claim that Africa has no indigenous written sources for its history, or that African oral traditions lack historiographic value. After the racial and cultural unity of the continent has been so clearly demonstrated, the attempt to exclude Ancient Egypt and Nubia from Africa cannot be sustained.

Some of the most unsupportable dogmas of colonialist historiography have been laid to rest. Cheikh Anta Diop has marshalled evidence in Vol. II, chp. 1, "Origins of the ancient Egyptians", to show that the ancient Egyptians were black, thus putting paid to the Hamitic Hypothesis. In fact, it is useful for the reader to contemplate for himself the two opposing theories put before the *UGHA* Symposium on the peopling of ancient Egypt. One, expressing the Hamitic Hypothesis, stated: "The people who lived in ancient Egypt were 'white', even though their pigmentation was dark, or even black, as early as the predynastic period. Negroes made their appearance only from the eighteenth dynasty onwards." The other, the Diopian thesis, stated: "Ancient Egypt was peopled, 'from its Neolithic infancy to the end of the native dynasties', by black Africans." (Vol. II, p. 59). The notion that people with dark or even black pigmentation were 'white' is so preposterous that it could only be advanced or held by minds bent on mischief. The internal contradiction in that thesis is enough to torpedo it and establish the other one, even without the scientific evidence marshalled by Diop.

The pastoralist dogma of British colonial historiography, which held that conquering pastoralists established states and aristocracies over sedentary agriculturalists, is exploded by B. A. Ogot's evidence from the Great Lakes region. He shows that not all pastoralists started out as rulers, nor did they all end up as rulers (Vol. IV, p. 513). Furthermore, "several small states were established in the interlacustrine region by Bantu-speaking agriculturalists before the pastoralists became politically important." (Vol. IV, p. 521)

Likewise, the colonialist myth of the Arab origin of Great Zimbabwe has not survived the presentation of evidence by B. M. Fagan. We learn that "unmistakeable Arab influence in either Great Zimbabwe's construction or in the Great Zimbabwe culture as a whole is almost impossible to detect." (Vol. IV, p. 542)

However, not all that needs expurgating has been expurgated. For example, Hellenic and Arabic names for Ancient Egyptian persons and places are still retained, whereas they should be replaced with the appropriate ancient Egyptian names.

Perhaps the most serious failure at expurgation is the continued use of the term "muslim" to denote both the Arabs and their African religious fellow travellers. Making the distinction clear at all times is important if the interactions between Arab invaders and their African victims are to be accurately presented, and if the anti-African role of Arabised Africans is to be clearly understood.

Exocentrism still crops up here and there. For example, we read that a queen of Meroe "had dealings with Augustus in a famous episode, one of the rare occasions when Meroe appears on the stage of universal history"! (Vol. II, p.290)

The worst case of exocentrism in a supposedly Afrocentric work is the Arabism introduced into Vol. IV by no less than the volume editor himself. It results in a sanitisation of the methods and meaning of Islamisation in Africa; and it leads to a minimisation of the Arab trade in African slaves. The overall effect is an unwarranted Arabist distortion of vital aspects of African history. The extent of this must be seen to be believed! Indeed, it amounts to a deliberate pro-Arab and anti-African propaganda in a work whose very aim is to present African history from an African point of view. Let us therefore look into it.

VI

In his introduction to the Volume, D. T. Niane asserts that "however many black slaves there were in Iraq, Morocco or the Maghrib in general, it must be emphasised that there is no comparison between" the trade in African slaves by Arabs and that by Europeans. (p.4) And he generally seeks to leave the impression that the former was insignificant. We are also told by him that "this trade could not be regarded as a haemorrhage, because what interested the Arabs above all in the Sudan was gold" (Vol. IV p. 619) This is a *non sequitur*, by the way, since even a tertiary interest could still be devastating, depending on its character. Contrary to such minimising claims, many statements appear in the book which, when taken together, lead to a rather different estimate of the size and impact of the Arab trade in African slaves.

On the same page 619, Niane himself reports that the yearly export of slaves from the Sudan to North Africa has been estimated at 20,000—a not insignificant figure at all. At 2 million a century, and given the many centuries the trade lasted, wouldn't that be a haemorrhage? We also learn a most illuminating detail from that same page. A 14th century Arab traveller, Ibn Battuta, travelled in a caravan that contained 600 women slaves who were being exported to the Maghreb. The demographic impact of such an export of reproductive capacity may not be dismissed as insignificant, especially since there is no evidence that what Ibn Battuta saw was an exception rather than a normal practice.

We later learn from another contributor that black slaves were, for centuries, re-exported from North Africa to Spain and other parts of Europe to serve as soldiers and domestics. One result was that by the 15th century, 83 per cent of slaves in Naples were blacks. We also learn that, from the 9th century on, sugar plantations were developed in Morocco, and that they relied on African slaves (p. 662). This is significant since it is commonly claimed that the Arab slave trade, unlike that to the Americas, was not for plantation labour, and so was not as hungry for slaves. If it turns out that black slaves were needed for plantation labour in various parts of the Arab world, or in the lands to which they were re-exported, then the characteristics of plantation slavery would have to enter the assumptions for calculating the numbers taken from Africa by the Arabs, and would revise the numbers upward.

One instance cited by Niane to minimise the Arab slave trade is a treaty whereby Nubia was obliged to supply Egypt with 442 slaves a year. That may appear insignificant until we realise that Nubia was only a small territory in the vast frontier zone from which the Arabs were supplied with African slaves. Secondly, that treaty lasted for some 700 years, and from time to time its obligations were increased. For example, when Sultan Baybars of Egypt put Shakanda on the throne of Makuria, he imposed terms of vassalage which required Nubia to supply 10,000 slaves. (p. 403). To reckon with such examples is to realise that the Arab trade in African slaves was not insignificant at all. And considering that it lasted for some 1,200 years before the European conquest of Africa put a stop to it at the start of the 20th century, there is little warrant to assume that the total numbers exported to Arab lands was dwarfed by the numbers exported to the Americas.

Regarding the spread of Islam, editor Niane asserts that

> In the Sudan, apart from the warlike episode of

the Almoravids, Islam spread slowly and peacefully in the interior. There were no established clergy or missionaries as in the Christian West. Islam, a religion of cities and courts, did not destroy the traditional structures. Neither the kings of the Sudan nor the sultans of East Africa went to war with the purpose of converting their people. Trade was the main consideration and Islam showed enough flexibility to ask no more of the conquered peoples than that they pay taxes; thus each was able to preserve its own personality. (Vol.IV p. 3)

As we shall soon see, this is pure Arabist propaganda: every claim in that introductory passage is actually contradicted by evidence in the body of the book, quite a few of them in the chapters written by Niane himself!

One obvious contradiction in the quoted passage deserves comment. How did Islam acquire "conquered peoples" in those places where it allegedly spread peacefully? Doesn't "to conquer" still mean to acquire by force of arms, to win in war? Or is there now something to be known as peaceful conquest?

Niane's claim for Islam's peaceful triumphs is contradicted, in his own detailed accounts, when we read (pp. 124-132) of wars between the Islamising Sundiata dynasty and the African traditionalist Kante clan in Mali. As a result of the victory of Sundiata, the Mali court became muslim. Some peaceful spreading that!

So there was no established clergy or missionaries of Islam in the Sudan? Well, what of this?:

[The victory of Sundiata] was also a prelude to the expansion of Islam. For Sundiata, whose ancestors had been converted to Islam in the eleventh century, made himself the protector of Muslims; the delegation sent to find him in exile had included some marabouts. (Vol. IV p. 132)

What were the marabouts? Did they not function, in Sundiata's time, as propagators of Islam? Had they no hand in getting Sundiata to make himself the protector of Muslims?

So Islam did not destroy traditional structures? But what of this?: Concerning the disappearance of Christian Nubia, we read of "the direct pressure of the Egyptian rulers on the weakening Nubian power", and of "the increasing penetration of Arab nomadic groups and their destructive effect on the Nubian social fabric" (p. 398) Or were these Arabs not muslim? We also read of the conversion of churches to mosques, and of "the Arabisation of the indigenous population" when the Arab muslims finally overran Christian Nubia. (pp. 408, 411).

If neither the muslim kings of the Sudan nor the Sultans of East Africa went to war with the purpose of conversion, then what do we make of this?:

> With Muhammad (1493-1529) and his successors, the Songhay wars against the Mossi were henceforth conducted in the name of Islam, the Mossi being 'pagans', like the inhabitants of Gurma. (Vol. IV p.214)

And if Islam asked no more of the conquered Africans than that they pay taxes while being left to preserve their own personality, what do we make of the case of Shakanda of Makuria who was placed on the throne by Sultan Baybars of Egypt, and then obliged to exact a yearly poll tax from those Nubians who refused to embrace Islam? Is that a case of being left to preserve their personality? If so, why was the poll tax not imposed on everybody, but only on those who refused to abandon their Nubian for an Islamic personality?

All in all, it would appear from evidence in the volume he edited, and even from the chapters he wrote himself, that the Almoravid "episode" of spreading Islam by war was not the exception but the rule throughout Africa. Even where traders began the process of Islamisation, when resistance finally came to a head, it meant war. So much for Niane's Arabist propaganda on the peaceful Islamisation of Africa.

But what did Islamisation entail? Did it allow the Africans to preserve their culture and personality? Consider the experience of Mali, as Niane himself reports it:

> The Wangara, always on the move from village to village, built mosques in various centres, like landmarks, along the kola routes. Because of the natural tolerance of Africans, they could say their prayers even in villages where the traditional religions were practised. Arabic became the language of the literate and the courtiers; Mansa Musa spoke it correctly, according to al-Umari, and can be regarded as responsible for the introduction of Muslim culture into Mali. (Vol. IV p. 622)

As the manifestation of "Muslim culture" in Mali, we are further told that "an African literature in Arabic came into being", and that "the rulers of the Sudan were surrounded by Arab jurists and counsellors". The latter would be tantamount to having African presidents today surrounded by European lawyers and advisers!—a situation which most Africans would oppose as neo-colonialist. Yet it seems perfectly all right with our Arabists. Thus, when the specifics of Islamisation are examined, it turns out to be cultural Arabisation, and even Arab political hegemony, quite contrary to what Niane, in that introductory passage, would have his readers believe about the preservation of African culture and personality. All in all, the march of Islam into Africa must be seen as no different from the later march of Christianity as the cultural and ideological side of the European onslaught on Africa.

For a work which is part of a project to Africanise African history, Vol. IV is to be seriously faulted on the following counts, all of which flow from the manifest Arabism of its editor. First, it minimises the role of war in the spread of Islam in Africa, probably out of a desire to satisfy the myth of Afro-Arab solidarity which was born of an anti-colonial alliance against the European conquerors of both Africans and Arabs. Secondly, it refuses to see Islamisation as a cover for cultural, and sometimes biological Arabisation; as the imposition of Arabic language, culture, religion, laws, customs and even rulers on African populations. Thirdly, it refuses to probe the role of white racism in the Afro-Arab encounter; and fourthly, it fails to present a focussed view of the price Africans paid for Islamisation, even though evidence of this great cost is scattered throughout the volume. Had the editor not evaded the issue, his introductory and concluding chapters might have commented on the destruction of African art, the inhibiting of the sculptural impulse by the claim that representation of the human form is idolatrous; and the squeezing of African cultural content out of African life, with the substitution of Arabic cultural content, under the pretence that Arabic culture is consecrated by Allah as a passport to heaven.

Had the pall of Arabism allowed Djibril T. Niane to see Islamisation as de-Africanisation, and to approach his project the way Adu Boahen approached his, Vol. IV might have been insightfully titled "Africa under Arab Colonial Pressure", or "African Resistance to Arabisation". Instead, it carries the bland title "Africa from the 12th to the 16th Century", which fails to highlight the central feature of that period of African history. And it is not as if Africans of the period did not understand Islamisation to mean de-Africanisation and Arabisation. They so understood it, and vigorously opposed it, as the resistance movements in Mali, Ethiopia, Nubia etc., make clear. One must conclude that, just as Sundiata, Mansa Musa and the other Arabising Africans of that era were eager to de-Africanise and Arabise themselves, so too are the African Arabists of today glad to do likewise to 20th century Africa and to African history.

Djibril Niane's Arabism is most serious in a work which seeks to authoritatively present an African view of African history. On his version of Africanising African history, the Anglo/Boers of South Africa would be welcomed into the fold of African peoples; and their racist, anti-African atrocities (such as the expropriation of African lands through the Bantustanisation policy, their apartheid, and such massacres as Sharpeville, Soweto, and Uitenhage) would be covered up under a blanket of Afro-European fraternity and universal Christian brotherhood. All in all, Djibril Niane's assiduous propaganda for Arab imperialism in Africa should qualify him for leadership in an Arab version of Britain's "Fake and Liar" school of African historiography. The sad thing, of course, is that he is not an Arab but an African.

Part of the responsibility for the failings in Vol. IV must lie with the entire Scientific Committee of the *UGHA*. Even if an editor's bias caused his introductory summary to convey an opposite impression from what is warranted by the material he summarised, it was up to the Scientific Committee, as the final vetter, to rectify the blemish. Why it let this one pass into print is a mystery. They probably need to be reminded that, for the success of the entire *UGHA*, all traces of exocentrism—whether Arabocentric or Eurocentric—must be expunged.

Part Three: Politics

The problem of the Twentieth Century is the problem of the color-line.

—W. E. B. Du Bois

Zionists, Arabists and Pan-Africanists*

My cousin says,
The Africans have no culture!
The Africans have no history!
The Africans have no religion!
The Africans have no one language!
The Africans are uncivilized!

He says,
It is his duty to extend
The Arab sphere of influence
Into Africa!

He claims that,
Egypt is already Arab!
Libya is already Arab!
Tunisia is already Arab!
Algeria is already Arab!
Morocco is already Arab!
Mauritenia is already Arab!
Somalia is already Arab!
Djebuti is already Arab!
Sudan is already Arab!
And soon,
Western Sahara shall be Arab!
Eritrea shall be Arab!
Chad shall be Arab!
And if God's willing,
Ethiopia shall be Arab!
Let the whole African continent
Become an Arab continent,
So that its people can be civilized!

* * *

* First published in *The Guardian* (Lagos) May 19 & 26, 1985.

> My cousin is deafened
> By Orouba[1]
> . . .
>
> And so,
> Like Zionism, or Apartheid,
> Orouba has become a racist ideology!
>
> —S. Anai Kelueljang

Last month,[2] Zionism was introduced into a controversy about Nigeria's divorce laws. A conference, held in Kano by the Muslim Sisters' Organisation, reportedly accused the National Council of Women's Societies (NCWS) of being "part of the global Zionist network."[3]

To so accuse the NCWS is to say that it is a partisan and agent of the state of Israel in its war with its Arab neighbours. Furthermore, by condemning the NCWS in such terms, the conference, perhaps unwittingly, was laying itself open to the charge of being Arabist, that is, a partisan and agent of the Arab states in their war with Israel. But why should the Arab-Israeli dispute be injected into a purely Nigerian question about the appropriateness of our divorce laws? Isn't it enough that we let it distort our foreign policy to the detriment of our fundamental African interests? Must we also import it to divide and fanaticise our domestic relations? To appreciate the absurdity of such importation, let us sort out a few things. Who are the Zionists, Arabists, Israelis, Palestinians, Arabs and Jews?

The Israelis are those Jews who have returned to the land of Palestine which they regard as their ancestral home; the Palestinians are those Arabs whom the Israelis have chased out in the process of repossessing the land and setting up the

---

[1] The cultural Arabisation of non-Arab people.
[2] April 1985.
[3] *New Nigerian* (Kaduna) April 12, 1985, p.1.

state of Israel there. The Zionists are a world-wide movement of Jews who support the state of Israel; the Arabists (if one may adopt the term) are a world-wide movement of Arabs who defend the claims of the Palestinians to the land on which the Israeli state has been set up.

But who exactly are the Arabs and the Jews; and why should Nigerians allow their dispute over a plot of land in the Levant, thousands of miles away, to shape our policies and lives? Simply put, Jews and Arabs are two sub-families of the Semitic branch of the white race. They are both indigenous to south-west Asia, even though, over the past two millennia, they have spread out into Europe and Africa, so that a majority of each group now live outside their ancestral region. Nevertheless, their primordial loyalties are still to their ancestral homelands; the Arabian peninsula for the Arabs, and Israel for the Jews.

In their intra-semitic land contest, the Palestinians and the Israelis are the principals; the Arabists and the Zionists are their seconds; while Arabs and Jews are their ethnic bases from where seconds are recruited. Non-Arabs and non-Jews who side with one or the other may be likened to fellow travellers, in this case of Arabism and Zionism. Since Nigerians, and indeed Africans, are outsiders to this dispute, what business do we have importing it to fanaticise our own disagreements? Wouldn't that be like sympathisers at a burial carrying the corpse home to stink up their own bedroom?

Some of us, as Pan-Africanists, do not welcome the injection of a quarrel between fanatical white semitic groups into the political and social affairs of black people. We think that neutrality, even of the "a-plague-on-both-your-houses" variety, ought to be our stand on the matter. To those mental slaves of Arabs and Jews who insist on defining our national concerns with reference to the white semitic world of south-west Asia, a few questions: Shouldn't "Nigeria First!" be our motto? Isn't it bad enough that we import so many things?

Should we import foreign quarrels too? And foreign fanaticisms? Have we no cultural self-respect or racial pride? And don't we have enough quarrels of our own to use up our contentious energies? If one white people takes land away from another white people, what headache of blacks is that? Why bother over that when we have not stopped white Arabs and white Europeans from occupying, and further encroaching on, lands belonging to blacks? Why should an African lamb feel obliged to support either the Jewish lion or the Arab leopard in their turf fight, when each is a habitual devourer of African lambs?

I can't quite see why Africans should side with the Arabs who invaded and occupied the supra-Sahara fifth of our homeland, and are still scheming, pressuring and manoeuvering to seize more from sub-Sahara Africa. If we let them, they could soon have forty per cent of our entire continent! If we were a sensible people, we would be telling them: "Oh, you want your Israeli cousins out of Palestine? You don't like your land to be taken over, your people dispossessed and expelled, by those you consider aliens, even if they are your cousins returning from a long exile? Well, then, how do you expect us to like it when you, who are not even cousins of ours, have taken over vast chunks of our land, and have expelled our people from there, such as the Beriberi, who fled Arab conquest in North Africa, crossed the Sahara, and have settled in Nigeria? If you Arabs have a principled objection to Israelis taking part of your land, why don't you uphold your principles by getting out of North Africa and hurrying back to Arabia where you came from? And why don't you hands off Chad, Sudan and Somalia for a start?"

As for us siding with the Jews, why? Haven't they, as part of the West, participated in the centuries of atrocities the West has committed against Africa and Africans?

Lest we foolishly ruin ourselves by partisanship in a dispute that is strictly none of our business, we ought to carefully scrutinise the history of our calamitous relations with Europeans and Arabs.

The highlights of European atrocities against Africa are the trans-Atlantic slave trade, the enslavement of Africans in the Americas, racism, and the conquest and colonisation of Africa, with all the massacres and humiliations which attended them. Being well documented and well remembered, these need no rehearsing here. But it seems that the atrocities visited on Africa by Arabs are not so well remembered; or if remembered at all, are minimised by most of us for all kinds of funny reasons, including Arab money and a psychological weakness for accepting unctuous Arab phrases about Afro-Arab brotherhood. Perhaps we ought now to refresh our memories about them, for our sanity and survival.

The Arab assault on Africa and Africans has been, like that of the Europeans, a bloody, expansionist saga of invasion, conquest, occupation, expropriation, slaving, racist contempt and discrimination. And it has lasted eight centuries longer than that of the Europeans! Whereas that of the Europeans began in the 15th century, that of the Arabs began in the 7th century. Before that, not one inch of African territory belonged to the Arabs. Then, suddenly, with the sword in one hand, the Koran in the other, and hunger for land and thirst for loot in their eyes, Arab hordes charged out of their desert homeland and overran Egypt. Their armies reached the north Atlantic coast of Africa, and all of supra-Sahara Africa fell under their hooves. Some of the aboriginal Africans of that region fled; those who didn't were swamped by Arab settlers, and culturally assimilated through relentless Arabisation.

For centuries thereafter, the Sahara marked the southern limit of Arab occupation of Africa. Then, by the first decades of the 16th century, the long resistance by the black kingdoms of Nubia collapsed. Arabs surged south of Aswan and took over that part of the Nile Valley that is today northern Sudan, destroying the African kingdoms they found there. Similarly, in the 16th century, Arabs moved south into Mauritania, ruled over the blacks, and Arabised their culture.

In the Nile Valley, Arab pressure to advance east from Nubia was, for centuries, checked by Ethiopia. Arab efforts to advance south and west continued until checked for half a century by the British conquest of the Sudan. But it was resumed after the withdrawal of European power following World War II.

The first skirmish provoked by the renewed Arab advance has been the protracted civil war in the Sudan. Its first phase lasted 17 years until a truce was arranged by Nimieri; its second phase, provoked by Nimieri's attempt to impose the Arab Sharia on the non-muslim blacks of southern Sudan, has not ended.

After 14 centuries of this pressure, Arabs occupy and rule on more than 7 million sq. km. of Sahelian and supra-Sahara Africa, and are itching to grab some 6 million more in the Chad and Nile basins; 100 million Arabs now call Africa their home, double the number in their entire southwest Asian home base that stretches from Syria and Iraq down to the Yemen. Anyone can verify all that by studying the maps. In contrast, by the way, the European whites now occupy only 2 million sq. km. of African land (Namibia and South Africa). So why are we so untroubled by the expansionism of the Arabs while we are quite rightly troubled by that of the Europeans?

Like the Europeans, the Arabs have massacred, enslaved and continued to discriminate against the African race. According to Vusamazulu Credo Mutwa, a Zulu recorder of the histories and customs of southern and central Africans, "Our historians mention that no less than a hundred tribes were wiped out completely in Tanganyika, Kenya, the Congo Basin, and Northern Rhodesia"[4] by Arab slavers.

[4] Credo Mutwa, *My People*, Harmondsworth: Penguin, 1971 (1964) p.227.

And down the centuries, African statesmen have cried out against the Arab slavers.

About the year 1391, Uthman Biri ibn Idris, King of Bornu, in a letter to Sultan Barquq of Egypt, complained:

> We have sent you as ambassador my cousin, Idris ibn Muhammad, because of the calamity we suffered. The Arabs who are called Judham and others have taken captive our free subjects—women and children and old people, and our relatives, and other Muslims.... These Arabs have harmed all our land, the land of Bornu, continually up to the present, and have captured our free subjects and relatives, who are Muslims, and are selling them to the slave-dealers in Egypt and Syria and elsewhere, and some they keep for themselves.[5]

And in the mid-20th century, Abubakar Tafawa Balewa, Nigeria's first prime minister, in his Hausa language novel, *Shaihu Umar*, portrayed the Arab menace in the late 19th century. In that story, the boy Shaihu Umar was kidnapped from his home near Bida, sold to Arab slave dealers, and taken to Egypt. His mother, Fatimah, who set out to find him, was herself sold off into slavery in Tripoli, Libya.

The social and cultural disfigurement provoked by the Arab slave trade was far reaching. Consider the following report by Mutwa:

> And there are also those, such as the Awemba of Central Africa, who were forced to defile the appearance of their womenfolk, as a last resort in their defence against those ruthless destroyers of my people, the slave-raiding Arabs. Even today the women of the Awemba are second in beauty only to those of the Tshokwe, and this made these

[5] Thomas Hodgkin, *Nigerian Perspectives*, London: Oxford University Press, 1975, p. 104.

women the target of any band of the slave-raiding aliens that came along. The Awemba hit on an idea that was copied by other tribes too. They pierced both the upper and lower lips of their women and fitted discs into the holes. This made the women hideous in the extreme, and it was hard for women so treated to talk, let alone eat, properly. The Arabs did not bother the Awemba much after that.[6]

Under Arab rule, blacks suffered slavery—as in Zanzibar before 1964 when a revolution overthrew Arab rule; and as in Mauritania till 1980 when slaves were liberated by decree, for the third time in 60 years! And not only have Arabs oppressed blacks under their rule: they have even discriminated against their black co-religionists down to this day. Example? In 1984, the Saudi government set up a council, "the Mutawif", to control the movements within the holy places of all pilgrims arriving at Jeddah from African countries other than Arabs. This was condemned as racist and discriminatory by officials of the Nigerian Pilgrims Welfare Boards, who also recalled an earlier move, back in 1977, to introduce a similar discriminatory measure.[7]

When all these experiences are taken together, it is clear that, as far as Arabs are concerned, all may be equal in Islam, but blacks are decidedly less equal than Arabs and other whites, and can be discriminated against and even enslaved with clear Arab consciences. In light of all that, we can better appreciate the following remark by Mutwa: "I find it hard to understand the role the Arabs are trying to assume nowadays—the pose of spokesmen for the black people, and even that of liberators. It will take more than honeyed overtures of friendship to make us forget what the Arabs did to Africa."[8]

[6] Mutwa, *op. cit.*, p. 226.
[7] "Haji '84 takes on racial undertones", *The Democrat Weekly* (Kaduna) June 10, 1984, p. 1.
[8] Mutwa, *op. cit.*, p. 227.

Given such detailed similarities in what Africa has undergone at the hands of the Arab and European branches of the white race, Pan-Africanists feel that we have no cause to be partisans in any dispute among whites, and least of all in that land dispute in the distant Levant between Zionists and Arabists.

In this matter, we need to be recalled to our senses by various Pan-Africanist spokesmen. As Marcus Garvey warned us:

> The attitude of the white race is to subjugate, to exploit, and if necessary exterminate the weaker peoples with whom they come in contact. They subjugate first, if the weaker peoples will stand for it; then exploit, and if they will not stand for subjugation nor exploitation, the other recourse is extermination.[9]

If we look without self-delusion at the careers of Arab and European intruders into Africa, we can confirm his statement for ourselves.

Marcus Garvey also admonished those among us who suffer from a spirit of subservience to the interests of whites:

> Remember always that the Jew in his political and economic urge is always first a Jew; the white man is first a white man under all circumstances, and you can do no less than being first and always a Negro, and all else will take care of itself. Let no one inoculate you with evil doctrines to suit their own conveniences. There is no humanity before that which starts with yourself, 'Charity begins at home.'[10]

And he further said: "Negroes the world over must practice one faith, that of Confidence in themselves, with One God: One Aim: One Destiny: Let no religious scruples, no

---

[9] Marcus Garvey, *Philosophy and Opinions* (Vol. 2), Edited by Amy-Jacques Garvey, New York: Atheneum, 1974, p. 13.
[10] *Ibid.*, p. 416.

political machination divide us, but let us hold together under all climes and in every country".[11]

In similar vein, Walter Rodney declared:

> Black Power is a doctrine about black people, for black people, preached by black people. I am putting it to my black brothers and sisters that the colour of our skins is the most fundamental thing about us. I could have chosen to talk about people of the same island, or the same religion, or the same class—but instead I have chosen skin colour as essentially the most binding factor in our world. In so doing, I am not saying that is the way things ought to be. I am simply recognising the real world—that is the way things are. Under different circumstances, it would have been nice to be colour blind, to choose my friends solely because their social interests coincided with mine—but no conscious black man can allow himself such luxuries in the contemporary world.[12]

Clearly, we need to eschew all perspectives which make the African interest subordinate to any non-African interest. We might as well begin by expelling the Zionist-Arabist conflict, with all its fanaticisms, from considerations of our domestic as well as foreign relations. And we should never again forget that Pan-Africanism, in the true and original sense of the term, is a movement for the redemption and rehabilitation of the black race, wherever they live in the world.

---

[11] *Ibid.*, p. 415-16.

[12] Walter Rodney, *The Groundings with My Brothers*, London: Bogle-L'Ouverture, 1969, p. 16.

Gaddafi: Arab expansionist[*]

> Would you please note one thing
> that Sudan which you preposterously claim to be
> an Arab nation in the heart of Africa
> has always been me and only me
> it's named after me—
> Sudan is me!
>
> —S. Anai Kelueljang

> These Arabs have harmed all our land, the land of Bornu, continually up to the present, and have captured our free subjects and relatives, who are Muslims, and are selling them to the slave-dealers in Egypt and Syria and elsewhere, and some they keep for themselves.
>
> —Uthman Biri ibn Idris, King of Bornu, (1391)

> I find it hard to understand the role the Arabs are trying to assume nowadays—the pose of spokesmen for the black people, and even that of liberators. It will take more than honeyed overtures of friendship to make us forget what the Arabs did to Africa.
>
> —Vusamazulu Credo Mutwa

Those who have all along suspected Libya's Gaddafi of conducting a campaign of Arab expansionism at the expense of Africans no longer have to deduce it from his adventures in Chad alone. His own description of his ambitions for Arab

[*] *The Guardian* (Lagos) May 12, 1985.

unification (*The Guardian,* Sunday May 5, 1985) gives his game away. It makes clear, to all but the wilfully blind, why he has occupied the northern strip of Chad, and why he has sponsored civil war to empower puppets who would help him annex all of Chad under an ostensible merger between Chad and Libya.

Hear "the leader" himself: "All the efforts to unite with Egypt, Sudan, Syria, Ethiopia and Chad were attempts to unite the Arab world as one nation." Please note: they were not attempts to spread socialism or radicalism or some ideology of universal human brotherhood and equality! They were simply projects in Arab nationalism. He goes on: "The Arab world is one nation, one people, they speak the same language, have the same origins, and about 98 per cent of the people have and practice one faith."

If an Arab is an Arab by virtue of race, language and religion, one must wonder when Ethiopians or Chadians became Arabs. And even if northern Sudan considers itself Arab, what of Southern Sudan? Presumably, in Gaddafi's Arab expansionist eyes, the Kanembu, Hausa, Fulani, Bulala, Sara, Chari and other blacks who constitute the overwhelming majority of Chadians are Arab, purely on account of some tiny minority of Arabs who now inhabit parts of the northern fringes of Chad. Likewise, the Oromo, Amhara, and Sidamo of Ethiopia; the Dinka and other blacks who constitute a majority of the population of the Sudan,—all these must presumably be considered of Arab stock, and their diverse languages must be classified as Arabic.

When Gaddafi declares: "The Arab world is very divided and badly needs to be united at whatever price", Africans must wonder if they are the price which Gaddafi is eager to pay. For it would appear that whenever Gaddafi covets a place, whoever lives there must be branded an Arab so that his act of Arab expansionism could be portrayed, at least to unmeticulous observers, as one of Arab unification. Incidentally, the Sudan, with only a minority of ethnic Arabs, already styles itself an Arab country, and is so regarded by much of the world.

But Gaddafi really bares the mischief in his mind when he says: "And for us, the unity of the Arab nation is one step towards a total unity of the African continent." Really? Is Syria perhaps now part of the African continent? Otherwise, how would Libya's unification with Syria be a step towards African continental unity? Perhaps what such talk of Pan-African unification by Pan-Arabists amounts to is the subordinate integration of Africa into the Arab world, the turning of Africa into a trans-Sahara annex of Arabia, as happened when various parts of Africa were classified as Overseas France or Overseas Portugal by European imperialism.

The implications of Gaddafi's pronouncements on who should be part of a unified Arab world are clear. His aim is to increase the territory of the Arab world by annexing well over five million square kilometers of the black African homeland; and to bring fifty-five million black Africans under Arab political power, and under Arab cultural hegemony through language and religion. Should Gaddafi have his way and effect a "merger" with Chad, Sudan and Ethiopia, the African lands occupied by Arab invaders would double; and the present population of "Arabs" in Africa would increase by well over 50 per cent.

In this Arab expansionist and hegemonic ambition, Gaddafi, despite all his reputation for radicalism and for championing the interests of "the masses", is no different from the Saudis whom he denounces as feudalists, conservatives and stooges of the Americans. Like the Saudis, he would like to elevate the Arab section of "the masses" by putting a subjugated Africa at their service. The only practical difference, so far, between Gaddafi and the Saudis is that, whereas his "mergers" have failed, the Saudi tactic has succeeded better. After all, only about a decade ago, the

Saudis pressured Somalia to declare itself Arab, and to embark on an intense campaign of cultural Arabisation as the *quid pro quo* for aid in fighting Ethiopia. Thus, if Gaddafi and the Saudis have their way, nearly sixty million blacks and five and a half million square kilometers of choice African lands, including most of the Nile basin, would become Arab possessions.

And from that strategic position in the African heartland, the Arabs would be poised for the next stage of their ancient mission to advance into, occupy and expropriate Africa from its black indigenes. This mission, we may recall, began with the hordes who burst out of the Arabian desert soon after Mohammed's death in the 7th century A.D. and overran Egypt, and later set out west till they planted Arab power and colonists all the way to the North Atlantic coast of Africa in what is today Morocco.

Despite all this, Gaddafi claims he is a liberator, not another in the long line of Arab expansionists into Africa! If, as he claims, it is his enemies who portray him as expansionist, I dare say they are correct, judging by his own idea of what is the Arab world.

The marvel in all this is not so much Gaddafi's tricky use of the rhetoric of radicalism and continental unification to camouflage his Arab expansionist programme. The real marvels are Africa's so-called radicals who seem so eager to be taken in by the man's posturings. One is compelled to wonder at their psychological condition: are they possessed by some racial death wish which compels them to hail and idolise a man whose policies would spell disaster for their own people?

Fortunately, the key to understanding their behaviour has been supplied by Ayi Kwei Armah. In accounting for some peculiar behaviour among Third World Marxists, he wrote:

> Intellectual orphans of the non-Western world,

those ideationally bereaved souls who have, after anguished searching, finally found in Marx and Engels their long-missed mental ancestor-figures, tend to get sharply upset when it is pointed out that Marx and Engels believed in the supremacy of Europeans over other peoples; that they were, to put it accurately, white racists. It is a crime to hurt orphans of any kind, and it would be a kindness to the intellectual orphans of the non-Western world to be able to report a lack of textual support for the charge of racism against Marx and Engels. But, in this case, the textual evidence is unkind to orphans.[1]

Likewise, there are African radicals who are cultural and intellectual orphans. Where, in their craving for ancestor-figures, they have attached themselves to some anti-Western rhetorical tradition, such orphans are genuinely upset if it is ever suggested that their radical foster-parents are racist or anti-African. For them to admit that is for them to feel cast back into the limbo of cultural orphanhood. They are genuinely upset when it is suggested that Nasser and Gaddafi and other Arabs who profess radicalism and Pan-Africanism also believe in the superiority of Arabs over Africans; that they are, to put it accurately, racists of the Arab semitic branch of the white race; and that they are devoted to promoting Arab penetration of the African continent, to expropriating African lands and resources, to politically subordinating Africans to Arabs, and to the Arabisation of African culture. It would be a kindness to such orphans to be able to report a lack of evidence for the charge of racism and anti-African expansionism against their Arab "radical" idols. But alas, as Gaddafi's own words and actions exemplify, the evidence is unkind to such orphans.

---

[1] Ayi Kwei Armah, "Masks and Marx", *Présence Africaine*, No. 131, 1984, p. 49

Let us stop fooling ourselves*

Sir,—There are several painfully wrong positions in your recent editorial and article about the Sudan, and in the piece on Botha vs the OAU (*Africa*, May 1985). They illustrate the suicidal folly of the reigning brand of Pan-Africanism, and prompt the question: Who do we think we are fooling but ourselves?

First, the Botha vs OAU article. Inventories of equipment and men are all well and good, but these are not the decisive factors in war. As experts on war, from Sun Tzu to Clausewitz, have emphasised, and as the universal insistence on appearing to wage a "just war" illustrates, the most important factor in judging the probable outcome of a war is the moral one. All else being equal, the side which feels the moral ground cut from under its feet will collapse. And even an army with superiority in every other area cannot long endure fighting if it loses on the moral frontier. Look what happened to the USA in Vietnam, despite its overwhelming superiority in equipment, population, industrial might, diplomatic and propaganda clout, and just about every other department.

Presumably, the objective of a war between the OAU and South Africa would be to liberate the blacks and give them democracy, civil rights, one-man-one-vote, etc. Right? But how do the African countries themselves rate on these issues? How many African countries practice democracy? Would their populace support a crusade to give to others something which they long for but don't themselves enjoy? Aren't they more likely to fight hard to give others some-

---

* Letter to the Editor, *Africa* (London) June 1985 (unpublished).

LET US STOP FOOLING OURSELVES

thing whose value they know from fond experience?

As for majority rule, which African country is not dominated by some minority—ethnic, religious, clannish, professional, or what have you? Which of these ruling minorities does not constitute a proportionately even smaller minority than the whites in South Africa? What moral legs can any African regime stand upon to launch a shooting crusade for majority rule in South Africa?

Regarding civil rights, freedom of speech, fair trial, humane treatment of prisoners, just ask Amnesty International or *Index on Censorship* for the records of African regimes.

You can't enthusiastically fight a protracted war to give the gift of freedom and democracy to others when you don't yourself have them. Human altruism is not known to go that far. You can imagine the demoralising impact on the African war effort if South African propaganda beams such reminders to the African population. And that they will undoubtedly do so was indicated by Botha himself, in his recent BBC world service phone-in, when he used Nigeria several times to show how black African rulers behave no differently to their black population than white South Africa does to its blacks.

When in the inventory of OAU forces, Libyan hardware is included, one is simply aghast at the extent of our wishful thinking. Libya? Where has Libya ever fought except to grab borderlands from weak neighbours like Chad? Has Libya even borne the brunt of any Arab-Israeli war? Can we expect Libya to fight for the liberation of blacks when most Arabs (however socialist, whatever their unctuous rhetoric about African unity and Afro-Arab botherhood) actually hold Africans in visceral, racist contempt? If Libyans won't die to liberate fellow Arabs like the Palestinians, how can we naively expect them to die for blacks?

On the political and military coordination of a high command, what grounds are there for anything but pessimism?

What happened to the OAU peace keeping force in Chad? Have African governments ever organised an international relief effort, let alone succeeded at it? What basis is there for hope in the logistical competence of African governments? Are they able to organise anything other than conferences, feasts, lootings and festivals? What ever happened to the All Africa Games? Haven't they all but petered out?

And what armies would fight under this mirage of a high command? These parade ground outfits, these local bullyboy squads only good for coups, mutinies, civil wars, border patrols, and for intimidating unarmed citizens and beating them up? Since when did coups become proper preparation for waging a major war with the regional superpower?

And who shall lead these troops? Our breed of coup generals and pogrom field marshals? The likes of Generals Doe and Afrifa, of Field Marshals Idi Amin, Bokassa and Nimieri? Have we forgotten that the strongest expression of opposition to Nkrumah's High Command and to war on South Africa has come from our Afrifa-style generals? Or that the idea of war against South Africa has been sponsored by civilians, and is usually dodged by African generals? For instance, didn't Nigeria's Major General Joe Garba, Rtd., recently say that a diplomatic war would end apartheid? Either he is now so thoroughly a diplomat that he naturally exaggerates the efficacy of his new profession, or he represents the preferences of an African military establishment which is most unwilling to fight real wars.

But really, do we expect that generals whose main eye is on the coffers of state, who have arrived at the keys to the coffers of state, would be eager to go into the field?

It is not that it is impossible for Africa to fight and defeat South Africa; it is rather that the will to battle South Africa has wilted, that we are distracted by other things, and should recognise that truth. After all, if ragtag peasant armies in Angola, Mozambique, Guinea-Bissau and Zimbabwe could defeat Portugal and Rhodesia despite the military, economic and diplomatic might with which NATO backed up these white powers, it is eminently possible for a continental black army to drive the white colonialists in South Africa into the sea from whence they came. But the social and political background from which such an army is recruited and supported has to be vastly different from what now obtains throughout Africa.

On the Sudan, there appears to be an enduring conspiracy to present a war against the Arabisation of Southern Sudan as if it was just another civil war, or some unfortunate disruption of Sudanese national unity, a unity which has never really existed. In the name of African unity, of a strange unity between Arab invaders and the Africans they have dispossessed and enslaved over the centuries, and now insist on ruling, the Sudanese Africans are expected to accommodate themselves to the North's permanent policy of Arabising and dominating the African population.

The problem in the Sudan is persistently misrepresented. It is not a Southern Sudan problem, contrary to what your story insists on saying. The chronic question in the Sudan, contrary to your editorial, is not "the South". Such a way of presenting the matter directs attention to the wrong quarter. The problem in the Sudan is the North; the crucial question in the Sudan is when will the North abandon its Arab expansionist mission? For the North insists on taking all of the Sudan into the Arab world; on presenting the Sudan as an Arab country; on Arabising the South by imposing the Sharia on it; on imposing Arab minority rule on the whole country, even though ethnic Arabs make up, at best, 39% of the population. Muslims may be a majority by now, but Arabs are a minority, yet Sudan is officially an "Arab" Republic, and belongs to the Arab League. Why?

Arab failure to respect the Addis Ababa Agreement of 1972 is not surprising. It should have been expected if we chose to understand the history of Arabs in Africa. How, for instance, did what is now northern Sudan become Arab in the first place? Do we think that the problem of the Sudan can be understood outside the context of that history? Given an expansionist policy now 13 centuries old, it is naive to expect Arabs to respect any agreement which blunts their ambition. They did not respect such agreements between black Nubians and the Arabs in Egypt when the African-Arab boundary was at Aswan. Which is why the frontline of African resistance has been pushed 1000 km south to Upper Nile Province. Arabs will never respect any such agreements until black power compels them to do so.

Your editorial helplessly speaks of fence-mending. What fence is there to mend? Or rather, the fence should first be erected between the Arabs and the Africans of the Sudan, by taking the African-Arab boundary back to Aswan.

Only then can the resulting fence be mended to keep both sides properly separated, and avoid the Arabs swallowing up the blacks.

If, as your editorial contends, the Sudan is Africa in microcosm, then it is no more than a microcosm of the tragedy of Africans refusing to acknowledge what is obvious—a persistent Arab policy of expropriating land, population and power from Africans in the latter's own homeland. And because the Africans refuse to recognise the obvious, they cannot devise measures to counter it. Instead, they aid and abet their own doom with pious nonsense about cooperation between predators and their prey. The tragedy is that it is the African prey who is praying for that cooperation and unification! A sheep which prays for unification with a lion by entering into the lion's belly is plainly suicidal and mad, and perhaps ought to be abandoned to its chosen fate.

On both these matters—the OAU waging war for the liberation of South African blacks, and the problem in the Sudan—if we don't have the stomach for what is plainly necessary, let us at least stop fooling ourselves. No one else is fooled by our antics, least of all the Arabs and the Anglo/Boers.

For a Black World League of Nations*

My plans [for the Pan-African Congress of 1919] as they developed had in them nothing spectacular nor revolutionary. If in decades or a century they resulted in such world organisation of black men as would oppose a united front to European aggression, that certainly would not have been beyond my dream. But on the other hand, in practical reality, I knew the power and guns of Europe and America and what I wanted to do was in the face of this power to sit down hand in hand with coloured groups and across the council table to learn of each other, our condition, our aspirations, our chances for concerted thought and action.

—W. E. B. Du Bois

As far as Negroes are concerned, in America we have the problem of lynching, peonage and disfranchisement. In the West Indies, South and Central America we have the problem of peonage, serfdom, industrial and political governmental inequality. In Africa we have, not only peonage and serfdom, but outright slavery, racial exploitation and alien political monopoly. We cannot allow a continuation of these crimes against our race.

—Marcus Garvey

* First published in *The Guardian* (Lagos) August 18, 25 and September 1, 1985.

What ought to be Nigeria's position on a proposal that has been making the rounds of African capitals for the past year or so, a proposal to create an Organisation of Black African States? I have long held that some such organisation is a geopolitical necessity, is long overdue, and should have been the natural culmination, in Africa, of the world-wide Pan-Africanist movement of the first half of the 20th century. Why that movement petered out by the 1950s, why such an organisation was not created when the black African countries got independence, and why an Afro-Arab forum, the OAU, was deemed an adequate substitute for that organisation, is a case study in African failure to uphold cardinal principles. One joke has it that Nasser slyly gave Nkrumah an Arab wife, and Nkrumah couldn't see straight after that on Pan-Africanism. Up till Manchester,[1] the Pan-African world, for Nkrumah, meant the Black World; after Fathia,[2] it meant the African land mass with its Arab and African dwellers. And with Nkrumah championing it, that has been the reigning version of Pan-Africanism ever since.

I am glad that at last an organisation that would reflect the proper sense of Pan-Africanism is being seriously considered, even if a quarter of a century late. Better late than never. However, now that we seem about to do it, we should take pains to do it correctly. Which is why I would suggest that the objective ought to be a Black World League of Nations embracing all black states in the world, not just those of Africa. Let me explain why.

The context of this discourse is the great and enduring competition between the major races of the human species. Whether some of us want to acknowledge it or not, that competition has been on for thousands of years under various disguises, and has been a decisive factor in international relations ever since the different races of the species came

[1] The 5th Pan African Congress, held in Manchester, England, 1945.
[2] Nkrumah's wife.

into conflict for land and the earth's resources. Those who ignore that competition—for land, resources, wealth, power and prestige—do so at their own peril: for what chance have they of winning a war who don't know, or choose not to acknowledge, that it is already on and far advanced?

In that long contest, there have been four main teams: the white or Caucasian race, the yellow or Mongolian race, the black or African race and the red or Amerindian race. We may, for now, leave out of account those populations produced by miscegenation between the primary races, such as the brown people of India—who are the result of some 4,000 years of miscegenation between white Aryan invaders from the region of Iran, and the autochthonous Dravidian blacks of the Indian subcontinent. In the four-way contest, the reds have had the worst of it, having been virtually exterminated. The blacks have had it second worst, having been invaded and decimated in their homelands, carted all over the place for enslavement, and dominated by all comers, especially the west-European and the semitic branches of the white race.

The yellows have come off second best, having been able to defend their east Asian homeland from all comers, without being exterminated, without being dispersed for enslavement. Those who have come off best thus far are the whites. From their relatively small homeland in west Eurasia, they have spread out and taken over more than half of the earth's land mass; with their seizure of so much land, their population exploded till they now make up well over one-third of humanity. Furthermore, they have imposed their political, military, economic and cultural power upon the whole earth, to the extent that whites control at least 95 per cent of the earth's known resources, and the two current superpowers are white.

Every white knows of this great, intra-specific competition for survival and advancement, and acts accordingly. In fact, their doctrine of white supremacy has acted as a morale booster for their team, and as an implicit reminder that there indeed is a contest going on. They are all committed to their side, which is why, whenever the chips are down, all white powers will gang up against non-whites; why Russia and the USA will patch up their allegedly irreconcilable and unto-the-death dispute over ideology, and defuse a Cuban missile crisis which would have wiped out the white powers and left the world to be inherited by the other races; which is why the atom bomb was used on Japan but not on Germany.

In contrast, most blacks seem unaware of the competition, and all too many refuse to accept that if you are black, your team is that of the black race; that the cardinal interest of your team is the survival, sovereignty, dignity and prosperity of blacks, and that any other position would be unnatural. It is this contest between the races which creates the agenda that makes necessary a Black World League of Nations. And the main point on that agenda is the very survival of the black race; and its second point is the condition in which the race shall survive—whether in dignity or degradation, prosperity or poverty, sovereignty or subordination. Which brings us back to Pan-Africanism before the Fathia factor.

The impetus for Pan-Africanism came from the humiliating fact that, by the end of the 19th century, the entire Black World, in the African homeland as well as the diaspora, lay under a blanket of white power. Only two African peoples—in Liberia and Ethiopia—had states of their own. But even these were impoverished satellites to white powers. That, in many ways, was the nadir for the black race. Things had declined from that high point where black Egypt was a beacon of civilisation to the entire world, to the point where the entire Black World had been overrun by white power. The aims of the Pan-Africanism which this terrible situation provoked were to roll white power off the backs of blacks; to create independent and self-governing black states; and through some unifying organisation, to get these states to create a power and a glory that would restore prosperity and dignity to the black race.

It was the spirit of that movement, as enunciated by Edward Blyden, W. E. B. Du Bois, Marcus Garvey, Claude McKay and others, which prodded on such African freedom fighters as Nkrumah, Kenyatta, Azikiwe and Senghor. They, in turn, galvanised countless Africans of their generation for the initial task of gaining independence for African countries. But alas, on leading their countries to independence, Africa's freedom fighters faltered on many points. They pretty much lost sight of the Pan-Africanist movement itself, and forgot the obligations its larger aims imposed upon them. Instead, the politically self-governing states became petty ends in themselves; the idea of black solidarity was abandoned, and a thorough confusion of identity caused the movement for an organisation of the independent states of the Black World to be diverted into the dead end of an Afro-Arab forum called the OAU. Even Senghor's effort to keep FESTAC all-black was defeated. And even such of those historic tasks as were still pursued—such as the ending of racism and apartheid in South Africa—lacked the clarity and cohesion necessary for their effective execution.

Yet, despite the floundering of the past 25 years, the unfinished agenda is still there, waiting for us. It cannot be willed away for as long as the contest between the races of humanity lasts.

And the outstanding points on that agenda? First, the fostering of a sense of the primacy of black identity, and the historic duties it imposes on all members of the black race; second, the expelling of white conquerors from southern Africa; third, the abolition of black slavery in both South Africa and North Africa, especially in Mauritania; fourth, stopping Arab expansion south of the Sahara, particularly through the defence of the northern frontline states of Ethiopia, Chad, and Sudan against encroachment and dismemberment by Arabs and their agents; fifth, the monitoring of the condition of the black diaspora, especially the black minorities in the Americas, Europe and Australasia, and the countering of anti-black racism wherever it occurs; and sixth, fostering black solidarity through the popularisation of the correct version of black history, through official observation of important events on the calendar of the Black World, and through celebrating the heroes of the Black World, from Menes to Mandela, Kamose to Kenyatta, Akhenaton to Azikiwe, Shabaka to Senghor, Nektharehbe to Nkrumah, Taharka to Tambo.[3]

These are some of the historic tasks which still await a world organisation of black states. What is needed is an organisation through which all black states, regardless of their internal arrangements, regardless of their other external affiliations, can get together, without outsiders, to

---

[3]Menes: The unifier (c. 3200 B.C.) and first pharaoh of Egypt.
Mandela, Nelson: (20th century A.D.) Freedom fighter and symbol of Black resistance to white domination in apartheid South Africa.
Kamose: (16th century B.C.) Egyptian noble who raised the revolt that eventually threw out the Asiatic Hyksos invaders and ended their rule.
Kenyatta, Jomo: (20th century A.D.) Freedom fighter and first president of Kenya.
Akhenaton: (14th century A.D.) Egyptian pharaoh and religious revolutionary, inventor of monotheism.
Azikiwe, Nnamdi: (20th century A.D.) Anti-colonialist leader and first president of Nigeria.
Shabaka: (8th century B.C.) Nubian prince who completed the conquest of Egypt, begun by his brother Piankhi, and established the 25th dynasty of pharaonic Egypt.
Senghor, Leopold Sedar: (20th century A.D.) A leader of the Negritude movement, first president of Senegal, and sponsor of the first World Festival of Negro Arts (1966)
Nekhtharehbe: (4th century B.C.) Last native Egyptian pharaoh during the brief reassertion of Egyptian independence before the second Persian conquest in 343 B.C.
Nkrumah, Kwame: (20th century A.D.) Anti-colonialist leader, first president of Ghana, and champion of Pan-Africanism.
Taharka: (7th century B.C.) 25th dynasty Pharaoh who resisted a determined Assyrian invasion of Egypt.
Tambo, Oliver: (20th century A.D.) Freedom fighter, leader of the African National Congress of South Africa.

work for solutions to the historic problems of the black race. From the foregoing, it should be clear that a Black World League of Nations is a historic necessity, and that setting it up is one of the historic tasks for the rest of the century.

Despite all that, we can expect resistance to the project from all sorts of Africans who are either confused about the implications of their racial identity, or are happily subservient to various anti-African interests. Predictably, some will retort: "Another organisation? Don't we already have the OAU?" Some others will say: "An organisation without our Arab brothers? Must we go it alone?" And yet others will demand: "An all-Black League? Wouldn't that be racist?" So, let me briefly answer some of these objections right away.

About the OAU, it must be candidly stated that it was inadequate from the start, that time has only made it worse, and that its inherent perversions have become manifest. As a coalition of Arab and African states, it perverts the fundamental goals of the very Pan-Africanism which was the impetus to its formation. It does so by including one branch of the white race, the Arabs, which had perpetrated, and still is determined to perpetrate, upon the black race the very atrocities which Pan-Africanism arose to oppose, namely, conquest, expropriation, slavery and racism. Had that principle which excluded a white, racist South Africa been applied with consistency and historical knowledge, it should have also excluded from the OAU all the Arab states of North Africa. But in the confused climate of the 1960s, in the euphoria of anti-European solidarity, Africans lost their bearings, got confused about what Pan-Africanism was really about, and with Nkrumah's help, allowed Pan-Africanism to be hijacked by the Arabs and emasculated within the OAU.

Once that initial perversion is comprehended, much of the OAU's subsequent erratic career becomes explainable. For instance, it is significant just how many of the issues which have bogged it down have been Arab issues, whereas other issues which ought to have preoccupied it have been left untouched lest Arab sensitivities be offended. Just consider Chad, the SADR, and the Ogaden war.

In Chad, the OAU was bogged down and compelled to squander resources to contain Libya's effort to grab and annex Chad, thus expropriating it for the Arab world. The conflict over the Saharaoui Arab Democratic Republic—which obstructed OAU deliberations on so many occasions and even kept it, for quite a while, from attending to the vital matter of Africa's economic collapse—is in fact a conflict between various Arab interests over which of them should gobble up a slice of Africa abandoned by Spain. And as for the Ogaden war, it became an instrument in the old Arab effort to dismember Ethiopia and Arabise the Horn of Africa when the Somalis were encouraged into it by Saudi promises to help on condition that Somalia join the Arab League. What is worse, this anti-African aspect of the conflict was not highlighted and opposed by the OAU; the premise of its conciliation efforts thus implicitly legitimised an unconscionable act of Arab expansionist brigandage.

Whereas the OAU had been bogged down by such issues, it hasn't found it possible to raise such issues as the enslavement of blacks in Mauritania; the Saudi-led Arab financing of the dismemberment of Ethiopia through muslim factions in Eritrea; or the African-Arab conflict within the Sudan. These topics have been taboo. An OAU where such issues as would top the agenda of a genuinely Pan-Africanist organisation cannot be raised; an OAU that is distracted by dissensions arising from Arab adventures against Africans, cannot claim to be the fulfilment of the Pan-Africanist dream of an organisation for ending the humiliations of the black race.

This perversion of including Arabs aside, the OAU, as is well known, is also under the thumb of the Western powers who still manage to wield more influence in it than all the African members put together. When these facts are taken into account, one must conclude that the OAU is conceptually and operationally a disaster for Africans. I would even go so far as to urge that that freak organisation be disbanded; for it is an impediment which is masquerading as a channel for African liberation and advancement.

To those who feel uncomfortable at the idea of breaking out of the Arab-African embrace; who think that solidarity with others requires that we sacrifice our separate identity and organisations, a question demands to be put: Don't those Arab 'brothers' of yours have their own separate Arab League? Have they disbanded it? Where is the Black World equivalent of their Arab League?

Whatever the merits and demerits of Afro-Arab solidarity on certain issues, that should not blind us to our need to have an organisation all to ourselves. To refuse to create a separate Pan-African organisation (in the original and proper sense of Pan-African as Black World), would be like sheep insisting that jackals always be present whenever sheep meet. That way, the sheep can never get to discuss how to rid themselves of the menace of sheep-eating jackals.

Objections, even violent objections, to any organisation exclusively for the black race can be expected from those Africans who are victims of the various pseudo-universalist doctrines which make white hegemony acceptable to its victims. For instance, African Christians, with their dream of a universal human brotherhood in Christ, in which all are equal without regard to race, are likely to look with revulsion at the prospect of a Black World organisation whose doors would be barred to their white co-religionists. So too African Muslims with their passionate desire for that Dar el Islam where there is no racial discrimination; so too African Marxists with their preoccupation with that abstract universal working class in which racial considerations are either abolished or taboo. Of course, like deluded people, they mistake their dream world for the real world and, like the mad, behave as if their dream world were already here.

But we need, all the same, to understand such absurd behaviour. Those white-sponsored universalisms have strong appeal for those blacks who are anxious to escape their racial particularity into some alleged universality. They are usually people who, overwhelmed by white supremacist propaganda, have come to accept that the black race is inferior, despicable, and only fit to be escaped from by anyone unfortunate enough to be born into it. And since they cannot remake themselves into whites (though many try by bleaching their skins and brainwashing their minds), the only way of escaping from the despised black race is into some universalist community and identity, created by whites, and left open to all comers who need a sense of proximity to the whites. It is of such people that Marcus Garvey said: "So many of us find excuses to get out of the Negro Race, because we are led to believe that the race is unworthy—that it has not accomplished anything. Cowards that we are! It is we who are unworthy, because we are not contributing to the uplift and up-building of this noble race."[4]

What such Africans will not face up to is that these versions of universal human brotherhood have failed to address the core of the historical problems of the black race; and that their proprietors have also inflicted—or proved unable to stop their racial brothers from inflicting—conquest, slavery and racism upon blacks. What these fake doctrines of universalism succeed in hiding from their African adherents is that their alleged colour blindness is but a gimmick to keep blacks from organising separately to tackle the problems imposed on them across the line of colour.

Those Africans who are so eager to flee into any of these allegedly universal, colour blind communities (Christendom, Dar el Islam, the world proletariat) tend to cower at the thought of being accused of "anti-racist racism" by their white friends. Let it therefore be made clear why such accusations are false.

[4] Marcus Garvey, *Philosophy and Opinions*, p.6.

Pan-Africanism does not claim that the black race is superior to any other and should rule others; *that* would be black racism. Pan-Africanism is simply concerned with the unification and upliftment of the black race, and with the development of its civilisation. Now, that does not constitute racism. Those who accuse Pan-Africanism of racism are actually opposed to the prospect of that black unity which would exclude whites from meddling in matters of vital interest to blacks, and so limit the ability of white racists to infiltrate, disorganise and dominate the Black World. The charge is predicated on the gratuitous error of equating the racial with the racist. To be racial is to be limited to members of a given race; to be racist is to believe in the inherent superiority of a given race. Thus, an organisation can be racial without being racist. This distinction is vital, and any attempt to gloss it over must be resisted. Glossing it over is what allows racists to weaken resistance from victims of their own racism by claiming that any anti-racist organisation must be multi-racial, thus enabling racists to join, undermine and sidetrack it from a determined assault on their cherished racism.

Some of those who accept the need for a separate Black World organisation may still prefer that it be called the African or Pan-African League of Nations. And they may do so from residual unease about using the racial term black. Those who are squeamish about being called black or negro are free to substitute the term African, provided they recognise the equivalence of the terms, and use them correctly. After all, an African is defined as a negro, a member of the black race, a native of Africa. Thus, a white African is a contradiction in terms. In particular, Arabs, being whites native to Asia; and Anglo/Boers, being whites native to Europe, are not Africans, whatever their pretensions, and they cannot legitimately be included in an African or Pan-African organisation. So long as that rule is clearly understood and is not violated (which it has been in the OAU), there should be no objection to the substitution of "Pan-African" for "Black World".

By the way, from the definition of African, the term black African is tautologous. Though the redundancy is judged useful for distinguishing Africans from the white settlers in Africa, it is dangerously misleading in so far as it lends credence to the idea that there is such a thing as a white African. Its practical harm, as in the matter of including Arabs in an African organisation, is ample reason for putting it out of use. A black African is simply an African; white settlers in Africa are simply white settlers in Africa.

While on this matter of language, we might as well attend to a misuse of the term black, which is spreading from the USA and Britain, to denote all non-white groups which suffer racial discrimination. Thus, Pakistanis in Britain are suddenly regarded as blacks. This metaphoric use of the term ought to be strictly discouraged before we are told, and find gullible Africans accepting, that Pakistanis, Mexicans, Vietnamese, and even Turks and Arabs, are blacks simply because they are discriminated against in Europe and America; and that they should therefore be admitted into any organisation of the black race.

Furthermore, to use black as a metaphor for victimage and being oppressed is to lend credence to the view that these are the natural lot of the black race. To be oppressed is not our natural lot; it has only been our lot in recent history; all races have suffered oppression at some time or other in history; and we would be stupid to allow black to be seen as the badge of victimage. Besides, the very point of a Black World League of Nations is to end the oppression of blacks, not to perpetuate it, not even in matters of symbolism. Black should therefore cease to be the symbolic colour of victimage, and should become the symbol, if anything, of victory against oppression. In fact, this matter of propagating correct usages of words like African and black, and of ending the racist associations which have accumulated on them, should be added to the agenda of the Black World League of Nations.

Having indicated at some length why a Black World League of Nations is absolutely necessary, and why objections to it are untenable, it remains simply to emphasise that, in the context of the competition between the races, if you are black or African, your team is the black race; and it is futile to pretend that it is not. It is naive in the extreme to think you can wish away your racial identity, and substitute for it some changeable class identity or an adopted religious identity. Furthermore, a rat doesn't cease being preyed upon just because it dresses up like a cat, and thinks it is a cat. What is done to rats will be done to it, until rats get together and cut off the claws of cats.

Nigeria, with its size and resources, with its pretensions to being the giant nation in the Black World, with its desire to be seen as a champion of black liberation, cannot afford to oppose such an organisation without thereby making it quite clear that it is the giant obstacle to the liberation of the black race. After all, the objectives outlined above for such a league are precisely some of the inescapable steps towards the liberation and rehabilitation of the black race from its centuries of subjugation and humiliation by others.

Part Four: Cultural control systems

The greatest weapon used against the Negro is DISORGANISATION.

—Marcus Garvey

Pan-Africanism and the Nobel Prize

> It is worse than stupid to allow a people's education to be under the control of those who seek not the progress of the people but their use as means of making themselves rich and powerful. It is wrong for the University of London to control the University of Ghana. It is wrong for the Catholic Church to direct the education of the black Congolese.
>
> —W. E. B. Du Bois

I: That Nobel Prize brouhaha[1]

What a brouhaha was kicked up by that *Newsweek* speculation about some African getting the Nobel Prize for literature in 1985! When the hopes were dashed, somebody asked what I thought of the prize not having gone to Wole Soyinka. Well, I was disappointed actually. In my view, the Nobel Prize and Soyinka's literary works deserve each other. It would have been an excellent case of the undesirable honouring the unreadable. I certainly wish them both better luck next time.

Actually, I've never thought much of the Nobel Prize. In "Olympics, Nobel Prizes and the Black World" (*Africa*, October 1980), I spelt out why I consider it undesirable for Africans—namely, its role as a bewitching instrument for Euro-imperialist intellectual hegemony, and the conceit that a gaggle of Swedes, all by themselves, should pronounce on intellectual excellence for the diverse cultures of

---

[1] *The Guardian* (Lagos) Sunday, November 3, 1985.

the whole wide world. Likewise, I am not one of those who stand in uncomprehending awe before Soyinka's literary works, and the reasons are made clear in *Toward the Decolonization of African Literature* (1980). Maybe, if Soyinka's works were even harder to make sense of, and even more pandering to Graeco-Roman mythology, they might have edged out the specimen of that hard-to-decipher species—the French *nouveau roman*—which got the Swedish Academy's nod.

As for all the heartaching in some circles, I don't see why any self-respecting African, who understands the cultural role of the Nobel Prize, should lust for a moment for the damn thing.

II: The Pan-Africanist case against the Nobel Prize[2]

An unexamined garland, they say, is not worth wearing: it could turn out to be a noose for leading us astray and strangling us. From the Pan-Africanist standpoint, every relation into which we were ushered at independence needs to be stringently evaluated. But many, alas, have not been. Only recently, following some passing remarks I made about its undesirability, did the pros and cons of Africa's relationship to the Nobel Prize become a matter of heated comment in the Nigerian press. The controversy makes it necessary to restate a Pan-Africanist case against the prize which I had put forward in 1980.[3]

Two principal arguments have emerged from those who think it desirable for Africans. They say an award to an African brings prestige to Africa; and that African recipients could use the $200,000 prize money, and that African countries could use the foreign exchange. But do these con-

[2] *The Guardian* (Lagos) April 13 and 20, 1986.
[3] "Olympics, Nobel Prizes and the Black World", *Africa* (London) October 1980.

siderations outweigh the Pan-Africanist objections to the prize? But first, let the case be heard.

To decide whether a prize is desirable or not, we need to look at the purposes for which it was set up, and at the mechanism for making the awards, especially the composition of the deciding committee. We also have to look at what kinds of works get it and what kinds do not, and what it encourages in aspirants.

The basic Pan-Africanist case is that, despite its universalist image, the Nobel Prize is not a genuine world prize; that is to say, it is not one organised by all the nations, administered by all nations, and free from domination by a parochial minority of nations. Beneath its universalist image, the Nobel Prize is, in fact, a local European prize. The standards applied in awarding it are European; the awards committees are European; and the awards are manipulated with full opportunistic regard for their role in fostering the hegemony of the West over the rest of the world.

As Jean-Paul Sartre said when he rejected the literature prize for 1964, "the Nobel Prize appears objectively as an honour restricted to writers from the West or to rebels from the East." And, needless to say, to fellow travellers from the Third World. For, when bestowed on persons from there, the prizes have, almost invariably, gone to persons who have accommodated themselves to the Western world outlook and served its interests. Rebels against the West and what it stands for rarely get it, unless, as with Pablo Neruda and Gabriel García Márquez, their dazzling achievement is such that to deny them the prize would betray the parochialism behind its universalist image.

The pro-Western bias of the Nobel Prize may elude those who accept its image as the world prize without peer for excellence in the fields it honours. However, what is judged excellent are works which a committee of Swedes considers significant for Western values and Western power. Each category of the prize can be shown to operate in that way.

The Peace Prize is for preserving the peace on Western terms, or for engineering a battle truce on terms compatible with the interests of the West, or for limiting the damage to Western interests from insurrections by the oppressed. Thus, when rebellions seriously challenge Western hegemony and white racism, the Peace Prize is brought out to manipulate them into channels least threatening to Western power. Cases in point are the awards to Martin Luther King, Albert Luthuli and Desmond Tutu.

When Martin Luther King was given the prize in 1964, he was in competition with Malcolm X for the allegiance of the Afro-American population. King was a Christian minister, and the apostle of a non-violent path to Afro-American emancipation from American racism. Malcolm X, in contrast, was a Black Muslim minister who was beginning to gather opposition to the non-violent campaign which he diagnosed as futile. Naturally, Malcolm X's way was far more threatening to white America and to the interests of the entire Western world than King's. By giving King the Nobel Peace Prize, the establishment of the white West intervened in the black rebellion, and gave a prestigious boost to that faction which they judged more tame and accommodating.

The awards to Luthuli (1960) and Tutu (1984) were politically quite similar. Like King, these two were spokesmen for the non-violent, multi-racial strand of opposition to apartheid in South Africa. They were in competition with leaders and factions which wanted, like Malcolm X, to fight apartheid by any means necessary, and until the white settlers were driven into the sea. In Tutu's case, he competes with the ANC militants and the young urban rebels. Conferring the Nobel Peace Prize on these "moderate" leaders was an intervention from the highest levels of the Western establishment to boost the prestige of the milder version of African rebellion, and enable it to keep its hold on the populace. All that may seem like passive but strategic manipulation; but the active manipulation of Peace Prize recipients was recently exhibited in the Tutu case.

While on a visit to the USA at the end of 1985, Tutu voiced support for the ANC, and pointed out that the anti-apartheid campaign could soon enter a more violent phase where black servants would poison their white masters. For airing such views, he was pounced upon by the US leadership and by a chorus of white South Africans. George Bush, the US vice president, claimed that such talk cast doubt on Tutu's commitment to non-violence. His standing as a Nobel Peace laureate was said to be under a cloud. On returning to South Africa, Tutu found it necessary to qualify what he had said: he declared that while he agreed in principle with the ANC, he did not agree with its methods; that he was categorically against violence, and his statement had been an analysis of the situation rather than a recommendation of violence, etc., etc. Thus was the good bishop tied up and restrained with the ribbons of the Nobel Prize.

The West's interest in keeping their opponents non-violent deserves to be understood. It is, after all, an ancient technique to saddle your opponent with a reputation which inhibits him from using his most effective weapon. Because the West is determined not to concede to anything but superior violence, it endeavours, through propaganda, to shepherd resistance into the non-violent path. Using such emasculating honours, they can hold a leader captive within the futile options of non-violence while going right ahead with their own violence. He, in turn, holds his followers in line, and prevents them from joining those who fight Western violence with a counter violence. Consequently, the armed opposition is smaller, and the Western system is safer.

While political manipulation by the Peace Prize is the easiest to demonstrate, the Prize for Economics is the most blatantly ideological. Its conception of economics is limited to theories and practices that help the Western capitalist system. These prizes have gone to those judged to have most usefully contributed to maintaining the system. The 1979 award to Sir Arthur Lewis, a black Anglo-liberal economist from the West Indies, merely confirms the point. His award was for analyses of economic processes in developing countries. However, those who have followed his career might well wonder whether it was not really for the great service he rendered the West by helping to lure Nkrumah's Ghana, via the Lewis Strategy for Ghana's "development", into a blind alley where she was set upon and robbed of some £200 million worth of reserves held in London banks. If so, his prize money works out as a commission of $1 for each £1,000 of which Ghana was robbed.

As for the science and literature prizes, their impact is simply to misdirect the efforts of non-Western scientists and intellectuals. The science prizes are given for "fundamental research", that is to say, for research of fundamental importance to the West. Whether or not such research is important for the rest of the world does not appear to matter. Given our neo-colonial subordination to the West, the best scientific minds throughout the "Free World" are drawn, by their training and the momentum of their disciplines, to research areas which might catch the eyes of the Nobel scouts. Those African scientists who are eager to prove themselves to the world (those who, it might be said, want to be "scientists, not African scientists") would rather work on biogenetic topics, for example, than on the problems of the tsetse or malaria control in Africa. The former, being important to the West for biological warfare, is granted an international prestige denied the latter.

The literature prize is similarly disorienting for those African Euro-assimilationists who make it the guiding goal of their career. In subtle ways, they (of whom it is said that they write for the Nobel rather than for us Africans) will accommodate themselves to the Western world outlook, to its prejudices and enthusiasms. Some may studiously avoid themes and treatments which might irk the West by exposing the savageries of their colonial intervention in Africa. If they combine that evasion with a relentless criticism of African barbarities down through history, the net effect of such portrayal is to confirm for Europeans their arrogant fantasy that the black man is the savage junior brother to the humane and civilised white man.

Other African writers, following the prescriptions of their Western mentors, may mimic some fashionable styles from Western literature. If their works are consequently incomprehensible to African readers, that does not matter to them so long as scouts for Western prize-givers are delighted. The result is a Euro-assimilationist literature which is bewitched by Western claims of cultural superiority, and which grovels for acceptance into the tributary streams of Western literature. Yet other African writers might contrive to make their Euro-assimilationist works appear authentic products of the African tradition by craftily giving them enough Africanesque patina and inlays to satisfy the Western tourist taste for exotica. Such works become sophisticated literary versions of airport art.

It is thus that the Eurocentric disorientations induced by the Nobel Prize divert some African writers and scientists from devoting their full energies to developing African science and literature. And it is thus that, in every category, the Nobel Prize channels the efforts of aspirants, and manipulates laureates away from their Pan-African responsibilities. Which is why the Nobel prize should be regarded by the Black World, not as a badge of honour, but as a disorienting gift from our racist, imperialist foes; which is why it should be repudiated.

In the light of the foregoing, can the arguments for the prize be upheld against the Pan-Africanist case? First of all, what good is a prestige which stuns and disorients us? Is it not a neo-colonial equivalent of the OBE which the British used to confer on those Africans whom our anti-colonial fathers dubbed the "Obedient Boys of the Empire"? Blacks who crave the Nobel Prize, like those who craved the OBE, must be seen as camp followers of Western imperialism. Admittedly, we have long suffered world humiliation and insult; but does grovelling for recognition from our insulters reduce or compound the humiliation?

Now about the prize money. Sina Odugbemi has argued that

> Any African who wins the $200,000 prize and refuses it is a monumental idiot. For he will deny himself the means of escaping into the bliss of full-time professional money. And apart from that, African writing could use the Nobel. It will be one big marketing score if it comes to our continent. We could use the foreign exchange the consequent greater attention will bring our efforts. Political as the prize is, the Blackist attack on it is misguided.[4]

The saddest part of Sina's argument is that it accepts that the prize is undesirably political, yet opts for the prize money because of alleged need. Africans may be poor, as persons and as countries; but are we so famishingly poor as to have to sell our political, economic and cultural autonomy? Certainly, no member of that African elite from among whom candidates might be selected could convincingly plead ravenous poverty of the sort that might justify selling one's mother.

Of course, anybody could use an extra $200,000. But money is not everything; it certainly is not the only thing. If it was, what would be the objection to the slave trade or to prostitution? By the way, such sacrificing of basic political and cultural integrity for money has long been the bane of

---

[4] "Wole Soyinka: bashers and fanatics", *Sunday Vanguard* (Lagos) December 29, 1985.

African society. For long centuries, hunger for money was used to excuse the selling of Africans by Africans to Europeans and Arabs for export and enslavement. Apparently, that destructive tradition is alive and well in some quarters.

May I observe that Sina's argument could be used to condemn John Fashanu for spurning a much larger prize money (£350,000 or some $500,000) when he declined an invitation to go play soccer in South Africa and so help apartheid to preserve itself. For that, most right-thinking Africans cheered him. No one who did so could accept Sina's argument, once made aware of the Nobel Prize's role in shoring up the Western imperialist system, once aware that the Nobel Prize is the august guardian of the ideological ramparts of the same system that gave us the Sharpeville and Soweto bloodbaths and the current massacres in South Africa.

If any African winner of the Nobel Prize should find its prize money irresistible, I believe a handful of Nigerian tycoons could be persuaded to contribute $500,000 to him, on the condition that he rejects that culturally undesirable prize and thereby helps to break its spell over Africa. I recommend the sum of $500,000 to compensate him, not only for the prize money, but also for whatever boost in book sales he would lose by turning down the prize.

What the Nobel is not

Wonders will never cease!

In late 1986, the intellectual and political elite of Africa reacted to the news from Stockholm as if it were an emancipation proclamation. It was as if the Grand Oracle of Culture, mouthpiece of the Great White God of Civilisation, had announced that the black race had at long last become the intellectual equal of the white race, and that a Nobel to Wole Soyinka was proof thereof. Like slaves hearing they were free at last, they clapped, they shouted, they danced for joy; some popped champagne and dived into bars and uttered amazing things. Those who could afford it trooped off to the Great White Altar of Culture at Stockholm, to be present at the immortal moment when the black race would receive its certificate of intellectual emancipation.

Wole Soyinka himself helped set the tone with his great cry of joy:

> This prize is a recognition of our culture and our traditions in Africa and I am very glad about it.[1]

From Accra, Nkrumah's Pan-Africanist capital, where Du Bois is buried and from where Pan-African sages used to proclaim the independence of the African personality, the current Ghanaian leader, J. J. Rawlings, chimed in:

> African literature has gained full international recognition and acceptance as a literary art form.[2]

---

[1] *The Independent* (London) October 17, 1986, p. 10.
[2] *West Africa* (London) October 27, 1986, p. 2248.

And in Harare, capital of Zimbabwe, Lewis Nkosi, eminent South African literary critic, announced:

> Africa has won a new sense of confidence. Until an African won [the Nobel], Europeans always felt we were second or third class citizens in the world of the arts.[3]

And from Lagos, capital of the biggest and richest independent black nation, President Ibrahim Babangida exulted:

> Wole's Nobel Prize for literature is a most powerful and thundering rebuttal of the slander often peddled by racists all over the world that the black man is intellectually inferior to other races. The racists must now eat their words.[4]

Like their leaders, ordinary Africans reacted as if the news was that Jack Johnson had wrested the world heavyweight crown and ended a previous all-white monopoly. "Isn't it wonderful," one wrote, "that a Nigerian was just named the world's brightest scholar in the creatively demanding field of literature?"[5] Another wrote: "I hope this Nobel award will not be the last to be given to an African in the next few decades."[6] Now that the celebration is over, let us soberly try to understand what fools we allowed Wole Soyinka and his Nobel prizegivers to make of us all.

The pity is not that an undesirable prize has once again been tossed into our midst: Who can restrain the Swedish Prospero from rewarding his African Ariels? Or stop Professor Higgins from honouring the mimic powers of his Eliza Doolittle?

The pity is not that the prize was accepted with joy by the

---

[3]*The African Guardian*(Lagos) October 30, 1986, p. 16.
[4]The *Daily Times* (Lagos) December 3, 1986.
[5]Sunday Ikenwoko Ezeh, *West Africa* (London) November 10, 1986, p. 2368.
[6]Obafemi Ilesanmi, *West Africa* (London) November 3, 1986, p.2321.

one on whom it was bestowed: Can one really expect a Nigger Tom to spurn a gift of laurels and bags of gold from the White Massa in the big Baas house?

The pity is that the descendants of those who invented writing; who gave Europe its alphabets; who taught Europe Chemistry, Philosophy, Architecture, Mathematics, Engineering and much else; who gave the world its oldest literature, have been reduced to pining so intensely for Europe to certify that their race has intellectual ability. It was like watching a grand old man dancing for joy because his own grandchild had finally recognised him as one equipped to procreate, and pronounced him a man at last! When a man throws a party to celebrate an insult, what does he deserve but pity?

But why did Africa react to the bestowal of a European prize on one of its writers as if it was an emancipation proclamation freeing the whole race from the stigma of intellectual inferiority? In doing so, Africans exposed several disturbing things about themselves: 1) that a generation after political independence, all too many of us are still sick with complexes which were inflicted on our psyche by European conquest and miseducation; 2) that many of us thoroughly misunderstand the nature and the significance of the Nobel, and so have mistaken its award to one of us as a declaration of our intellectual emancipation, whereas indeed it is no such thing; 3) that in so far as we acknowledge our complexes, we still misunderstand what it would take to cure them.

The assertion of African inferiority, drummed for so long into the African psyche by colonial propaganda, has bred a pathological longing for European validation of what we are and what we do. The notion, spread by imperialism, that Europe, as political master of the world, knows best and is the rightful arbiter and definer of all things, has led all too many of us to believe that we are not whatever we are unless Europe says so: they claimed we were inferior, and we believed that it was so; if they now say that we are their equals, then it must be so; and if tomorrow they once again claim that we are inferior to them, then it will be so. The situation is to be determined by their say-so! Having swallowed this view of things, we crave their seal of approval for whatever we do. And at the first sign of our being accepted into their company, we give vent to a boundless joy: "Massa says we smart! Massa says we smart! Rejoice, all you niggers, rejoice!" And we overlook the little fact that such a reaction does not release us from our complexes, but merely testifies to its presence.

Most adults have probably observed individuals who are afflicted with this sort of disease. After their advances have been snubbed by a woman, some men will endure any indignity, stomach any insult, sink into the mire of self-abasement, and even squander their fortune in a marathon siege on that woman's affection. If they eventually extract a word of praise, a smile or a kiss from her disdainful lips, they react with boundless joy. When we watch such a man, we know he is sick, we know he is in bondage, no matter how much he struts and boasts about being his own man. Alas, our cultural counterpart of his sickness was not eradicated by political independence; it remains with us to this neo-colonial day. The reaction to Soyinka's Nobel is public proof of that. The intensity of our euphoria indicates just how much work needs to be done to restore self-confidence to the African elite by the year 2000. The job will be difficult, but, by our illustrious ancestors, it will be done.

Over the years, the Nobel has conned its way into acceptance as the world prize for intellectual excellence. But it is neither a *world* prize nor a reward for excellence; rather, it is a western European reward for those who render specific kinds of service to Western power and Western global hegemony. Were it indeed the intellectual heavyweight crown of the world, then an African winning it would prove a point about the ability of Africans—and that might help to diminish African feelings of inferiority by demonstrating to ourselves that what our alleged superiors can do we too can do.

However, the Nobel Prize is not an intellectual world cup; it is not an intellectual version of the world heavyweight crown; it is not an intellectual equivalent of an Olympic gold medal. A black being awarded a Nobel is not like Jack Johnson winning the heavyweight crown for the first time ever. A black being awarded a Nobel is not like Jesse Owens setting four world records in one day, or carrying off four Olympic gold medals before Hitler's very eyes, thus making nonsense of the myth of Aryan superiority. A black being awarded a Nobel is not like Nigeria's Golden Eaglets winning the Under-17 World Cup in Beijing, the first time it was competed for, to the televised chagrin of the white officials there. Now, why is a Nobel Prize different from all these?

When black athletes win in world competitions, they do so before a world which knows the rules and can measure the victory margin with its own eyes. Such is not the case with the Nobel. One does not win a Nobel; it is bestowed on one. All we hear is an announcement that some Scandinavian cabal, in its mysterious wisdom, has decided thus and thus. All that the public is admitted to is the ceremony held for the alleged winners in a contest whose rules and venues and officials are shadowy.

It is all rather like what used to happen in colonial days. Our African fathers, like others in the British Empire, would wait for the King's New Year's Honours List—the king of England, that is! They would wait to hear if any African would be named a knight of England! And if any was, they rejoiced. How the British king chose his knights, he never told us. What one had to do to be picked for that knighthood, we never were told. What services one had to render to British interests were not disclosed to the public.

But one thing some of our fathers (the nationalist, anti-imperialist crusaders among them) knew in their marrows: rulers do not honour those who injure their interests; they reserve their honours and rewards for those who render them exceptional service. An award of a knighthood to an African by the British monarch was therefore an advertisement that that African was a valued servant of England's emperor-king. He was therefore a presumed agent of anti-African interests. If you were an O.B.E., you were dubbed an Obedient Boy of the Empire; and you were certainly not to be trusted or hailed by the African victims of, and crusaders against, that same empire.

Similarly, when a black gets his Nobel today (his Neocolonial O.B.E. Lollipop), it does not mean that he has rendered exceptional service to the interests of Africa, or to those of the Black World. Anyone conversant with the intellectual and political history of the Black World can easily name 20 black thinkers and activists who have made first-rate contributions to black progress in this century, but who would not conceivably have been considered for the Nobel Prize. Can anyone soberly imagine that the Nobel scouts would consider giving their prize to such of our first rank writers and activists as Marcus Garvey, W. E. B. Du Bois, George Padmore, Amilcar Cabral, Malcolm X, Agostinho Neto, Kwame Nkrumah or Samora Machel? Or to Aime Cesaire, Cheikh Anta Diop, Richard Wright, Frantz Fanon, C. L. R. James, Okot p'Bitek, Alex Haley, Sembene Ousmane or Walter Rodney?

Let us compare the above men, whose contributions to the Black World are incontrovertible, with the type to whom Nobel Prizes are awarded. Where, I ask you, would Arthur Lewis and Wole Soyinka stand among those giants? Wouldn't they both disappear between the toes of a Garvey or Du Bois? If either man is to be regarded as a pre-eminent black intellectual, on whose say-so would that be? That of the Black World or the White?

Let me reiterate: The Nobel Prize is not an intellectual world cup or belt or medal. When it is bestowed upon a black, it does not mean he has won a championship fight on our behalf; it does not mean he is the best and brightest of the blacks in his field; it does not mean he is an intellectual counterpart of Jack Johnson, or Jesse Owens, or Nigeria's Golden Eaglets. All it means is that, in the view of the West's Establishment, he has done great work for them. It means that, like the African O.B.E.s of colonial times, he has been acknowledged as a valued servant of Western hegemony.

To end all doubt, all reasonable doubt about that, we can examine the careers of those blacks on whom Nobels have been conferred, and see what each did for Western hegemony in order to earn it.

Let me first call in evidence one of that minority of African intellectuals who dissent from the general euphoria about Nobel awards. Pitika Ntuli, an Azanian poet and sculptor of the Soweto generation, has said:

> When one speaks of Nobel Prizes, what crops up into my mind is: Who are given these peace prizes and why? I am confronted by a series of coincidences. When it was offered to Luthuli in 1960, it was half a year after the Sharpeville massacre, when our people decided to take up armed struggle. They offered it to Tutu after the current series of massive uprisings in our country started in 1984. And we also remember that when it was given to Martin Luther King, it was during the wave of Black consciousness in the United States of America. It is a political weapon to silence the people in order to contain them. I denounce anybody who accepts this kind of prize.
>
> It is not surprising that Wole Soyinka received the literature prize. First, we've got to look at the people who offer the prize. What is their politics, what is their interest, and what are their views on the ordinary people on the continent? Wole Soyinka writes for those types of people; he is not writing for us Africans. I am a highly sophisticated man, with two masters' degrees, and I

write; but I need an interpreter to read his *Interpreters*. Soyinka's contribution is to mystify the actual issues in our countries. I am suspicious.

The coincidences spotted by Pitika Ntuli are more than coincidences; his suspicions do not prove groundless when investigated. Martin Luther King, Albert Luthuli and Desmond Tutu were specifically given Nobels for leading or shepherding, along non-violent lines, the Afro-American campaign against racial discrimination and the anti-apartheid campaign in South Africa. They had rendered a crucial service to Western hegemony by containing those insurrections by the oppressed which could have smashed Western power. Had such leaders emerged in Vietnam to guide them into non-violence, might they not still be ruled by France, or by American puppets like Ngo Dinh Diem? Would Rhodesia have become Zimbabwe if the Zimbabweans had not abandoned non-violence? Had the ANC embarked on armed struggle back in 1960, might Azania not be a free country today?

Before these non-violent gentlemen appeared on the scene, Ralph Bunche had received his Nobel Peace Prize in 1950. Why? He had successfully negotiated an Arab-Israeli truce in Palestine in 1949, a service to Western hegemony in that part of the world. He was later berated by Afro-American militants for standing aloof from his own people's freedom movement; and he was eventually shamed into participating in the Selma and Montgomery Civil Rights Marches of 1965.

Sir Arthur Lewis got his Nobel specifically for his analyses of economic processes in developing nations. These were the analyses upon which he based his advice on economic development to several African, Asian and Caribbean governments. What was the product of such advice? Let me illustrate with what it helped the West to do to Ghana in the late 1950s.

The Lewis Strategy persuaded Nkrumah's government that it needed £2 million a year of *foreign* investment if it was to achieve economic "take off". To get that investment, Ghana had to gain the confidence of foreign investors by several measures, including keeping a healthy foreign reserve in London. Ghana was therefore persuaded to leave her £200 million worth of reserves deposited in London so as to inspire investors with enough confidence to bring £2 million a year into the country.

But why any *foreign* investment at all? If £2 million a year were taken from those reserves and invested in Ghana by Ghana, it would still take a century to exhaust them. That would be ample time, one would think, to achieve "take off," and time enough to do so without a penny of foreign investment. But with the expert Lewis guiding the thinking of the Ghana government, it proved unthinkable to repatriate part or all of that £200 million.

Before long, as the price of cocoa, Ghana's chief export, was driven down by operators of the London cocoa market, and as the prices for Ghana's imports rose, and as the cost of trade invisibles like freight and insurance increased, Ghana developed balance of payments deficits which wiped out her foreign reserves. When it is understood that the alleged, but groundless, need for foreign investment was simply a way to constrain Ghana to behave in ways advantageous to the British (such as leaving her reserves in London where they could be raided through a balance of payments scam), it will be seen that, in plain language, Ghana was set up to be robbed by none other than the Lewis Strategy. For such advice—lucrative to the West, and damaging to the countries which accepted it on the fraternal authority of a black economic expert—Arthur Lewis received both a knighthood (1963) and a Nobel (1979).

If the Nobel given to each and every one of Soyinka's black predecessors was a reward for services rendered to Western hegemony—services detrimental to the Black

World's interest—might his own be an exception? What service might he have rendered the West to earn his Nobel? A citation might go like this:

1) Right at the start of his career as a literary personality, with his cry of *Tigritude*!, he led a coup against Negritude, and helped to expunge Black nationalist consciousness from the emerging academic literature of Nigeria. Through his campaign, the following sort of writing was driven out:

> Naked woman, black woman
> Clothed with your colour which is life, with your
>   form which is beauty!
> In your shadow I have grown up; the gentleness of
>   your hands was laid over my eyes.
>   . . .
> Naked woman, dark woman
> Oil that no breath ruffles, calm oil on the athlete's
>   flanks, on the flanks of the Princes of Mali
> Gazelle limbed in Paradise, pearls are stars on the
>   night of your skin
> Delights of the mind, the glinting of red gold against
>   your watered skin
> Under the shadow of your hair, my care is lightened
>   by the neighbouring suns of your eyes.
>
>   —(from "Black Woman", by Leopold Senghor)

That kind of writing (which declared that black is beautiful, which recalled the dignity of ancient Africa, which used images from Africa's fauna and flora) was execrated for the parochial "sin" of Negritude and anathematized. In its place, the following kind of writing was given pride of place:

> Hirsute hell chimney-spouts, black thunderthroes
> confluence of coarse cloudfleeces—my head sir!—scourbrush
> in bitumen, past fossil beyond fingers of light—until . . . !
>
>   —(from "To my First White Hairs", by
>   Wole Soyinka)

That sort of writing (which pejoratively likened the black man's head to a scourbrush—taken from the toilet bowl, perhaps?—dipped in coal tar, and to the chimney spout of hell's fire belching the soot of burning souls; which looked at the black body with negrophobe eyes; and which outdid the racists in pouring contempt on blacks) became the exemplar of the universalist values of Tigritude literature. For his voluntary cultural servitude in blocking the march of Negritude into Nigerian academic writing, and for that exquisite display of self-contempt by shouting in print ("my head sir!") that his own black head is a scourbrush dipped in coal tar, a Nobel for Wole Soyinka!

2) He served loyally as an apostle of Euro-modernism, spreading in Africa its literary ideology that poetry must defy understanding. He helped to install the Hopkins' Disease, with its impenetrable verbal structures, as the official style of poetry in African universities and schools. By precept and example, he taught Africa's academic writers and critics to devalue clarity of thought and felicity of diction and to cultivate jargon. Some samples:

> In paths of rain, in rock grooves, may
> These rare instants of wild fox-fires
> Write on moments, lives.
>
> —(from "In Paths of Rain", *Idanre*)
>
> Metal on concrete jars my drinklobes
>
> —(from *The Interpreters*)

He taught them that this is the civilized way to curse:

> Giggles fill water-hole
> Offsprings by you abandoned,
> And afterbirth, at crossroads
>
> —(from "Malediction", *Idanre*)

And for lack of seven types of ambiguity per line, for lack of mangled syntax, for lack of obscure allusions for the reader to puzzle over, he taught that traditional African curses, like that below from the Limba of Sierra Leone, be dismissed as trite, prosaic drivel:

> The one who took the hen,
>   —If it is an animal in the bush, a wild cat, let it be caught;
>   Wherever it goes, may it be met by a man with a gun;
>   May it be found by a hunter who does not miss;
>   If it meets a person, may it be killed.

By his prominent example, he taught African academic writers to take Euro-modernist professors as their primary audience: give them plenty of obscurities to puzzle out, and your reputation as a great poet will be made. For installing the Hopkins' Disease in the academic literature of Africa, a Nobel for Wole Soyinka!
3) He imported the spirit of European Romanticism into African literature. He made fashionable the shamanist conceits, demi-god pretensions and alienated poses of the self-marginalised Romantic poets of the West. He taught his followers to pour "divine" abuse on whoever dares to criticise whatever "divine" mess they spread out on a page; on whoever dares to demand that they write in accents which the ordinary African reader could understand. For infecting African writers with Euro-Romantic conceits, a Nobel for Wole Soyinka!
4) By other such contributions, he fostered (in African poetry and drama especially) an obscurantist mediocrity which could take another generation to root out. For harming in these ways the development of African literary culture, a Nobel for Wole Soyinka![7]

---

[7] For a detailed discussion of the pro-imperialist aspects of Soyinka's early career, see *Toward the Decolonization of African Literature* (1980), chp. 3, especially pp. 196-238.

In other words, just as Sir Arthur Lewis implanted ideas which helped Britain to run down Ghana's economic inheritance, so did Soyinka sponsor literary attitudes which helped the West to stunt the growth of Africa's authentic literary traditions.

Since honours inspire emulation, his new status as Nobel Laureate promises to entrench many of the traits for which he is known. What messages have been signalled, through his Nobel award, to African writers and intellectuals who aspire to getting Nobels? What extent of cultural servitude might have been encouraged by bathing Soyinka in the aura of the Nobel? Let us try and fathom that by comparing the message in his works with those in the works of Leopold Senghor, Ngugi wa Thiong'o, Chinua Achebe, Okot p'Bitek and Sembene Ousmane.

By honouring Soyinka rather than Senghor, the message is that Tigritude may earn you a Nobel, but Negritude will certainly not; that if you show that you are a negrophobe Negro (by, for instance, portraying the black body in images which Botha and Verwoerd would wholeheartedly approve) you might get a Nobel, but if you celebrate black beauty and the dignity of traditional Africa, no Nobel will be tossed your way.

By honouring Soyinka rather than Ngugi, the message is that denouncing Nkrumah's nationalism and others of its type (*Kongi's Harvest*) may earn you a Nobel; but reviving the nationalist Mau Mau view of white settlers (*Weep Not Child, The Trial of Dedan Kimathi*) will certainly not.

By honouring Soyinka rather than Achebe, the message is that presenting what Soyinka himself has called "a jaundiced view of the much-vaunted glorious past of Africa,"[8] (*A Dance of the Forests*) may earn you a Nobel; but standing up for the validity and integrity of pre-colonial African societies (*Things Fall Apart, Arrow of God*) will certainly not.

[8] Quoted in James M. Markham, "Soyinka, Nigerian Dramatist, Wins Nobel Literature Prize," *The New York Times*, October 17, 1986.

By honouring Soyinka rather than Okot p'Bitek, the message is that paying imitative homage to Euripides and ancient Greece (*The Bacchae of Euripides*) and playing the ape to Shakespeare and Hopkins (*Idanre, A Shuttle in the Crypt*) may earn you a Nobel; but denouncing servile mimicry of Western traditions (*Song of Lawino, Africa's Cultural Revolution*) will certainly not.

By honouring Soyinka rather than Sembene Ousmane, the message is that if you avoid fictionalizing themes like African resistance to colonial rule, if you evade portraying from the African standpoint the atrocities committed against Africa by European conquerors, you may earn a Nobel; but if you insist on celebrating African revolt against colonial exploitation (*God's Bits of Wood*) you certainly will not.

Considering that works by Senghor, Ngugi, Achebe, Okot and Ousmane are far more popular with African readers than works by Soyinka, the message in honouring Soyinka rather than any of them is that pandering to the prejudices of the Nobel scouts may earn you a Nobel; but writing, first and foremost, for the African readership and their interest will certainly not.

As I see it, the significance of the recent ceremony in Stockholm is not that African literature and culture have been recognised by Europe; it is rather that the European Prospero, in an effort to shore up the props of his hegemony in Africa, lifted up his African Ariel and declared: "This is my adopted son, with whose mimicry I am well pleased. If any of you would please me, let him follow his example." And I dare say that in lifting aloft this model Ariel from Africa, Prospero couldn't have made a better choice.

Let me make it quite clear that I would not wish a Nobel on any black whom I respect. I am therefore far from suggesting that Senghor, Ngugi, Achebe, Okot or Ousmane should have been given Nobels at any time. In fact, the Nobel would have to abandon its strategic objective in order to go to any of them. Soyinka, I believe, is the African writer of his generation whose career best deserves it. The cultural servitude to Europe for which the Nobel selectors would reward a Soyinka is precisely why he would not qualify for any reward devoted to the African or the Black World interest; and the African cultural nationalism which would bar a Senghor, Ngugi, Achebe, Okot or Ousmane from a Nobel Prize is precisely why they would be honoured by any prize devoted to the African or the Black World interest.

And so, when Soyinka claims that his Nobel is a recognition for African culture, I disagree and I reply: It is not African culture which has been recognised by his Western masters, but his own personal services to Western cultural hegemony over Africa. By quickly packaging his private reward as a recognition for African culture and traditions, he was attempting to legitimize in black eyes his acceptance of a quisling prize.

And when J. J. Rawlings claims that African art has been recognised through Soyinka's Nobel, I disagree and I reply: African art is not in need of Europe's recognition; if anything has been recognised by Europe, it is simply Euro-assimilationist art from Africa—that orphan without a home, that sophisticated version of airport art which is marketed to academic tourists, i.e. works which ape the European tradition while incorporating African decorations to make them exotic.

And when Lewis Nkosi claims that recognition by Europe is cause for confidence for African art, I disagree and I reply: self-confidence is gained, not from Europe's acclaim, not by collecting decorations from Europe, but from knowing and appreciating and matching the solid achievements of our ancestors. Can you imagine Kimathi or Chaka gaining self-confidence by being offered the British Military Cross, and by marching off to receive it from the hand of some monarch in London? On the other hand, Bokassa has his chestful of French decorations; but what sort of self-confidence did he derive from all that?

And when Ibrahim Babangida claims that allegations of black intellectual inferiority have been rebutted by the award of a Nobel prize, I disagree and I reply: If anyone wants to rebut the malicious aspersions on our race, let him look to Ancient Egypt, to the pyramids and their treasures, to what our ancestors bequeathed to the world, and not to the antics of an Eliza Doolittle aping his Western mentors.

After the above glimpse into what each black recipient of the Nobel has done to get it, I have a question for all those blacks who feel like applauding when a black is awarded a Nobel: If the British Queen had given a knighthood to Bishop Muzorewa, Prime Minister of "Rhodesia-Zimbabwe," would Mugabe be expected to cheer? And if President Gorbachev of the USSR were to bestow a Lenin Prize on Arthur Scargill, Tony Benn, or some other prominent leader of the British Left, would England burst out in applause? If not, why not?

Let me end by asking the numerous Ariels and Nigger Toms among us to listen and pay heed:
1) Stockholm is not the intellectual capital of the Black World. It is not the venue for electing and anointing the intellectual leaders of the Black World.
2) The official voices of the West do not speak in the interest of the Black World. Therefore, who in his right mind would consult them when choosing intellectual or any other leaders for the Black World?
3) The authority of the Nobel oracle stops at the boundaries of the Western World. Attempts to extend it to the Black World are a pretentious joke. Consider this: Suppose a committee of Papuans or Swazis presumed to tell Europeans who to regard as their best thinkers and writers, how would their presumption be received in Europe?
4) Do not be misled: the Nobel is not what it purports to be. The Nobel Foundation, with its glittering prizes bestowed by its satellite academies, stands at the validating apex of that

Western school system which colonialism implanted in our societies. As one of our African sages, Cheikh Hamidou Kane, has warned us: "Better than the cannon [the colonial school] makes conquest permanent. The cannon compels the body, the school bewitches the soul." We must therefore understand that gifts of Nobel Prizes are more deadly than a spatter of bullets from Botha's tanks and machine guns. We should never disregard that warning from Hamidou Kane. And we should be most wary of these heirs of the Greek legacy when they come to us bearing their most dazzling gifts.

5) We should never forget that Africans are now in the sixth century of a protracted war with Western Europe. Any sensible people would treat with automatic suspicion an honour bestowed by their antagonists on any of their generals. Either that general is a quisling, or the enemy are up to some deadly mischief. Either way, they would insist on rejecting, or at least discountenancing, the alleged honour. A Nobel award to any African, therefore, is not a matter for African rejoicing.

The Olympic Games and the Black World[*]

> Like drunken men
> You stagger to white men's games,
> You stagger to white men's amusements.
>
> Is *lawala*[†] not a game?
> Is *cooro*[††] not a game?
> Didn't your people have amusements?
>
> —Okot p'Bitek, *Song of Lawino*

Does the Black World need the Olympics? I think not. I say this in spite of the billing given the Olympics as the world's most important amateur athletics competition; and in spite of our penchant, induced by our experience of colonial aspersions, for "putting Africa on the map." It is my contention that the Olympic Games are neither in fact nor name the World Games they pretend to be—that is, they are not games organised by all nations, governed by all nations, and free from political domination by a parochial minority of nations. Since the Olympics are indeed controlled by a Western world deeply antagonistic to black people, they ought not to be regarded as an athletic competition indispensable to us. Besides, the point is not to put black nations on the map as it exists, but rather to remake the map.

[*] A version of the original essay from which this is excerpted appeared in *Africa* (London) October 1980, as "Olympics, Nobel Prizes and the Black World."

[†]*Lawala* is a hunting game. [††]*Cooro* is a board game.

As we reflect upon the Moscow and Montreal boycotts, it is crucial to realise that the Olympics are a Western institution in which the rest of us are half-tolerated paying guests. Why do I say that? Consider the following facts. The Olympics, inspired by an ancient Greek festival, were founded by a Frenchman and headquartered in Switzerland. All presidents of the IOC have been Westerners; all the Olympic events, except judo, are either Western in origin or are played in their Western versions; the rules of eligibility (such as amateurism for athletes, and independence from governments for national Olympic committees) are tailored to the characteristics of Western capitalist society, and have little relevance to the characteristics of socialist society or to the economic realities of poor Third World countries. Furthermore, most Olympic sites have been in the West, and when they have not (Mexico City; Moscow) the West has found grounds for displeasure at having to compete outside their own turf. If the sites in Japan seem like exceptions, bear in mind that Japan is a highly developed member of the Western capitalist bloc, and that Japanese are regarded as honorary whites even in apartheid South Africa.

But why would Westerners lead a boycott against an institution they regard as their property? Are they losing control of it? Does it no longer serve their hegemonic purpose? One revealing reason cited by the boycotters is that it was a mistake to award the games to Moscow at all! Why do they feel so, since the USSR is a member of the Olympics? When we cut through their rhetoric about Afghanistan, about freedom, about Russia taking advantage of the Moscow Games to make propaganda for its way of life, it becomes plain that the boycott leaders have three geopolitical motives for their campaign.

First, holding the games in Moscow offends their sense that the Olympics are their property. If holding them in the despised Third World (Mexico City) was bad enough for their sense of propriety (recall the controversy that arose over that), how much worse must they feel about holding them in the headquarters of their socialist rival?

Second, this is happening in a period when Western domination of the games (as measured by harvests of gold medals) is on the wane; when the USSR has led in golds in Olympic after Olympic, with East Germany, its ally, repeatedly pushing the USA down to third place. While the USA dominated the events, it viewed its victories as testimony to the superiority of capitalism over socialism. In fact, it continues to hold the view that Olympic victories bring credit to the social system of the victors, as witness this recent remark by Herb Brooks, coach of the US hockey team at the 1980 Winter Olympics: "Our victory over police state teams shows that our way of life is better." With such an attitude, no wonder they would rather destroy the Olympics than see them contribute to the prestige of their Soviet rivals.

Third, in the battle for minds waged between the capitalist and the socialist blocs, the prospect of thousands of visitors from around the world viewing the Soviet Union at first hand, or of millions seeing it through TV coverage of the games, could be unpalatable to the guardians of the capitalist bloc. What if the world is curious to see how the poor and the ethnic minorities are treated in the USSR? Do they live in slums like Harlem and Watts? Are the streets safe—without rape, muggings, stray bullets, police riots and other harassments endemic to the US? Are there in Moscow staggering contrasts in living conditions like those in New York between Park Avenue posh and gutted Harlem tenements? What if Western TV cameras found nothing of that sort to beam to the "Free World"? What impact might that have on the poor in Harlem, Rio, Lagos, Nairobi, and Manila? Could an important reason for the boycott be that President Carter doesn't want the world to see Moscow for themselves?

By appreciating the high risk to Western prestige which the Moscow Games have posed, it is easier to see why the guardians of capitalism would violate their habitual strictures against mixing politics and sports (which they brandished against the black nations at Montreal), and themselves use the politics of Afghanistan to wreck the Moscow Olympics. Given their hegemonic Eurocentrism, with its attendant racism and anti-communism, they would gladly purge the Olympics of those they regard as irksome or overshadowing guests. With their boycott of the Moscow Games they are saying to the Soviet Bloc: "We won't have you participate in *our* Olympics if you are going to dominate it and eclipse us. If we can no longer shine in it, we'll wreck it." With their refusal to bar New Zealand from Montreal, even when faced with the black boycott, they were saying to the Black World: "The Olympics are *ours*. If you cannot stomach our racism, you can get out! And good riddance!" In fact, one Olympic official at Montreal put it bluntly when he said of the black boycott: "We have gone on without them before; we can go on without them now."

If we are outraged by that attitude, we ought perhaps to ask ourselves what we expected a host to do when a guest, reluctantly invited, tolerated with ill grace, walks out of a banquet just as it is about to begin, because he cannot stomach what one of the sons of the house is doing. Did we really expect the host to cancel his feast? Viewed thus, it becomes clear that we should go beyond the tantrums of boycotts. We should instead work out a long range response to Montreal. To do that, we should probe the deeper politics of the Olympics, and consider what relationship, if any, a self-respecting Black World should have with it. For that, a look at the long history of racism in the Olympics, and at the implications of the Moscow boycott, should help.

Even though IOC rules expressly forbid both racism and politics, they have prevailed at the Olympics all along. But when the Black World attempts, as at Montreal, to expunge white supremacist politics from the Olympics, we hear talk that we are "polluting" the Olympics with politics. The white supremacist bias of the IOC has a long history. In 1912, when the decathlon and pentathlon were first competed for in the same Olympic Games, both were won by Jim Thorpe, who came to be widely regarded as the greatest athlete of all time. But he was not a white man; he was an American Indian. So, the following year, the white men who set the rules contrived to strip him of his titles. They struck his name from the roster of Olympic champions, took back his medals, and retroactively bestowed his decathlon title on one Swede, and his pentathlon title on another. White supremacy, you see, had to be upheld in athletics.

Again, when Adolf Hitler elaborately staged the Berlin Olympics (1936) as a showcase for Nazism, and as propaganda for "Aryan superiority", the IOC did not stop him; nobody opted to boycott it; and after it was over, the Berlin Games were not struck from the records. The participating countries probably agreed with the Nazi myth of Aryan superiority, though some may have been amazed that it was thought to be in need of demonstration. But their show was ruined by Jesse Owens and nine other blacks from the USA. With Hitler watching in mounting anger, they collected 8 gold medals, 3 silvers and 2 bronzes. Jesse Owens, in perhaps the best deflation of the Aryan myth, set four Olympic records, including one in the long jump that was not to be surpassed for 24 years! Hitler, the point of his show destroyed, was visibly chagrined.

The IOC tolerated Hitler's show of racism. But when, in 1968 at Mexico City, Tommie Smith and John Carlos, in protest against racism in the USA, gave the Black Power salute as they stood on the victory stand, they were summarily dismissed from their team. The IOC officials guarding the political virginity of the Olympics acquiesced. So, you see, it is all right with the IOC to have the Olympics politicised in favour of white supremacy, but all wrong to have them politicised against white supremacy.

In a world divided by racism, where black champions are

only grudgingly accepted by whites, it is not surprising that New Zealand was not asked to withdraw from the Montreal Games, even after the massive boycott by black nations. The IOC and its supporters probably welcomed that boycott as an opportunity for the "Great White Hopes" to snatch back the titles that were held by blacks. Now, is an institution with so consistent a white supremacist bias one in which the Black World should participate?

Once the motivations and implications of the Moscow boycott are understood, the Black World's long term response to Montreal should be directed, not just at racism, but also at the Eurocentrism and hegemonism of a parochial institution which pretends to be a world institution. In fact, efforts being made to capitalise on the Moscow boycott and move the Olympic Games to a permanent site in Greece should prompt the Black World to withdraw altogether from the Olympics. Why should we consent to journey, every four years, to salaam at the shrine of a racist, hegemonic version of athletics?

In this business of subtle cultural control, Western hegemonists have reasons of domination for wanting the world to go to Greece to compete for prizes in physical prowess. For them, it is not enough that Western institutions should arrogate to themselves the function of arbiters of excellence for the whole world; they also want them to be visibly domiciled in and unalterably identified with the West, thus reinforcing the prestige of those who house and manage them. This is why advantage is being taken of the Moscow boycott to secure a permanent site in Greece (that alleged fount of Western civilisation) for the Olympics.

The fundamental question which the Black World needs to answer is this: When shall we stop tolerating our being treated as guests in international institutions? In the euphoria of independence, we allowed ourselves to be persuaded that joining the U.N., joining the Olympics, striving for Nobel Prizes, were some of the dignifying rites of passage from colonial status to full membership in the world community. We have integrated the U.N. and the Olympics; we have even collected some Nobel Prizes. But the owners and managers of these instutions repeatedly make it clear that we are barely tolerated guests. If we dislike such treatment, as our boycotts and protests amply demonstrate, it is up to us to build international institutions that would be more to our taste. We must realise that though integrating another man's restaurant may be an important step towards social equality, it is not the same thing as being an equal partner in owning and managing it. In the wake of President Carter's boycott campaign, with its attendant disarray in the Olympics movement, the situation is ripe for non-Westerners, blacks especially, to force the creation of a genuine World Games to replace the Olympics. In preparing to press for that, we of the Black World should examine our options. Let me outline three.

If we are convinced that the Black World needs to participate in some form of World Games, and believe that the Olympics should be transformed, not abolished, we might want to dilute its Eurocentrism. According to IOC rules, the honour of hosting Olympic Games goes to a city, not a country. How about staging the Olympics in a city of the Black World, with all the black nations joining to fund the event? Though the present tradition of national financing might be invoked to block such multi-national staging of games (e.g. by those who want to move the games permanently to Greece) there is actually nothing in the rules to prevent it. If Canada could force the exclusion of Taiwan from Montreal, why should the black hosts not then exclude all of South Africa's fellow travellers in racism? Would the West react with a boycott? If they did, they would wreck the Olympics over the issue of their own racism. I, for one, would not be sorry to see that. But even if the West did not boycott it, I doubt that a black-hosted Olympics would be more than a sop to our sensitivities. Like the U.N. Security Council session held in Addis Ababa in 1972, it would not affect the real issues: Western definition, domination and control of the institution, and their promotion, through it, of their Eurocentric world outlook.

A second option would be for blacks to withdraw from the Olympics until they are satisfactorily reorganised, renamed the World Games, purged of Western domination of their committees, rules, rites, name and aims. Such a withdrawal should be accompanied by the setting up of that Third World Games which has long been dreamed and talked about. It would then be the responsibility of a Third World Games Organisation, in concert with the Olympic Games Organisation of the West, and with its Soviet Bloc counterpart to negotiate terms for founding a genuine World Games. If and when this genuine World Games Organisation is formed, its sponsoring organisations would serve as guarantors of its good, non-racist behaviour.

A third option would be for the Black World to unconditionally withdraw from the Olympics, as from a congenitally tainted thing, and then initiate a World Games Organisation, and invite all the world to join on non-racist, non-hegemonist terms. What is involved here is the seizing of initiative. Those who persist in believing that global initiative, in all matters, must be left to the West might shrink from so bold a step. It should therefore be pointed out that only an anti-racist initiative, preferably from the Black or Third World, could create a genuine World Games. Moreover, such initiative would be as vitalising for the psyche of the Black World as was the Angolan trial of white mercenaries. It would free from the thrall of Western definitions yet another corner of our sense of how things ought to be. Initiative exercised in defining significant parts of our relationships in the world, will, I submit, do far more for our sense of dignity and self-respect than all the tantrums, protests and outpourings of moral outrage we now tend to resort to.

Part Five: Literature

> Writers and artists must play and are playing their part in the forefront of the struggle for decolonization. It is their task to remind the politicians that politics, the governing of the City, is only one aspect of culture and that cultural colonialism, in the form of assimilation, is the worst colonialism of all. It is their task to analyse the total situation of the respective peoples and, as part of this, to say what must be retained from the values and institutions of their traditional civilization and, most important of all, to say how, through the leaven of outside influences, these can be brought back to a new life.
>
> —Leopold Sedar Senghor

Literature and nation building in Africa[*]

> Men act out of their images, they respond, not to the situation, but to the situation transformed by the images they carry in their minds. In short, they respond . . . to the ideas they have of themselves in the situation. The image sees . . . the image feels . . . the image acts, and if you want to change a situation you have to change the image men have of themselves and of their situation.
>
> —Lerone Bennett

> The ancient prophets were, in fact, poets commenting on the social and political issues of their time. They were not engaged in foretelling some distant future, for no mortal can 'know' what he has not yet experienced. They sang of love and hate, expressed joys and sorrows, and shed bitter tears to wipe away corruption of power. Literature is concerned with matters of state as well as domestic affairs. It is a direct criticism of life.
>
> —Okot p'Bitek

The central aspect of the historical project in present-day Africa is nation building. Its ruling objectives are the defence of African societies and the renaissance of African civilisation. These require the fostering of national spirit and the transmitting from generation to generation of the

[*] Prepared for the Second African Writers' Conference, Stockholm, April 1986.

achievements of African civilisation. In previous eras of African history, as in other parts of the world, literature and orature have made indispensable contributions to such objectives. Unfortunately, African literature of the late 20th century seems to lack an articulated awareness of such national and civilisational purposes, and so seems devoid of a vital focus.

A wilderness without signposts is a playground for misleaders; similarly, an African literature without a clear set of national and civilisational goals is open for hijacking by interests hostile to African civilisation. If this unacceptable situation is to be remedied, African writers and critics need to meticulously examine the implications of nation building for their work.

First, the business of fostering national spirit. Western "universalists" are prone to decry African literature for being "ethnic", "local", "political" and what not, even though such attributes are vital in fostering national spirit. Since Sweden is home to an institution which poses as one of the centres of "universality", let me illustrate the value of such literature by an example from its northern European locality.

In his "Politics of Ethnopoetics", an American poet, Gary Snyder, illustrated how publication of ethnic literature reinforces a people's sense of identity:

> A young doctor named Lonnrat set himself to walking widely through the northern parts of Finland, collecting the remaining fragments of songs and epics and tales that the people were still telling in the early 19th century. He strung these together in an order which he more or less perceived himself, and called it the Kalevala. It became overnight the Finnish national epic and helped the Finns hold up against the Swedes on the one side and the Russians on the other. It may well be that Dr. Lonnrat's walking around in the

summertime is responsible for the fact that there is a nation called Finland today.[1]

A series of questions is posed for African writers by that example, namely: Are they consciously producing works that could similarly foster national spirit in Africa? If not, how ought they to set about doing so, and what ought they to desist from doing?

On the matter of a renaissance of African civilisation, we ought to note that a civilisation usually produces a body of literature, codified during some high point in its evolution, which transmits its fundamental values and outlook for the guidance of subsequent generations of its members. Even after a civilisation has vanished, this body of works conveys its spirit to whoever reads it. Apart from factual accounts, such a body usually includes creation myths, national and heroic epics, religious texts embodying the civilisation's cosmography, treatises on political and personal conduct which embody its moral temper, as well as poetry, plays, songs, and other imaginative works and entertainments.

Some civilisations, at some point, anthologise the best of such works, and hold them up as the flower of their intellectual life. Perhaps the most famous of such anthologies is the *Old Testament Bible*, which was compiled sometime in the 7th century B.C. to serve Judaic society and culture. Its influence has, of course, spread far beyond Judaic culture. Through Christianity, it helped to shape European civilisation; and through its influence on the Koran, it helped shape Islamic civilisation.

Similar compilations from other civilisations are the *Vedas, Brahmanas, Upanishads, Mahabharata, Ramayana* and other fundamental books of Hindu civilisation; the *Kojiki* and the *Nihongi* of Japan; *The Book of Songs* and the Confucian Classics of Chinese civilisation; and *The Greek*

---

[1] *Alcheringa/Ethnopoetics*, New Series, Vol. 2 No. 2, 1976, p.18.

Anthology which preserves the intellectual glories of Hellenic civilisation.

If one attempted to compile an anthology that would similarly transmit the spirit and achievement of African civilisation, would the contribution from 20th century African literature be up to par? And again, if not, why not? And what should African writers do to remedy that, and what should they desist from doing?

To answer these questions, we need to explore the relation between identity, consciousness and action; the role of culture in nation building; literature's contribution to national culture; and apply all that, and more, to the specifics of African history and civilisation.

Identity, consciousness and action

In his long poem, "Harlem Gallery", Afro-American poet Melvin Tolson retells a Zulu tale about a hunter who found an eagle eating dung, along with a flock of chicken, in a barnyard near a buffalo trail. The hunter picked up the eagle, carried it to a mountain top, and tried to teach it to fly. Throwing it into the air, he cried: "Aquila fly! You are not a chicken but an eagle!" But the eagle, alas, tumbled to the ground. Several times the hunter tried; each time the eagle flopped to the ground. Then a falcon flew past them, crying and soaring in the breeze. Its dormant instincts awakened finally, the eagle stretched its wings and, after a few false starts, soared off toward the sun.

This tales makes two things clear for us: the supreme importance for action of a consciousness of one's correct identity, and the value of those who prompt us to overcome our false consciousness. It can also be applied to illuminate the challenges facing Africa and its literature. Explaining, prompting and supplying inspiring examples are among the ways in which literature, and orature before it, have affected human action. In contemporary Africa, though the acknowledged historical project is nation building, it is being hindered by a false consciousness of our identity, our history, and our capabilities. Therefore, the challenge for African literature today is to play, as it were, the hunter to Africa's Aquila.

Nation building and national culture

In the context of nation building, it is useful to look at culture as that fabric of mental, emotional and physical activities whose threads hold a people together within and across generations. It does so by shaping their feelings, by ordering the routines of their days, by defining their interests, by determining and interpreting their experiences, and by inculcating in them the values and beliefs with which they conduct their lives. National culture defines the range of what they wear, eat, talk about, aim for, argue and fight over; it organises the memories they share, the games they play, and even the disputes they feel party to. It determines their religious rites, work procedures, leisure habits, culinary styles, economic attitudes, judicial practices, manners, customs and other behavioural regulations. Because national culture is the fabric which orders the life of a nation, it can be said that nation building is but the building of a national culture.

For example, when Chaka created a new nation, the Amazulu, out of fragments of the nations he conquered, he made them renounce their clans and languages, and he made them join his regiments and become Amazulu. He built a capital, instituted social reforms, trained his regiments in new arts of war, taught his nation new greetings, and gave them a new name. According to Thomas Mofolo, in his fictionalised biography of Chaka, Chaka's chief object was to make them Amazulu in heart and soul. He therefore composed many beautiful songs and praises, which caused his warriors when they heard them to weep and be carried away with enthusiasm.

As Chaka well understood, the fundamental task of the nation builder is to detach the primary loyalty of its members from all other groups (subnational as well as supranational), and to attach it to their new nation and its symbols. This has always required the making of new myths of origin, the invention of national heroes and heroic traditions, and the legitimation of the new national system of authority. Thereafter, preservation of cohesion among the members of the nation becomes a matter of reaffirming allegiance to the symbols of that national identity.

Literature and national culture

Among the creators and preservers of national culture are, of course, those who fashion the national mind and shape the attitudes of the citizenry. Literary artists, who fictionally rehearse the nation's history and experiences, who exercise its imagination and direct its feelings, contribute enormously to national identity. But literature helps principally by serving as a medium for the dialogue among a people about their history and destiny; and by husbanding and keeping efficient a national idiom for communication and expression. The national idiom provides a system of attitudes, references, allusions, metaphors and images by which thoughts, feelings and experiences can be powerfully conveyed between the members of a nation.

Incidentally, this idiom is much more than a national language, in so far as two or more nations which speak the same language (e.g. Britain and the USA) almost invariably evolve different idioms to accommodate the peculiarities of their national histories. Over time, as their experiences diverge, even the same phrase would come to evoke different images, memories, attitudes, and feeling in members of the different nations.

Literature modifies and enlarges the national idiom, and

helps teach it to members of the nation. Consider the basic texts of England's literature, from Chaucer, through the King James Bible, to Shakespeare and beyond. Those brought up on these texts absorb a compendium of images, attitudes, and values which imparts to them the fundamentals of both the Judeo-Christian and the specifically British cultural heritage.

The case of the Jewish nation is perhaps the most spectacular. Their national anthology, the Bible, has helped hold them together in spirit and identity for millennia, despite their physical dispersal among hostile nations around the world. Their myths of origin, their heroic epics, their religious poetry, their fundamental moral code, etc., are all included in that anthology. Through it, individuals are initiated into their Jewish identity, and indoctrinated in their national idiom.

Beyond the husbandry of national idiom, literature serves nation building by performing three functions: it makes affirmations, it evaluates, and it explores.

Regarding its explorative function, it should not be overlooked that nation building is the willed enactment into history of some myth or idea of a nation. It is a creative enterprise, much like rebuilding, according to some new design, an old city going to ruin. It thus requires an exploration of the potentialities of the situation. Imagining what a nation could be like, what life in it might feel like, would seem a natural task for persons whose stock in trade is the inventing of lives for individual characters, and of plausible worlds for sets of characters.

Regarding the affirming function, nation building requires that national enthusiasm be sparked and maintained for as long as the project lasts. The thoughts and feelings of the participants need to be kept keen by repeatedly affirming the attractive goals and the sense of destiny. This, it would also seem, is yet another task tailor-made for writers. After all, their stock in trade is the making of myths, the guiding of thoughts and the triggering of sentiments.

As to its evaluative function, one of the major obstacles to historical action is a divergence between the world and the picture of it we carry in our heads. If you believe that you are a chicken when in fact you are an eagle; or if you believe that you are in chains in a guarded dungeon when in fact you are unfettered and in a boundless plain, your sense of your possibilities will be drastically different from what they really are. By holding a mirror before us, thus enabling us to evaluate the actual workings of our lives and society, literature can help us to remove such impediments to desirable action as are placed by time-honoured beliefs, bad habits, delusions and confusions.

African nation building: context and constraints

If African literature is to discharge the above functions, African writers must be well acquainted with the specific context and constraints of African nation building. Otherwise, the dialogue conducted through them might stray from issues central to the African historical project. What then are these constraints, and what is the context of the project?

Today, Africa is in the neo-colonial phase of a transition from its non-industrial past towards some autonomous industrial civilisation of the future. Among the disabilities imposed by the historical legacy of the past 500 years are the following:

1) A pulverised political and cultural landscape, with some 40 fledgling black nation states, and hundreds of ethno-linguistic groups, all sandwiched between white-occupied regions of the continent: the Arab occupied North, and the European occupied south.

2) Economic poverty, with each under-productive and poorly integrated economy buffeted by natural and man-caused scourges like drought, famine, epidemics, inflation, cash

crises, and the dislocations of wars.
3) Weak state-systems with under-defined, or even undefined national purposes; with confused identities, flimsy national sentiments, shaky loyalties, unformed national character, muddled national outlook, and no agreement on the fundamentals of national morality.
4) A population with false historical and cultural consciousness.
5) A hostile and contemptuous world which is determined to put disintegrative and impoverishing pressures on a continent already so divided and so poor.

Against that background, the cardinal aim of the African historical project is to produce, out of that mess, and as quickly as possible, a civilisation in which Africans can take justifiable pride; and societies which will be sufficiently strong that no other people or state could ride roughshod over them, let alone invade, rule or exercise hegemony over them.

Literature's part in the project

Literature could help by supplying reminders of why the project is essential, what its ultimate goals and intermediate objectives are, and by continually assessing the state of the project. This it could do by relating its affirming, explorative and evaluative functions to the specifics of the project.

African literature's most important affirming task is to assert our African identity and bring out its historical significance. Essentially, the job is to din it into each of us that "You are an eagle, not a chicken!" Thus, against all non-African communities which would like us to adopt their identity, and so give our primary loyalty to them (Christendom, Islam, the Free World, the Socialist World, the various European "Commonwealths", etc.) African literature must affirm, validate and give concrete meaning to our Africanness, and proclaim the high destiny of African civilisation.

The second affirming task concerns the African nation states. Since the sovereign unit within which each African lives out his life and serves African civilisation is indeed some African state or other, his African cultural identity needs to be anchored on his national identity. Thus, each national-patriotic literature must promote loyalty to the nation state, to its institutions, and to the destiny of its people.

In its evaluative function, it is incumbent on African literature to present portraits of African life as it is lived today, and as it was lived in the past, taking pains to expose the inadequacies, and to celebrate the triumphs.

Protest literature, that brand preoccupied with inadequacies, ought to help us see our barnyard life for what it is, and to show us why we should not continue with it. With that in mind, African protest literature would need to examine how we got into the historical mess, what keeps us bogged down in it, and how we came to accept it as our natural condition. It would look into our experiences under colonialism and neo-colonialism, and cast light on the nature of the humiliations and amnesia Africa has endured under foreign conquerors. In particular, it would probe the enduring white racist antagonism (both Arab and European) to Africa, the psycho-economic sources of their antipathy, its modes of operation, and what the correct African responses should be.

In contrast to protest literature, celebrative literature would commemorate important events in African history and African life. Among them would be Dingaan's defeat of the Boers, Menelik's rout of the Italians, Ethiopia's long resistance to Arab expansionism in the Nile Valley, the victories of the anti-colonial struggles of the 20th century, and even African triumphs in sports, such as Nigeria's stunning victory in the first Under-17 world cup competition in Beijing.

Our history aside, evaluative literature must look into ongoing social transformations and illuminate the drama of clashing interests. It would have to present the emergent struggling to be born, and the decadent resisting demise. It would convey the moral crises which these struggles provoke in the lives of different sections of the population. It would have to make the reader see the issues, factions and personalities; make the reader feel the moral dilemmas, enthusiasms, anguish, pains, triumphs, tragedies, nostalgia, mistakes, disappointments, surprises, rage, horrors, as well as the joys of the adventure. It would have to probe the psychological recesses of individuals caught up in the drama. It would need, for instance, to make us feel the causes and cruelties of clan feuds; the atrocities of gang warfare between business and political factions; the duels between the propagandists for conflicting interests. It would also lead us to the springs of motivation, individual and collective, from which these actions arise.

In its explorative function, African literature could help us probe the possibilities of our future by drawing out the implications of our historical identity and our circumstances. Just as the eagle could fly after its species instincts were reactivated, Africans could fashion a major civilisation today if challenged by the cultural heights first reached by the blacks who created the Egypt of the Pharaohs.

The attainments of Ancient Egypt, symbolised by the pyramids, were predicated upon the construction of a united kingdom out of the fragmented polities of the lower Nile Valley. Once again, Africa is engrossed in the task of fashioning modern nation states by unifying pre-existing polities. If our African identity means anything to us, it should oblige us to make these modern nation states of a calibre comparable to the Egypt of the Pharaohs.

Similarly, for any modern nation state to identify with ancient Ghana, or Mali or Zimbabwe or Ethiopia or Meroe or Songhai or Nubia should have implications for the quality of civilisation it sets out to build. It cannot be content with being a poor, crude, weak or anarchic nation state.

If we mean to rise to the challenge of our past and create a dazzling modern civilisation, literature could help us enlarge our sense of cultural possibilities. Such a literature would explore how nation states are built and sustained, how prosperity is created and maintained, and how the scientific outlook and technological ethos are made to permeate society. This would require African literature to become venturesome in spirit, not just nostalgic or protest ridden. It would have to carry our imagination to mountaintops and challenge us to stretch our wings by summoning possibilities before our imagination. In other words, Africa literature would have to invent alternative ways of life, not just science fiction which addresses itself to technological possibilities, but also works of culture fiction, as it were, which image futuristic versions of society, both utopian and dystopian, for us to contemplate.

And if we are to cultivate the social and personal virtues indispensable for this renaissance of African civilisation—virtues such as courage, foresight, probity, integrity, steadfastness, prudence, thrift, inventiveness, loyalty—then African literature would have to be consciously didactic. It would have to supply us with an abundance of appropriate fables, proverbs, exemplary tales of heroic and unheroic behaviour which, from being told and retold, would form the ethical fibre of the new African who would accomplish the African project.

But where is this revived historical adventure to take place? On what turf? Placing Aquila in its proper environment would, for us, be equivalent to getting us to actually see with keen eyes the features of our continent. Our literature ought to put us in intimate touch with the landscape on which our historical drama takes place. African literature should supply us with works through which we breathe and smell and taste the dust of our land; works which open our senses to our continent's flora and fauna, to its geology and ecology. To familiarise us with our patch of earth is to deepen our sense of attachment to it, is to strengthen our bonds to others who have the same cause for attachment to it, and is to give us a psychological springboard from which to defend it against all invaders and expropriators.

Perhaps the most important explorative contribution African literature could make is by helping us realise that nation building, as well as the making of civilisation, is a willed act, and not the product of fate or of immutable laws of history. It is probably useful to note here the intense philosophical discussions of will, and the literary portrayal of strong-willed achievers in other societies when they were gearing themselves up for the enterprise of nation building and industrialism. The wilful achievers in Shakespeare's drama, for instance, were models to an age of Englishmen undertaking the building of Britain. These dramas were thus a psychological school to an age. So too were the myriad novels about rags-to-riches adventurers which came to prominence with the industrial revolution in England and France. Even the novels of romance, in which the wilful and designing female wins the manor and its lord, belong to the species of literature which cultivates a tradition of willed action. For an Africa undertaking nation building while spiritually smothered by all manner of fatalistic beliefs, lessons in the willed enactment of plans and myths would not be superfluous. This could stimulate the self-confidence and risk-taking which are necessary for spectacular achievement.

Carrying out the above tasks does not require imaginative literature to degenerate into treatises. Literature would attend to these matters in the normal course of playing out before us the drama of human events and desires. After all, like the hunter's remarks to the eagle in the Aquila tale, literature does its work through the seminal remark, the cataract removing statement or question, the provocative shift in viewpoint, the revealing image, the evocative and inspiring example, the allure of the beautiful, and the stirrings of vigorous emotions which prepare people for the catharsis of action.

Through stories of politics, war, love, peace, economic adventure, etc., literature would present us with a full repertoire of individual and group behaviour. It would direct our attention to our possibilities through historical novels, heroic epics, as well as through cautionary tales, satires, proverbs, dilemma stories, stories of exemplary lives, etc. By doing so, works of African literature can contribute to the dialogue among Africans about their history and destiny.

Euro-assimilationism in African literature

Having looked into what needs attending to if African literature is to do its duty by African nation building, it is time to turn to what needs to be discontinued.

I am presently involved with two anthology projects, one covering 50 centuries of Pan-African literature and orature (from 3000 B.C. to the 20th century A.D.); and the other of 20th century African literature. From the evidence of the materials assembled, the best of the surviving works from other eras seem significantly superior, both aesthetically and in nationalist spirit, to much of the works of 20th century African literature.

In my view, taken as a whole, 20th century African literature displays a certain thematic narrowness, a certain stylistic unrobustness, a feebleness of rhetorical power. These deficiencies are due in part to alien mentors who have narrowly and outlandishly defined both what African literature should concern itself with, and what it should sound and read like. They are also due in part to the phenomenon of Euro-assimilationism among African writers and critics.

Chief among these mentors are the bourgeois Euromodernists who are determined to turn African literature into a mediocre mimic of Euromodernist literature, and the proletarian revolutionary internationalists who are baying for Marxist agitprop.

The Euromodernists claim that didacticism in literature

is unaesthetic and out of date; their African wards go along and eschew didactic writing, even though African orature and pre-colonial literature are full of such, and even though contemporary Africa could use didactic literature. The Euro-modernists also claim to prefer obscurity and convoluted style; their African wards obediently devote themselves to serving such fare, even though African orature and pre-colonial literature are characterised by clarity, wit and eloquence.

The proletarian internationalists, for their part, demand Marxist agitprop to the exclusion of virtually all else; their African wards serve it up and disregard, and even denounce, the many other themes drawn from African life which African literature could present. These proletarian internationalists, in their monomania for Marxist catechism, deprecate matters of style and technique; their African wards obediently neglect technique and denounce attention to it as the sin of "formalism".

But for all their differences and antagonisms, both gangs of cultural missionaries energetically denounce Afrocentric literature as lacking "universality", as being ethnic, sociological, topical, etc. And both groups are keen to reduce African literature to a tributary or overseas addendum to Western literature. Their disorienting demands would merit little attention but for the fact that some Euro-assimilationist African writers and critics echo and try to satisfy them. As we have shown in *Toward the Decolonization of African Literature*,[2] these Euro-assimilationists were spawned under colonialism. They have multiplied their kind through their entrenchment in the educational apparatus of Africa, and through the prestige manufactured for them by Western critics. As a result, the number of African writers and critics devoted to Pan-Africanist literature is far

[2] Chinweizu *et al.*, *Toward the Decolonization of African Literature*, Enugu, Nigeria: Fourth Dimension, 1980; Howard University Press (1982) and Kegan Paul (1985).

smaller than it should be.

What, it may be asked, distinguishes the Euro-assimilationists from the Pan-Africanists? Pan-Africanist writers and critics make the African readers their primary audience; the African interest guides their choices of themes, treatment and critical standpoint; they defend African civilisation and the best of its values; they repudiate and combat Western imperialist propaganda against Africa; and they accept that the mission of Pan-African literature is to renew and extend the African tradition so it can serve African survival and civilisation.

The Euro-assimilationists, in contrast, make the Western readership their primary audience; their themes, treatment and critical standpoint are decided by the tastes, interests and prejudices of their Western audience; they malign African civilisation by ignoring its best values and concentrating on its worst aspects; they lend their African imprimatur to Western slander against Africans and African civilisation; and they are either unaware of, or reject the anti-hegemonist mission of Pan-African literature.

The difference between the Pan-Africanists and the Euro-assimilationists was summed up the other day in Lagos by a journalist who said that there were those who wrote for us Africans, and those who wrote for Nobel! It is thus that the basic conflict between Africa and the West over the latter's imperialism and hegemonism is reproduced within 20th century African literature as a conflict between these two factions.

If the factors which keep 20th century African literature from living up to its Pan-African responsibilities are to be corrected, Euro-assimilationism must be ended. This, in turn, requires putting an end to the enormous power held over African writers and critics by the cultural sirens of the West.

African writers and the sirens of the West

In the absence of an articulated cultural purpose, such as is implicit in national anthologies of the sort considered above, Euro-assimilationist writers have been unable to resist distractions beamed at them by historically anti-African interests. These operate primarily through Western critics and Western prize givers. These are the two sirens I wish to discuss here.

After their induction into the Western tradition by the schools and universities which shape their minds and styles, Euro-assimilationists pass into the control of Western critics and reviewers who stage-manage their reception by the Western readership, and who whip up for some the reputations that bring them to the notice of prize givers in Europe and America. As keepers of the gate to Western acclaim and prizes, these critics and reviewers wield enormous power over these Euro-assimilationist writers.

Three things strike Pan-Africanists about them: namely, the eccentricity of their terms of appraisal, their monumental ignorance of African literary matters, and their intellectual incompetence. As we have shown in the book *Toward the Decolonization of African Literature*, their ranks are crowded with mediocrities who drip racist condescension in virtually every remark they make. They insist on judging African literature by the aesthetic criteria and political interests, not of Africa, but of the West, which is much like judging a game of *okwe* by the rules of draughts on the assumption that both are board games. Their cockeyed and jaundiced view of African literature results in startlingly odd judgements.

Some, for instance, have declared 20th century African writers geniuses for writing like Shakespeare. One would have thought that anyone writing Shakespeareanisms in the late 20th century was not a genius but an anachronism of some Rip van Winkle sort. Some have ignorantly attempted to pick for us who we should consider the greatest representative of African literature. Their candidates have turned out to be those Euro-assimilationists who have pandered most to the tastes and prejudices of their Western imperialist masters.

Some have gone as far as to tell us who is the most formidable literary force to have emerged from Africa. And they have ignorantly imagined that it is anyone born in this century. Evidently, these alien literary kingmakers have never heard of the Africans who invented writing and wrote literature in the 4th millennium B.C.; nor have they heard of the Africans who composed such glorious and still fresh classics as "The hymn to the Aten", "The lion in search of man", "The eloquent peasant", and "The satire on the trades"; nor are they acquainted with the power of African epics like *Da Monzon*, *Sundiata*, or *Amda Seyon*.

Some have even been arrogant enough to fabricate pantheons for us, and to brazenly tell us who should be on them. Imagine how any African or Chinese would be received in the West if he should presume to pick for the West who they should regard as their greatest writers!

All in all, the performance of these Western "authorities" on African literature may be likened to that of some ignoramus who declares authoritatively that tomcats are tigers. One feels embarrassed, and a bit outraged, to realise that it is nitwits who can say such things who have concocted literary reputations for Africans, and are obediently followed by Africa's Euro-assimilationists. But, of course, their authority derives, not from the excellence of their own minds, but simply from the neo-colonial structure of relations between Africa and the West. Overthrowing that bizarre authority is part of the tasks of Pan-Africanism.

Bluntly put, these cultural sirens of the West are doing insidious damage to African culture. With their praises and prizes, they distract a significant number of African writers from their Pan-Africanist obligations, and turn them into producers of an assimilationist literature that is the equivalent of airport art. By that I mean works which firmly belong in the European tradition, but are given enough Africanesque patina and inlays to make them classifiable as African. Such airport art from "overseas Europe" does not advance the African tradition; it bastardises and exploits that tradition to earn foreign acclaim. When Western critics and prize givers see them, they shower themselves with disguised self-praise: "Ah, we have taught some African monkey to mimic Shakespeare; some African primitive to contract the Hopkins' Disease. How extraordinary of us!"

You may well wonder why these issues should be raised at a writers' conference in Stockholm. Well, I can think of no better forum for addressing both those African Euro-assimilationists who need most reminding of the nation-building obligations of African literature, and the Western sirens under whose spell they are misled. After all, in Stockholm is the altar from where the most powerful of Western sirens, the Nobel Prize, calls out to African writers.

The crucial issue is this: Africa does not need the cultural disorientation and subservience which Western prizes promote. By its origins and operations, even the most globally prestigious of these prizes, the Nobel Prize, is a local European prize, and should go back to being just that. If it wishes to become the international prize it gives the impression of being, it should stop lending itself to hegemonic uses. Its terms of reference, its selection procedures, and its award committees should then all be internationalised. Not to do so would continue the nonsense that a bunch of Swedes, who are parochially devoted to Western hegemony, is competent to pronounce on intellectual excellence in all the diverse cultures of the world.

It is, of course, most unlikely that the West would agree to a genuine internationalisation of the Nobel Prize. That would end their control of it, and end their ability to use it for hegemonist purposes. But should that ever be seriously about to happen, one can expect the West to abandon the Nobel organ, and in much the same way that they have been abandoning UNESCO since, under its African Director-General, it ceased being an obedient instrument of the West. With that in mind, it is up to the rest of the world, in a bid to stimulate a long-overdue New International Cultural Order, to publicly withdraw allegiance from the Nobel Prize, and so reduce it to its proper minitude as a local European prize.

Deriding the Derridians[*]

> In art we have no lessons to learn from Europe. We are here on our own ground. All the lessons from African art must be retained as contemporary European art itself has retained them.
>
> —Leopold Sedar Senghor

Good evening! I have two problems right now: I am full of sleep; and we are all full of food. By my body clock, it is 5 a.m.; and after the long days of conferences, and the dinner, I don't know how many are in the mood to listen to the kind of talk I've been asked to give. But it is a pleasure to be here, even though I got to the conference late.

When I was asked to talk at this banquet, I protested vigorously, because I am not good at post-prandial prattle. But I was told that it is in the tradition of this association to have people discourse on some serious topic after the conference dinner. So I was obliged to comply, though I cannot guarantee any seriousness in the tone of my talk.

What I orginally intended to talk about was Euro-Marxism. I was going to make observations on two recent books: Emmanuel Ngara's *Art and Ideology in the African Novel*, and Georg M. Gugelberger's *Marxism and African Literature*. But after listening to what has gone on at this conference, I don't think I should talk about that. It seems to me that the critical theory dominating discussions here is

[*] A post-prandial deconstruction of Critical Theory, being an edited transcript of a banquet speech to the African Literature Association at its conference at Michigan State University, East Lansing, Michigan on April 18, 1986.

the structuralist and post-structuralist variety. By the way, I have observed that, with great hubris, this variety parades itself as Critical Theory, as if it were the one and only critical theory in the world. Well, it isn't. However, in keeping with the usage at this conference, I shall mean by critical theory the structuralist and post-structuralist variety; and in keeping with the theme of this conference, I shall talk about critical theory and its own political commitment. And I want to do so from a Pan-Africanist point of view, since we are talking about African literature and criticism in this organisation. For reasons of time, I shall compress my remarks, and largely limit myself to raising questions. I am sure there will be other opportunities to discuss the questions in appropriate detail and with whatever rigour is deemed necessary.

Before I go on, let me say that I am not opposed to theory. I spent my undergraduate years studying mathematics; and I can't think of anything as abstract and theoretical as pure mathematics. I am saying this because it seems to be one of the tactics of critical theorists to talk as if opposition to their particular brand of theory is opposition to theory. Well, there are theories and there are theories and there are theories. And as the sciences show, theories come and go; and the main danger to avoid is theory for theory's sake, or theories which do not justify themselves in terms of practical results or theories whose foundations are decrepit.

Literary theories, in my view, like all theories that demand our attention, have to demonstrate a certain explanatory power in their domain. Theories are constructs of limited scope. They establish certain frameworks within which certain issues can be investigated. And there are questions that are permissible within them, and others that are not. So, when we want to consider the merits of structuralist and post-structuralist critical theory, it would be interesting to ask what questions can be raised within it, and what questions it rules out or is unable to accommodate. I am raising this matter because I doubt whether certain issues that, in my view, are central to the Pan-Africanist position, can be raised within the framework of critical theory, or in works of literature which heed the prejudices of critical theory.

Their range of internal questions aside, theories ultimately justify themselves by their results. How good are the results when they are applied to the issues for which they are concocted? And it seems to me that, in the case of structuralist and post-structuralist critical theory, I can do no better than to cite Anthony Appiah's comments on its unfruitfulness. In his contribution to *Black Literature and Literary Theory*,[1] an anthology edited by Henry Louis Gates, Jr., Anthony Appiah argues, and I believe convincingly, that what little it has to say that is of literary value can be said without resort to the technical apparatus it finds it necessary to mobilise. So, if we can do the work for less effort, I don't see why we should bother with all that unnecessary technicality.

Another question that ought to be raised about critical theory is its relationship to the real world and to real world problems. I had an instructive experience many years ago when I was a graduate student in philosophy. For a long time I listened to my professors talking about sense-data theory, and elaborating an intellectual structure that, I think, arose with Bertrand Russell. It was very interesting. But at one point I said to myself: but where does this set of problems come from in the real world? It turned out to be based on a cluster of examples of apparent difficulties. I'll give you one of them.

If you take a stick and put it in a glass of water, and the stick is longer than the column of water in the glass, and you take a look at it, you will find that it looks bent. There is a perfectly satisfactory explanation in physics for why it looks bent even though it is straight. But sense-data theory takes

---

[1] London: Methuen, 1984.

off from that point, disregards the scientific explanation, and goes on to elaborate an alternative set of intellectual constructs for explaining appearances which differ from what we think reality is. That was one of the experiences which led me to give up philosophy. The procedures of sense-data theory did not make sense to me; and what it considered problematic I thought had perfectly acceptable explanations in classical physics.

Why am I raising that example? It is a preface to some questions about the procedures of critical theory which I find bemusing. Let me cite a few of them. All the critical theorists here can correct me if I've gotten part of their assumptions and procedures wrong.

Consider the notion of texts, and the way texts seem to be approached. If I don't get them wrong, critical theorists seem to presume that texts have an independent communal life, and speak to one another, and read one another, and echo one another, and do to one another various things that humans are traditionally expected to do to one another's minds through written materials. What bothers me about all that is this: when I think of the real world, and observe how manuscripts and printed books sit on shelves or on coffee tables, I do not see them participating in the kinds of activities which seem to be presupposed in the locutions of critical theorists. And it seems clear to me that critical theorists are making the elementary mistake of endowing lifeless objects called texts with some of the properties of the human minds which create the texts.

This attempt to give ontological autonomy and active powers to literary objects strikes me as coming, in part, from those anxieties that used to trouble the social sciences, namely, to imitate the assumptions and procedures of the prestigious physical sciences. In other words, they are the anxieties of those who deal with a world in which things, alas, are not the way they are postulated to be in classical physics or chemistry. There it is postulated that atoms have an existence and activism independent of the human observer, and that the investigator's task is to apply the human mind, through theorising and making experiments, to find out how things are and what they do in their autonomous realm. If you happen to believe that the classical physical sciences are the most prestigious branch of the human pursuit of knowledge, and that their epistemological procedures are the best for exploring the nature of things, you might be tempted to imitate them by importing their assumptions and procedures into other fields of knowledge. You might then be tempted to endow the objects of humanistic and social science studies with the kinds of autonomous activism which have proved successful in the physical sciences. But such assumptions and procedures are not applicable in every domain, as the social sciences found out. The world they investigate is much too protean for the basic regularities assumed by the classical physical sciences. Furthermore, social relations, being creatures of human activity, cannot be plausibly said to have the autonomous existence and activism postulated for the objects of the physical world. Thus the failure of the attempt to import into the social sciences the basic assumptions and procedures of the physical sciences might have been predicted. However, and unfortunately, since their main motive was to acquire the prestige of the physical sciences, failure only heightened the anxieties and complexes of the social sciences, leading them to go in for a jargon which echoed the physical science vocabulary. This was a desperate move to cover up their failures. Now, it seems, literary studies have been tempted to the same enterprise.

Despite this fashionable effort to endow literary objects with autonomous existence and activism, it seems to me pretty self-evident that texts do not talk to texts, books do not read books, texts are not objects capable of interacting with themselves in some hermetic compartment out of touch with writers, readers, hearers, etc. To presume that they are (as I think, from the manner of their locution, critical theorists do) is to take the human dimension out of literary activity. Which is stark folly, for whatever else critical theorists may refuse to concede, they must concede that texts do not write or read themselves.

Another aspect of their procedure that I find bemusing is the type of emphasis that is placed on language by some tendencies within critical theory. While the way language is used is indeed a legitimate matter of literary interest, to make the technical manipulation of language and its formal structures the primary interest risks turning literary studies into a footnote to linguistics. One is not surprised, therefore, to find Chomskyan generative and transformational grammars, with surface structures, deep structures, transformation rules, tree diagrams and all, invading, in the hands of critical theorists, the literary business of relating works of literature to society and to those intellectual issues that used to be the concern of the humanities.

Yet another aspect that I find bemusing is what I believe has been imported into critical theory from hermeneutics. It seems to me, and I stand to be corrected, that texts are approached as if they are arbitrary codes. Therefore, reading a text, for people who so approach books, consists in deciphering the code and inventing some "real" meaning which might have been left out, or was even unintended, by the text maker. Reading then turns into the job of inventing multiple determinations for the so-called indeterminacies in the phrases and sentences of the text. It seems to me that this reduces the game to one in which the figurative, the fanciful, rather than the plain meaning of the words becomes the centre of significance. It is almost as if the point of the writer (if he is at all admitted into the interchange between the autogenous texts) is to write one thing and mean something else, or to leave his meanings in the interstices between what he has actually written. When arbitrary code-breaking takes over the literary enterprise, it seems to turn the game into one of secretive communication. Unless you are an initiate, you are liable to be misled by what the text appears to say.

I don't know how many writers actually set out to write arbitrarily coded messages. But perhaps that they do not is irrelevant, in so far as texts, once created, are supposed to do their thing without too much concern for, or relationship to, writers and readers. But those of us who are ordinary readers and writers are liable to have problems with a critical enterprise which makes these kinds of assumptions. I personally find it all peculiar.

I should like to now say a few things about the political commitment out of which, in my view, this crazy enterprise has proceeded. On the face of it, critical theory, as one of the species of formalism, would seem to have no political commitment. But I am not sure that that is true. I would rather argue that it belongs to that school of intellectual enterprise which is finely disguised to defend the political interests of an entrenched imperial system. Its ability to do so comes from the fact that it excludes from its discourse all kinds of issues which that particular imperial enterprise might find embarrassing to have raised in literature. In other words, critical theory aims to sanitise literature by excluding certain issues. It functions as one of the gate-keepers, the policemen, at the cultural frontiers of an imperial system. How does it do that?

It is fashionably believed by some academics that literature is an autonomous, autogenous realm, self-contained, divorced from the rest of life and society. Advocates of this literary purism include Northrop Frye and Harold Bloom. Northrop Frye, in his *Anatomy of Criticism*,[2] claimed that "poetry can only be made out of other poems, novels out of other novels". He also declared that "literature shapes itself, and is not shaped externally." In a variant of these claims,

[2] Princeton University Press, 1957.

Harold Bloom, in his *Anxiety of Influence*,[3] declared that "the meaning of a poem can only be another poem". Such easily demolishable claims, if believed, could effectively insulate literature from politics and society. And this could be done in a very interesting way.

If literature has no social origins, no social context, no consequences in the real world; and if it exists in an autonomous, self-contained realm of its own, it becomes easy to insist that you exclude from it such annoying, unorthodox and perhaps embarrassing questions as are raised by colonialism or feminism, and on the grounds that they touch upon political and social matters which would sully the purity of literature. Those who then participate in a literary culture thus attenuated, can live in a world of the mind undisturbed by those annoying, unsettling and devastating questions which are raised by the larger world.

From those who subscribe to such literary purism, we receive injunctions against the so-called sociological, anthropological, ethnic, journalistic and topical aspects of African literature. In fact, the critical literature on African writing is full of such denunciations. If we heeded them, we would never write or talk about some of the most crucial issues in African life and history in our novels, poems and plays.

It seems to me that critical theory is tainted with literary purism through assumptions like the autonomous existence and activism of texts, and through the mountain of jargon and technicalities whereby it insists on approaching works of literature. If texts are autonomous and insulated from the goings on in the world in which writers and readers live, it is hard to see how you could legitimately put political and social issues to the texts without violating their hermetic autonomy. To be able to do so, you would have to abandon the assumptions implicit in the locutions of critical theory. Thus, adherence to the tenets of critical theory means that

[3] New York: Oxford University Press, 1973.

issues connected with colonialism, neo-colonialism, feminism, etc, may not be raised in works of literature or in critical discourses on them.

To bring this talk to a close, let me re-emphasise the issue of the Pan-Africanist viewpoint. Incidentally, the Pan-Africanist viewpoint is not a recent development; nor is African literature a newly emergent literature. A lot of the discussion of African literature erroneously assumes that African literature is of recent origin. It is not. African literature is fifty centuries old: five thousand years. And within that long tradition there have been all kinds of tendencies and all kinds of guiding values from whose perspective the fads which Euromodernism has been propagating sound silly.

When I say that African literature is 50 centuries old, let me note that some of the oldest works extant in the African literary tradition are the Pyramid Texts carved on the walls of the pyramid tombs of the Nile Valley. If you read them, you will be amazed. Other ancient works of the African literary tradition are still available. Some of the satires are fresher today than most of what contemporary African writers are producing. Their admonitions, their invocations, and their love poetry are simply exquisite. So too their praise poems. Yet, Eurocentric critics of African literature are either ignorant of them, or wilfully try to exclude them from the tradition within which contemporary works must be inserted and evaluated.

But more important for the evaluation of critical theory are the kinds of values which have regulated the long African tradition of literary production and intellectual discourse. On that, let me quote from a recent essay by the African novelist, Ayi Kwei Armah:

> As far back as our written and unwritten records go, it has been the prime destiny of the serious African artist to combine the craft of creativity

> with the search for regenerative values. To this neo-colonial day, the best African artists are obsessed with the philosophy and history of our people, with our values and how we express or betray them in our present lives, with how we strengthen or frustrate them in our planning for the future. Nekht, the ancestral scribe, is a seeker after values, principally justice, and on that search his sister Thuau, also an artist, is totally with him. The purpose of Thoth, the divine writer, is a matter of values: Justice. Asare and Aset, known to the West as Osiris and Isis, made the cultivation of humanizing values a permanent aim of the arts and sciences. Ptahhotep, Kagemni, Ani, Neferti—all in their works were concerned with philosophy, with values.[4]

From the standpoint of cultivating humanising values, how should critical theory be looked at? What are the values that critical theory has been serving? Are they humanising values? Are they capable of serving African society and African civilisation, especially at this historical juncture? If the answer is yes, then, of course, critical theory could be of value when applied to African literature. If the answer is no, then it is, at the least, called into question, and attempts to perpetrate some of its intentions on African literature would have to be reconsidered.

For my part, I find it hard to reconcile a political commitment to Euroimperialism with the defence of African society and the promotion of African civilisation. I find it difficult to concede that imperialism is a humanising project. On technical grounds, the nature of the critical theory game presupposes that human beings do not mediate between these allegedly autonomous texts. How, I wonder, can something be humanising which bars humans from its setting and processes?

[4] "Masks and Marx", *Présence Africaine*, No. 131, 1984, p.35.

All that notwithstanding, I've heard it argued at this conference that one of the contributions of critical theory to black liberation is to enable black scholars who take it up to stand on an equal footing with Western scholars by being able to brandish their own variety of it, and so demonstrating that blacks are capable of "doing theory". In effect, the claim is that if *they* can practice all that technical hermeneutics, *we* too can. I am not sure that this is particularly valuable. To practice critical theory on that basis seems to me to concede everything to Western hegemonism. It keeps those who do so in the trap of living up to Western criteria, because when you are proving that you can do whatever they can do, even when what they say they are doing is patently absurd, it doesn't seem to me that you have escaped from the hegemony of their culture.

Yet, it seems to me, escaping their cultural hegemony is what Pan-Africanism is all about. For ultimately, the job of Pan-Africanism in this century is to liberate the African from the authority of foreign traditions in every department of culture and life. That does not mean that Africans should reject foreign traditions; it simply means that we do not accept their authority. The crucial part of the entire hegemony business in culture is to get you to accept, without question, without doubt, the authority of alien traditions that are quite often in conflict with your interests and your well-being; and therefore, the crucial part of the liberation business is the dismantling of the authority of all foreign traditions, especially those which are unsound or incompatible with African survival, well being and dignity.

It is on these grounds that, if I had time to elaborate, I would put in a Pan-Africanist defence of African literature against inroads by Euromodernist critical theory. Thank you.

African literature and Marxist criticism[*]

> Marxism, in its approach to non-Western societies and values, is decidedly colonialist, western, Eurocentric and hegemonist.... Marxists in Africa exhibit a desire to institutionalize western communist hypotheses as the only correct philosophy.
>
> —Ayi Kwei Armah

> It is principally its *method* which we must retain from European socialism.
>
> —Leopold Sedar Senghor

> Africans must learn to use Marxism, but Marxism must not be allowed to use Africans!
>
> —Samora Machel

> The Nigerian intellectual is an expert in foreign ideologies. Take the Marxist for instance. Although he defends Marxism with fanatical zeal and is sure it can be transplanted here, he is quite ignorant of the indigenous political system that has kept his people going for millennia. What is more, he does not want to know.... Socialism was here long before Marx wrote *The Capital*. But the Nigerian Marxist lacks the initiative to research into how our socialism and extended family system operated.
>
> —Elechi Amadi

---

[*] A review essay on Emmanuel Ngara, *Art and Ideology in the African Novel*, London: Heinemann Educational Books, 1985; and Georg M. Gugelberger, ed., *Marxism and African Literature*, Trenton, N.J.: Africa World Press, 1986.

AFRICAN LITERATURE AND MARXISM

I*

African Marxist critics often display towards African writers the frustrations of a sergeant-major whose mindless orders go unheeded. However, their charges that the writers are "bourgeois" and lack "commitment" seldom make clear the source of the friction between them. One of the merits of Emmanuel Ngara's *Art and Ideology in the African Novel* is that, without setting out to do so, it exposes for probing the root cause of that friction.

Ngara's examination of the African novel in the light of Marxist aesthetic theory makes two things clear. First, Marxism has had little influence on contemporary African literature, for only a handful of literary works satisfy Marxist criteria for socialist art. Second, Marxist aesthetic theories have little to offer for the study of African literary style, which is why Ngara has to resort to non-Marxist stylistic criticism to evaluate the works of African novelists.

In Part One of his book, Ngara distils from the pronouncements of Marx, Engels, Lenin, Trotsky, Stalin, Gorky, Mao, Lukács, Cauldwell and Eagleton several criteria for determining the socialist character of literary works. These are, that a book must have as its theme some kind of class struggle (for instance, collective bargaining between proletarians and their exploiters, the development of proletarian or peasant revolutionary consciousness, armed struggle); it should deal with the plight of the working class, not that of a race or nation; it should espouse proletarian internationalism, promote egalitarianism, prefigure and enthuse about the coming of socialism; and so on. Stylistically, it should restrict itself to critical realism (the truthful portrayal of typical characters in typical circumstances, particularly in the manner of Tolstoy or Balzac), and to socialist realism as outlined by Gorky and Zhdanov.

* This part was published as "More than Marxist", *TLS*, June 13, 1986, p. 663.

Unsurprisingly, few works of African literature succeed in so severely restricting their themes and techniques as to satisfy these criteria. Having, in Part Two of his book, examined the works of Achebe, Ngugi, Armah, Sembene, Maillu, La Guma, Gordimer and others, Ngara concludes that only a handful of African literary works qualify as socialist art. The rest, even those by admittedly radical African writers, fail the test for such assorted blemishes as liberalism, nationalism, Pan-Africanism, racial consciousness and indulgence in metaphoric and mythic realism.

Most African writers are, evidently, unwilling to play down, or avoid altogether such crucial aspects of human reality as sex, race, nation, or personal ambition. In illuminating anti-imperialism, ethnic rifts, corruption, unstable nation states, false versions of history, or the murderous ambitiousness of rulers, most African writers feel obliged to employ any techniques they find serviceable. They therefore find it strange that the aim of socialist art is not to illuminate African lives and conditions through truthful and accomplished works informed by Marxist analysis, but rather to package African lives and experiences in ways that conform to Marxist formulae and dogmas, and to incite enthusiasm for a socialist future, regardless of the actual experiences and preoccupations of Africans.

Ngara's book, though, is valuable in that it assembles Marxist dicta and tests them against African literature. Had it pushed its investigation to the point of explaining the very slight influence that Marxism has had on African writing, it would have been a much more valuable work.

II

But why are Marxist critics so unsympathetic to the broad range of themes evident in African literature? Why are they hostile to African openness to diverse literary styles and techniques? Georg M. Gugelberger's *Marxism and African*

Literature supplies grounds for answering these questions. It suggests that this is primarily because Marxism and African nationalism, which the mainstream of African literature serves, are devoted to different political constituencies some of whose vital interests sharply conflict. Secondly, Marxist aesthetics, and the aesthetics of African literature, derive from different traditions which emphasise different principles. However, given its universalist pretensions, Marxism finds it hard to concede to African literature the right to pursue interests and use devices not sanctioned by Marxism. As a result, Marxists display towards African literature a Eurocentric hegemonism that is the left-wing counterpart of the imperialism for which Euromodernist critics are notorious. African Marxist critics, like African Euromodernist critics, fail to take sufficient note of this, and, in effect, act as native auxiliaries of European cultural imperialism.

The political constituency of African literature is the Black or Pan-African World. Pan-Africanism, which African literature manifests, aims to defend the African race and to advance its civilisation. It is committed to the survival, prosperity, dignity, independence and cultural renaissance of the African peoples throughout the world. Marxism, in contrast, has for its constituency the global industrial working class or the world proletariat. It is committed to getting this class to rule the world through a revolution that would install its dictatorship over all other classes.

These constituencies do not much overlap: only a tiny fraction of Africans belong to the industrial working class. And even if all African wage and salary earners were added to swell the numbers of the African proletariat proper, they still would form a tiny fraction of the African population.

There is also a profound conflict between their historic projects. Africans do not wish to be dominated by the European proletariat any more than by the European bourgeoisie, both of whom have together dominated and devastated Africans of all classes for five centuries. Today, the rule of the world bourgeoisie is so organised that the African petit-bourgeoisie is subordinated to the European bourgeoisie. If the present distribution of power among the continents of the world should persist, it is difficult to see how, whenever world proletarian dictatorship arrives, the African proletariat will escape being subordinated to the European proletariat. Perhaps sensing that Africans would not take kindly to such a prospect, Marxists seem particularly ill-disposed to anything that might sensitise Africans to it. They therefore hasten to cry down any theme (such as those which highlight racial or continental divisions) whose exploration in literature would cast light on the need to redress the distribution of power between Europe and Africa, regardless of what class rules.

In aesthetics, the inheritances of the two constituencies are different. What the Marxists would have us accept as the aesthetic of the world proletariat is but a pseudo-aesthetic derived by Marxist intellectuals from aspects of local European experience. African literature, however, derives its aesthetic from African experience and traditions. Which is not to say that the African and European aesthetic traditions have nothing in common, for they do. But Marxism turns its back on much of those common aspects, and instead substitutes political and economic criteria for the aesthetic. And they would like African literature to do likewise by repudiating its own rich aesthetic inheritance, and by adopting that philistine pseudo-aesthetic which Marxism has obtained by ignoring the core of the European aesthetic tradition.

The philistinism of the Marxist pseudo-aesthetic needs to be seen to be believed. The Nigerian Marxist sociologist, Omafume Onoge, says:

> Marxist critics are necessarily class partisan. . . .
> Marxist critics are always concerned, in the final

analysis, with the assessment of artistic visions in terms of their practical relevance to the struggle for ever more democratic forms of social existence. (Gugelberger, p. 60)

Partisanship for the proletariat, and this insistence on making aesthetic assessments on the basis of how a work helps the political struggle of the proletariat, tend to make Marxist literary criticism thin on what are commonly considered aesthetic concerns in both the African and the European traditions. It tends to ignore, or denounce as "formalism", questions of beauty, of style, of technique, of sensibility, of appropriateness and so on—things which, in most of the world's traditions, are regarded as being at the heart of aesthetics. An "aesthetic" theory which ignores these core aspects can only be a pseudo-aesthetic.

In its passion to transform everything into class politics, Marxist criticism thinks it has made an aesthetic judgement once it determines whether a poem, story or play is "progressive"; or whether it serves the bourgeoisie or the proletariat; or promotes the "revolutionary" dreams of the petit-bourgeois intellectuals who claim to represent the proletariat. As political missionaries for the proletariat, Marxist critics approach works of African literature with such questions as these: What does it say about the dominant ideology? Does it supply an attractive image of the industrial workers? Does it paint an unflattering picture of employers and other enemies of the proletariat? Does it beat the drums for socialist revolution? To answer such questions, for them, is to make aesthetic determinations. Such is their philistinism.

Reducing aesthetics to class politics leads Marxist critics to some curious verdicts. For example, Omafume Onoge thus pronounces on one of Leopold Senghor's poems:

> We find that whereas, for Césaire, it was the

> genocidal violence of the colonizers that impressed him about the Congo, for Senghor it was the primeval essence of the River Congo. In spite of the pressing heritage of King Leopold's bestiality, Senghor found time for the startling gaiety of 'Oho! Congo Oho!' and the projection of an ultra-romantic past which does not intersect with the brutal colonial reality. Given the reality of the violent changes consequent upon colonialism, the tenor of Senghor's retrospective explorations is an *undignified* retreat. (Gugelberger, p. 29)

Presumably, then, nature poetry and poetry about the pre-colonial past are ruled out by Marxist pseudo-aesthetics unless they stray from their theme to denounce colonial brutality. This is as if literature must have just one attitude (anti-colonialism) and one tone (outrage); as if the celebration of nature, of its gifts and beauties, were incompatible with anti-colonialism. From such an outlook, you wouldn't think that soldiers at anti-colonial war fronts ever had time for love or laughter; or for contemplating a beautiful flower or a soothing sunset heralding a night's rest. What an amazing narrowing of sensibility by political monomania!

In another display of curious judgement, Tunde Fatunde, another Nigerian Marxist academic, says of Yambo Ouologuem's *Bound to Violence*:

> Yambo Ouologuem presents the working people as an amorphous mass belonging to a single social class in society. Of course he is correct to show vividly how this class was oppressed by the feudal lords of Nakem in alliance with Arab and European slave traders who came under the umbrella of a so-called civilizing mission, but he gives the impression that the working people are lacking in any spirit of rebellion to that oppression. They re-

fuse even to attempt to cut the parasitic sucker binding them to the local and foreign exploiters. And thus in *Le Devoir de Violence* there appears the *eternal* omnipotence of African lords and foreign colonizers. (Gugelberger, pp. 113-114)

What could Fatunde possibly mean by this charge, since there indeed are incidents in which the working people of Nakem show the spirit of rebellion to oppression? Didn't Barou, the blacksmith, rebel when he was approached to commit murder for the Saif? Wasn't he intimidated, with the choice of either doing the deed or himself dying from the bite of an asp, before he capitulated? One wonders just how many of our academic militants have ever been faced with such a choice and yet persisted in their rebellion! And wasn't Barou later killed for having dared to show rebellion in his initial refusal?

If Barou's type of resistance doesn't count in the eyes of militant Marxism, could the charge then amount to this: that no slave revolt or jacquerie is enacted in the novel? If so, was such a revolt recorded in the history fictionalised by the novel? If none was recorded, wouldn't the charge amount to faulting a historical novel for not falsifying the history it is presenting? But even if the chronicles did record a slave revolt, would its inclusion be mandatory regardless of the theme and structure of the story the novel has chosen to tell? And, by the way, how would the absence of worker revolt from a particular novel show "the *eternal* omnipotence" of their lords?

Such considerations would reduce Fatunde's charge to a complaint that a presumed aesthetic obligation to present the proletariat as ever and always militant was not met by Yambo Ouologuem. Which would amount to a demand that literature should falsify its portrait of the world, or give up all other interests, in order to oblige Marxist dogma and its revolution.

It would be useful to investigate whether the African proletariat, let alone the larger African population, would subscribe to the pseudo-aesthetic evident in such pronouncements as are made by petit-bourgeois African Marxists who presume to speak for them. There is indeed evidence that African proletarians would not endorse such judgements. Reporting on what happened at the Kamiriithu Youth Centre in Kenya, during the invention and scripting of the play *Ngaahika Ndeenda* by a proletarian and peasant collective, Ngugi wa Thiong'o, an African Marxist writer who has actually carried his practice from the ivory tower into a community of African proletarians, writes:

> When it came to song, dance and ceremony, the peasants, who of course knew all about it, were particular about accuracy of detail. Their approach was very serious. They were also particular about language which, of course, is another element of form. They were concerned that the various characters, depending on age and occupation, be given the appropriate language. 'An old man cannot speak like that' they would say. 'If you want him to have dignity, he has to use this or that kind of proverb.' Levels of language and language-use and the nuances of words and phrases were discussed heatedly. . . . The participants were most particular about the representation of history, their history. And they were quick to point out and argue against any incorrect positioning and representation of the various forces—even the enemy forces—at work in the struggle against imperialism.[1]

This suggests that the African proletariat would neither reduce aesthetics to class politics, nor decry poems about

---

[1] Ngugi wa Thiong'o, *Decolonising the Mind*, London: James Currey, 1986, p. 54.

nature which did not incorporate anti-colonial sentiments. They would not accept an aesthetic which took no interest in stylistic matters, let alone one which denounced such interest as "formalist"; nor would they agree to a romanticisation of the proletariat which falsified history. In this, the African proletariat would share the principles of the African aesthetic tradition wherein the aesthetic and the political are held distinct, and the beautiful is not reduced to what is politically desired. The mindless political partisanship in Marxist pseudo-aesthetics would be abhorrent to a tradition in which the beauty of even an enemy is acknowledged, as in the ancient Mali epic *Da Monzon*; in which it is recognised that beauty is an independent power, which is not extinguished even by the most villainous politics; in other words, that aesthetics is not reducible to ethics.

Once the constituencies of Marxism and African literature are differentiated, and once the implications of their different historic projects and aesthetic inheritances are drawn out, it becomes clear that the two will disagree on quite a few matters. What is surprising then is that Marxists should insist that African literature should not pursue its own interests, but should serve as a drummer boy for a Marxist world revolution that is not incontrovertibly in the African interest.

When thwarted in their aim to commandeer African literature for their purposes, some Marxist sergeant-majors feel impelled to provide lofty warrants for their commands. They then appeal to the allegedly universal authority of Marxism. This, they hope, will overcome what they consider the misguided particularism of Africans. Some even go so far as to deny the possibility of an African aesthetic on whose authority a universalist Marxist pseudo-aesthetic might be repudiated. Georg M. Gugelberger, for example argues that "most African critics have confused geography and ethnicity with ideology" (p. vi), but that "criticism, philosophy, logic, ethics, etc. can hardly be reduced to black and white, Europe versus Africa, but can be conceived as class related, i.e. supportive of one class while being harmful to another" (p. 3). And whereas he asserts that "it will be patently impossible to arrive at a separate (alias African) aesthetics" (pp. 13-14), on the other hand he says "it is doubtful that we can ever arrive at . . . a criticism based on rejection of European critical concepts." (p. 3).

Those familiar with similar claims by Euromodernists will recognize the Eurocentrism and hegemonism implicit in the above statements. Translated into plain talk, Gugelberger is saying to Africans: "Don't be ethnic, don't be Afrocentric, don't be parochial. There cannot be an African aesthetic anyway, only the Universalist aesthetic, made in Europe, which Marxism has fashioned to serve the world proletariat."

To decode Gugelberger's meaning, please note that if an African aesthetic is impossible, and if criticism without European concepts is impossible, then the only aesthetic which Africans could use in criticism must contain European aesthetic concepts. Thus Africa, the aesthetic orphan, is part of the domain for which the European aesthetic generously plays stepfather! To support the universal sway of the philistine Marxist brand of this European aesthetic, Gugelberger claims that criticism and philosophy have a class character but lack a geographic or racial character. Now, really? If the propositions of criticism and philosophy can have a class character, why can't they have national, racial, cultural or continental character as well? What is so special about class divisions and antagonisms that they can affect ideas whereas national, racial, cultural, continental and other divisions and antagonisms cannot? Do these other divisions and antagonisms lack the materialist or economic origins which class divisions and antagonisms are said to have within Marxist theory? Only those who refuse to investigate the matter could believe that.

Gugelberger's claims indicate that white Marxists can be

against black racial consciousness, against African ethnic and national consciousness just as much as white non-Marxists. But they will couch in spurious universalist and class terms their parochial European opposition to Africans examining African issues in the light of African cultural traditions, racial experiences and historic needs. Which means we must beware of left-wing imperialism.

III

Two things ought to be clear by now. From the list of the luminaries whose dicta supply the Marxist aesthetic canon (Marx, Engels, Lenin, Trotsky, Stalin, Gorky, Lukács, Zhdanov, Cauldwell, Eagleton, etc.), and from the fact that their dicta are derived from the narrow European experience rather than from the diverse experiences of all the peoples of the world, it is clear that Marxists are trying to foist a fundamentally European tradition on African literature; and they are doing so without as much as examining its compatibility with African interests. Worse still, that particular tradition is demonstrably philistine and pseudo-aesthetic, for in its political monomania, it would dismiss genuinely aesthetic criteria as "formalist", and replace them with partisan political ones.

Alas, it is on the spurious universal authority of this impoverished branch of the European tradition that Africa's Marxist Ariels would hobble African literature.

An implication of all this is that African Marxists in their very Marxism, need to have their minds decolonised. This is especially important because they are so convinced of the inherent anti-imperialism of their creed that its unconscious Eurocentrism and cultural imperialism, like a hidden abscess, can cause more damage than if made visible. Unless they dispell the notion that every idea in the Marxist canon has binding authority everywhere, they will not be able to sort out what is valid and scientific from what is not, what is Hegelian theological claptrap or sheer European prejudice from what is not, and they will not be able to select what may usefully be applied in Africa from what may not.

Responsibilities of African literary scholars and critics[*]

Why should there not be 'African humanities'? Every language, which means every civilization, can provide material for the humanities, because *every civilization is the expression, with its own peculiar emphasis, of certain characteristics of humanity.* How can an African elite play its part in bringing about a renaissance of African civilization out of the ferment caused by French contact if they start off knowing nothing about that civilization?

—Leopold Sedar Senghor

Egyptian antiquity is to African culture what Graeco-Roman antiquity is to Western culture. The building up of a corpus of African humanities should be based on this fact.

—Cheikh Anta Diop

Introduction

Good morning, Ladies and Gentlemen. I have been asked to talk about the responsibilities of African literary scholars and critics. I wish to do so from the standpoint that a literature has responsibilities to the society that produces and consumes it, and that, therefore, literary critics and

---

[*] An expanded version of a Keynote Address to the Sixth Annual International Conference on African Literature and the English Language, at the University of Calabar, on May 9, 1986.

scholars, who try to mediate between a society and its literary works, also have responsibilities to that society.

Since my remarks will amount to a criticism of the shortcomings of our literary critics and scholars, I bet I will be accused of being a prescriptive critic. So let me anticipate that accusation by asking whether there is any other kind of critic? The charge of being prescriptive is usually made by those who do not like what a critic is saying; to those who like what he is saying, he is not being prescriptive at all, he is an affirmer of what common sense recommends.

However, there is a sense in which all criticism really is prescriptive. If critics tell you what they like and what they don't like, and why, they are prescriptive in so far as those who write and wish to be read by them, and want to please them, would do well to take note of what they like or do not like. To that extent all criticism can be said to be prescriptive.

But I understand that people who make that charge do not mean it that way at all. They usually imply that a critic is ordering writers about, legislating for them, making mandatory recommendations to them. But I doubt whether that is ever true. A critic is not a legislator; any writer is quite free to disregard what any critic says if he does not agree with it. Ultimately, a critic makes suggestions, and a suggestion is not a command. In my view, a critic is an advocate, urging certain practices and interpretations, and arguing against others. If the case he makes is persuasive, then, of course, he will be heeded. But even when a critic's views become widely accepted, it is through persuasion, for in the last resort, he speaks only for himself, though others may add their assent to what he has said.

In so far as I am embarking here on a criticism of literary critics, I would like to hope that those whose stock in trade is to criticise can themselves cheerfully take a little bit of criticism. On the other hand, I feel sure that, in so far as criticism is not legislation, the criticised critics will disregard what I am going to say should they not find it sensible.

What is the place of the critic and scholar in the web of relationships between writers, readers and society? Though one might be hard put to discern it from the manner of some critics, scholarship is not an intellectual or cultural boss over literature. Rather it is a servant. Scholars and critics must therefore be seen, not as bosses to be served by writers and worshipped by the readers, but as glorified kitchen help and stewards. As I see it, the writers are the cooks; the readers are the guests invited to the feast; and the proper roles of scholars and critics are, first, to help the cooks in the kitchen by preparing materials, insights and suggestions which writers may use in their cooking if they like; and second, to set the table and hand to the guests the salt and pepper of their commentary to enhance the flavour of the dishes. It would therefore be very useful to all parties to bear in mind that though critics and scholars could be very important for the production and consumption of literature, their roles are secondary, not primary.

The responsibilities I wish to talk about fall into three groups: first are the responsibilities of criticism and scholarship to writers and to readers as producers and consumers, respectively, of literature; second are their responsibilities to the society, culture and civilisation to which the writers and readers belong; and third are their responsibilities to the practice of scholarship and criticism. Many of the points I shall make are commonplace, but there is value, I believe, in putting them together so we can get the benefits of a comprehensive view of these responsibilities.

Responsibilities to African writers and readers

These responsibilities derive from certain considerations about literary activity in a society, which I shall now outline.

First of all, in my view, literature is simply the written part of a dialogue which people conduct among themselves about their history. Their lives, not some abstract categories or theories, are the stuff of that history. And among the aims of a society's literature are the following: to help deepen and expand its people's awareness of their world by illuminating corners of their experience; to clarify their history and identity, and thus prompt them to correct action; to throw light on that society's moral problems and supply inspiring examples. This list, of course, is not exhaustive.

Secondly, a literary work, by itself, is like a diamond in the dark. It needs light from the reader's mind to make it sparkle. The richer and stronger the light from the reader's experience, the more radiance the work will give out. Criticism can play the role of an illuminator which, by its commentaries, situates the literary work within the history of the primary audience to whom it is addressed; which places it within the literary tradition of that group, and discusses the moral, social, philosophical and other issues to which the work draws attention. This localisation is imperative because specific works of literature are products of specific social histories, and the best way to appreciate them is to put them in the context of their specific societies.

On that view, criticism and scholarship have to try to illuminate a work, not for the benefit of theory, but for the benefit of the specific people to whom the literature belongs. In the case of Africa, African critics and literary scholars have an obligation to illuminate African literature for the benefit of the African people.

In yesterday's Writers' Forum, we had a valuable example of criticism in action. We discussed T. M. Aluko's *Wrong Ones in the Dock* in the light of our experiences and of the stake we have in Nigerian society, rather than in an attempt to serve structuralist theory borrowed from elsewhere, or British curiosity about Nigeria, or some such foreign interest. We could feel the electricity in the room. Everybody knew what we were talking about, had a personal stake in the matter, so nobody fell asleep. When criticism recognises that such is its primary job, we shall all find reason to appreciate what our critics proceed to do for us. They then would be less vulnerable to the charge that they are parasites on our writers.

Thirdly, a literary scholar is a professional reader who uses a literary work to illuminate the world, and the world to illuminate the work. As a professional reader, a literary scholar is expected to have trained his sensibilities, to have fine tuned his emotional and intellectual antennae so he can gather the best stimulus from both the work and the world. If he gets more out of a work than the average reader, it is presumably because he brings more to it. And to read the work through his eyes is to see it through lenses which magnify and give a clearer resolution of what is presented.

Fourthly, given that a literary scholar is someone who gets to write what he thinks about what he and you and everybody else have read or can also read, what makes his comments worthy of our attention? What gives authority to his pronouncements? Critics cannot blithely assume that simply because they have gone through some academic training they have earned the authority to address the writers and readers. I believe that it is the quality of their comments, the value of what insights they offer, that earns them our attention. Any critic can flourish 25 PhDs if he has them, and we shall be unimpressed if his remarks are foolish or obtuse. But when he tells us something that helps us to see a new and vital dimension to a work, we shall appreciate him even if he never went to school.

Fifthly, the professionally trained literary critic or scholar is expected to bring a broader range of ideas, facts and issues to bear, and in a systematic and logical way, upon what he reads. In particular, he is expected to bring the fruits of his systematic reading, and of his systematic observation of life and society, and of his systematic thinking on literature and society to bear upon each work he discusses. I keep emphasising "systematic" because I have the impression that the comments we get from our critics tend to be unsystematic. One rarely gets the sense that they have considered the many different sides of an issue, or that they have looked into the presuppositions that they ought to have looked into before venturing to make comments. However, what a literary scholar says of a work is expected to reflect the thoughtful care which his training is presumed to have accustomed him to. And whereas an incoherent or disorganised statement by somebody who has not gone through the discipline of scholarship might be routinely overlooked, we have a right to demand that trained experts conduct their discussions in a coherent and systematic manner.

Sixthly, let us assume that a critic has done his work of looking at society and at a work of literature, and has come up with something he wishes to tell us. Like any other reader, he is expected to be able to say what he likes and dislikes about what he has read; but he is also expected to be able to say why. And his training is expected to equip him to demonstrate his reasons for his responses to a work, so we can evaluate the cogency of his remarks. When he pronounces on the value of a work, he is expected to show grounds for his evaluation. Its artistic worth, its intellectual merit, its place in the field to which it belongs, its contribution to the intellectual life of society are some of the aspects one would expect a critical and scholarly evaluation of a work to report cogently upon. Such are the qualities which would make a literary scholar's pronouncements worth listening to. If he doesn't demonstrate them, I think he should not be surprised if he is ignored by readers and writers alike.

What responsibilities derive from the foregoing considerations? Generally speaking, a literary scholar's comments on any work have two constituencies—the consumers of literature and the producers of literature. The demands of these two constituencies are not necessarily the same. Whereas the consumers are generally more interested in what the work will do for their intellectual enjoyment and for their perception of life, producers tend to show great interest in the technical devices and tricks with which the work was put together.

Accordingly, the consumers expect the literary scholar to interpret a work in ways that make it resonate with meanings and lessons for them. In so far as a literary work embodies or expresses ideas, the literary critic or scholar is expected to reflect on the validity of such ideas, to work out their implications and probable impact on society and individuals. Consumers therefore expect him to perform, not like a code-breaking clerk, but rather like a professional musician who plays a piece of music so that they hear and enjoy it far better than when they play it for themselves, by bringing out its nuances and special qualities.

Producers, in contrast, expect what is really shop talk for technicians. However, since a literary scholar's shop talk has to be sound and highly instructive if practitioners are to pay him any attention, those scholars who are themselves not competent writers are not likely to bring first hand experience to their comments on the problems of literary craft, and so are not likely to command the attention of literary craftsmen.

However, it must be noted that there have been excellent technical commentaries from scholars who produced no fictional works of their own. But then these are exceptional people who display the qualities of a natural coach. A football coach doesn't necessarily have to be a good player himself. But he must be a good observer, a good analyser, and a good instructor with a sharp sense for what works and what doesn't work. From watching and reflecting on many games, he develops a knack for looking at what his trainees are doing on the field and then inventing devices and stratagems that they, the players, might find advantageous to adopt. So, though I can sympathise with writers who disdain critics who do not themselves produce competent works of literature, we must recognise those who, without being poets or dramatists or story tellers, are nevertheless able to tell us useful things about the technical side of literature.

The literary scholars' responsibilities to these two constituencies may be summed up by saying that it is their obligation to help to improve the writer's craft, the reader's powers of appreciation and discrimination, as well as everybody's artistic taste and ability to relate literature to society and society to literature. Now, how well have African scholars and critics carried out these responsibilities in the past generation?

We may appreciate the spectacular shortfalls in their performance by asking a few questions. Where are the African equivalents of I. A. Richards' *Practical Criticism*—a book which conducted experiments to help people learn how to read poetry with some expectation of understanding and profit? Where are the African equivalents of Ezra Pound's *How to Read* or his *ABC of Reading?* Where are the African equivalents of Mayakovsky's *How Verses are Made?* After all, poems, like tables and chairs, are made: they have a technical side and are not just the mysterious and effortless discharge of "genius". Which was why Mayakovsky (one of the foremost Russian poets of the early 20th century) thought it necessary to write a book to instruct the would-be poet on how verses are put together. Where, also, are our counterparts of F. R. Leavis's magazine *Scrutiny* which devoted itself to the job of relating specific works of England's literature to the tradition from which they sprang, and to various of England's social and philosophical questions?

The absence of such works from a whole generation of African critics suggests that they have not bothered to evaluate what they were taught at Western universities—and at their Eurocentric African counterparts—for its serviceableness to the African situation; nor, it seems, have they applied their learning in ways that would address the specific needs of our literary culture.

To the extent that, as readers and as writers, we look around and find little of help from our professional critics and scholars, we are entitled to wonder what service they are really giving us. What we find them churning out are papers on the kinds of questions and analyses that are in vogue in Western literary academia. Observers of the output of our critics and scholars will be familiar with titles like the following: symbolism in ABC; surrealism in DEF; tragedy, history and ideology in GHI; proletarian consciousness in JKL; structuralist poetics in MNO; deconstructive degeneration in PQR; semiotic hermeneutics in STU; myth and *langue* in XYZ and so on and so forth. These are simply dull echoes of what they learned in school when they were studying Western literature. They simply transport the same questions and try to perpetrate the same analyses on African literature.

Which may be fine if there were nothing better for them to do with the resources Africa puts at their disposal. My reservation about such goings on is that such papers do not address questions which African writers and readers want addressed today. It all seems like a waste of time and resources when we have a crying need for somebody to tell us the finer points of how to write, and of how to get the best out of a work of literature in order to relate it to our own lives.

Critics interested in the health of literature should not forget that ultimately, as David Maillu has argued, people read literature for their own practical needs. Therefore, those whose careers depend on a thriving literature would do well to encourage literature to answer to these needs. For you to pick up a book after class or work, in your home or on the train or bus, you have a practical problem that you want to solve. Maybe you want to kill time, you want to be amused, you want to learn about what happened in some country at some time and there is a work of fiction that enables you to immerse your mind in that situation. Critics and scholars would be more useful to our literature when their comments and papers address issues that encourage writers to satisfy the numerous needs of readers, and readers to derive satisfaction from the works of our writers.

Our critics are themselves not immune to practical considerations for reading and writing on literature. Indeed, African critics churn out such papers for the practical reason that they want promotion in their academic jobs, and given the neo-colonial tradition entrenched in our universities, they can most readily get promoted by writing on such obtuse topics. The basic problem seems to be that the practical reasons which dictate what African critics and literary scholars write about African literature have not been reconciled with the interests which drive African writers to write, and non-academic African readers to read African literature. We would be appreciative when the kinds of papers they need to write to get promotion become such as answer to the needs of African writers and readers.

Until the university authorities bring this about writers, in particular, will be justified in their present view that critics and scholars are parasites who use what writers produce as raw materials for advancing their careers, but who give nothing useful back to the writers. Readers, for their part, would justifiably dismiss them as irrelevant, self-centred idlers supported by their taxes and other contributions.

Responsibilities to African society and civilisation

I should emphasize that I am here talking about African literature, and that what is pertinent is the responsibility of African critics and scholars to African society and civilisation, not their responsibility to the universe. As is apparent to most people, African society is afflicted with numerous ailments, and African civilisation is in disarray. If Africa is to get back on the road to health and resurgence, and if there is anything that literary scholars and critics can contribute to that, then they have an obligation to do it.

First among what they can do is to promote a kind of literature which will illuminate our history for our own society; a literature which will thereby serve the well-being and self-respect of the African people. Many of our writers are already doing this, the rehabilitation of the African and the restoration of his self-respect having motivated many of them to undertake to write. The curious thing though is that African scholars and critics have not been as supportive of this undertaking as they ought to. All too many have followed their Western masters in denouncing African writings which try to revive the dignity of the African, especially those which project a version of the African past that is more realistic than that favoured by our colonisers.

As Elechi Amadi told us the other day, some critics think that we have a surfeit of novels that deal with the African past; and he rightly warned them to resign themselves to very many more works on the African past. In support of Elechi Amadi's position, let me point out that in other societies, writers constantly turn out historical works of all kinds—biographies, histories, fiction. Such works are every year written about events that happened as long ago, in some cases, as a thousand or two thousand years. Yet their critics do not tell them that they have a surfeit of works that deal with their past.

Why are sensible societies rightly fascinated with their past? And why should Africans write and read even much more about the African past? The past is all that we have; and to wipe out our past through amnesia is to wipe out all that we have, all that makes us what we are. Those who would teach us amnesia about our past, especially while doping us with accounts of the past of other peoples, cannot have our best interests at heart. They, in effect, wish us to commit social and cultural suicide by turning into zombies.

Our knowledge of the African past has been mutilated by centuries of propaganda by foreign invaders and conquerors; it is therefore imperative that we discover the authentic version of our past. Until we do, we shall remain the zombies which centuries of Arab and European colonisation have made of us. It is exceedingly important for our mental health and social progress that we appreciate that we did not emerge from a historical vacuum yesterday, and that our roots do not lie in Europe or Arabia. As Chinua Achebe once said, our history did not begin with the colonial conquest. So, whatever we may be doing today, we need to bear in mind that we are part of a long tradition. If we are to reconnect ourselves with that long tradition, scholarship has the monumental responsibility to help us recover that tradition, document it, criticise it, celebrate it, and make it generally available to us. Then our writers can have the materials to relate to; our readers can read them and have them as a common background from which to absorb what our writers produce.

Most people have heard about the European renaissance. It was a period when the scholars of Europe went about digging up as much of the ancient materials from Greece and Rome as they could find. They critically examined them, analysed them, commented on them, celebrated and disseminated them. The result was that, within a few generations, a barbarous and ignorant Europe had recovered the culture of the Greeks and Romans and made it their own. And once they made it their own, it became easy for them to move forward. If they had not assembled that heritage, and internalised it, they might be still floundering today trying to figure out the Archimedes principle, or those principles of drama which Aristotle had written down.

The example of the European renaissance is pertinent to us because, unless our scholars do similar work on the African heritage, we are bound to find ourselves locked into the European tradition which colonialism imported and entrenched in Africa, with all manner of disastrous results. I remember once finding on a notice board on one of our

Nigerian universities a syllabus for a drama course. I read through the list of books and found it started with Aristotle, passed through Shakespeare and ended with contemporary Nigerian dramatists. It struck me that whoever compiled that list was unaware that there was something anomalous about it. As far as that African professor was concerned, contemporary African drama was supposed to anchor itself on that of ancient Greece, and via that of modern Europe! There was no sense that the roots of African drama may have absolutely nothing to do with Aristotle and his theories, or that the taproot of contemporary African drama lies in a traditional African drama which is still alive today. Such obtuseness suggests that before we can encourage some of our scholars to break out of their neo-colonial Eurocentrism, we have to persuade them that there is an African intellectual tradition that is old and distinguished, that is second to none in the world, and that they have an obligation to recover it for us. I'll elaborate on that later on.

The second of these responsibilities is to help us to uphold the cultural independence of the Pan-African World, and to defend it from all foreign imperialisms and hegemonies. It may not be clear to many just how much our independence is in danger. Part of the trouble is an ignorant complacency which plays into the hands of the foreign enemies of African civilisation. For instance, those of us who have been campaigning for decolonisation in various areas of African culture are often told that colonialism is over, and so why all the talk about decolonisation? Just a few months ago, in January 1986, Adewale Maja-Pearce ended his review of *Toward the Decolonization of African Literature* in the *New Statesman* of London with this gibe at the authors: "Colonialism is over, but perhaps they haven't heard the good news." Which makes one wonder whether Mr Maja-Pearce has heard of what has been going on in South Africa, or Namibia, or Mozambique, or Angola. Or are those, perhaps, not parts of Africa? Or is their decolonisation of no concern to other Africans, or to the entire world?

But that aside, we were reminded by Elechi Amadi the other day that there is political colonialism, there is economic colonialism, and there is intellectual colonialism. The generation of our fathers fought for political decolonisation from the West. They won a large measure of success, which is why we can talk of African governments operated by Africans. Whether or not we like what they do is another matter. But whatever mess we may be making of it, we at least do have the political independence to do so.

Most people now concede that Africa groans under Western neo-colonial economic domination. So, even if some lull themselves into the belief that Western political colonialism is over, no alert observer can maintain that their economic colonialism is over. In contrast, Western intellectual colonialism is so insidious and pervasive that most people seem quite unaware of its existence. This is for a quite understandable reason. As Cheikh Hamidou Kane said of the colonial school: "Better than the cannon, it makes conquest permanent. The cannon compels the body, the school bewitches the soul."[1] And most Africans have been so bewitched intellectually by their Eurocentric education that they think that those who call to them to cast off the spell must be mad. Which makes the job of reversing the impact of a century or more of intellectual colonisation doubly hard, but doubly necessary. The work awaits this generation, and we all need to get on with it.

It is not out of any foolishness that we should get this job done. Whether we wish to acknowledge the fact or not, there are three hegemonist forces engaged in a new scramble for Africa right now, a whole century after the infamous Berlin Conference. Most of our ancestors probably had no inkling of what was being hatched at Berlin against their indepen-

---

[1] Quoted in Ngugi wa Thiong'o, *Homecoming*, New York: Lawrence and Hill, 1973, p.45.

dence; but we cannot pretend ignorance of the new scramble. The three foreign hegemonist interests are as follows: There is the West, which we all know about and which most anti-colonialists focus exclusively upon. There is the Soviet Bloc, which only some will admit as being interested in hegemony over Africa, regardless of accumulating evidence of such interest. Then there is the Arab world which, using oil money and Islam, has revived its ancient mission to take over and Arabise Africa. Most Africans seem to prefer not to recognise this at all.

Twenty-five years after most of Africa attained independence from Europe, the crusade to Arabise Africa is gathering momentum. And Arabisation means the abandoning of African names, clothes, languages, customs, religions, architecture, social organisation, political norms, etc, and the substituting of Arab ones in their places, usually under the guise that they are Islamic, not Arabic. The uncontested campaign to Arabise Somalia, and the hotly contested campaign to Arabise Southern Sudan ought to be well known. I shall supplement those examples with one more.

While the OIC affair was being hushed up in Nigeria, a meeting took place in Istanbul, Turkey, between some scholarship students from several East African countries (Kenya, Tanzania, Somalia and Ethiopia) and some officials of the Islamic Bank. According to an eyewitness, it was, for most of it, a routine affair in which stipends, progress reports and other matters of the students' welfare were discussed. But before the meeting ended, the Islamic Bank official introduced a Saudi Arabian official who proceeded to remind the students not to forget that the fundamental purpose for giving them scholarships to study engineering, science, administration, etc, was so they could go back and Islamise their states and Arabise their countries. Now, this is no idle talk, for, in the last two decades, several African countries have been pressured to turn themselves into Islamic states, or into Arab republics and to join the Arab

League. And Arab money has financed civil strife and secession movements in some countries, such as Ethiopia, which refuse to capitulate to Arab pressure.

Those who, despite contemporary evidence, prefer to believe that our relations with the Arab invaders and colonisers of the north of our continent is one of brotherhood and cameraderie should be advised to go and re-read African history, and to discover what Arabs did to Africans between the 7th and the 19th century, before the Europeans overran the entire continent and interrupted them.

While the pressure of Arabisation mounts, our Western oriented schools continue to be centres for European intellectual colonialism. In the field of literature, according to Elechi Amadi,

> The average literature graduate knows four times as much foreign literature as African literature. The fear here is that unless this lop-sided syllabus is maintained the graduate in literature could not be considered educated by foreigners. Yet the average British graduate in literature knows nothing at all about African literature. He may take it later on as a specialist course.[2]

In the field of philosophy, a silly debate goes on about whether there really is something to be called African philosophy, and whether it should be accommodated within the philosophy curriculum of African universities! By the way, by philosophy they mean universal philosophy, which in practice means the Western European philosophy tradition from the pre-Socratics of Greece to the positivists, existentialists, etc. of the 20th century West. In the course of examining the debate between Africa's universalist and

---

[2] "Background to Nigerian Literature" (unpublished paper) 1986.

Africanist philosophers, Ghana's Kwasi Wiredu raised a central issue: "It might accordingly be held", he wrote, "that the attitude of the African universalist boils down simply to an unthinking willingness to submit himself to instruction in the philosophies of other cultures before attending to those of his own. Why may he not reverse the order?"[3] Now, why indeed not? After all, isn't charity supposed to begin at home? Or isn't self-knowledge the core without which all other knowledge is hollow?

Commenting on the fashionable disorientation in African education in these neo-colonial times, A.B. Assensoh, in a letter in *West Africa*[4], said:

> It is ironic that while non-black Africanists were spending time studying African history, literature and other cultural subjects, some of us, as *bona fide* Africans, were busy studying the works of John Milton, Shakespeare, Karl Marx, Engels and pure European or American History for university degrees, with pride.

With such exocentrism, and with these Eurocentric curricula and syllabuses, is it any wonder that Africa's neo-colonial schools and universities persist in bewitching the souls of Africans, and turning out zombies instead of Africans knowledgeable about their culture and confident in themselves?

If charity is to begin at home, then the sensible procedure is for Africans to master African literature, philosophy, history and cultural traditions before venturing out to study those of other lands. The colonial education system mischievously inverted this common sense procedure, and stuffed the heads of its African victims with European traditions to the almost total exclusion of the African. And even

---

[3] Kwasi Wiredu, *Philosophy and an African Culture*, Cambridge: Cambridge University Press, 1980, p.27.
[4] February 10, 1986, p.306.

now, at the mere suggestion that this disorienting procedure be abandoned, Africa's neo-colonial zombies howl in terror.

Euro-imperial universalists oppose the Africanisation of curricula in Africa because an African child who is first given a thorough grounding in the African cultural tradition, before being exposed to those of other lands, is not likely to be intimidated into awe of European culture, and is far less likely to be inducted into servility towards European culture. Knowledge of African nursery songs, ancient African epics, drama, fables, stories, parables, and a correct appreciation of their worth, would fortify him against hegemonist propaganda. He would display a cultural confidence born of sound knowledge of the glories of his African civilisation, and he would be less prone to genuflect to the culture of Europeans, Arabs or whoever else. Which is why those who wish to alienate and enslave him take pains to infect him with a sense of cultural inferiority, by first cutting him off from his African traditions, and then feeding him overpraised alien imports.

To correct this great and lamentable weakness in his cultural foundations—this gap in his self-knowledge through which hegemonists enter to seize his soul—the African must be first exposed to and grounded in the African tradition, and brought to appreciate its full scope and glory. And that point brings me to the next obligation of African literary scholarship.

The third of these responsibilities is to bring about a renaissance of African civilisation. Many might wonder what there ever was that should be given a rebirth. Most people may not know, or might find it emotionally impossible to accept that, in written form, the African intellectual tradition is fifty centuries old. Colonial propaganda, by suppressing that fact, has helped to make it easy to bewitch our souls with lies about Africans being eternal primitives who have never done anything that was worth noticing or admiring by anybody, and lies about the history of Africa being simply that of foreign invaders and their doings in Africa.

For demonstrating the antiquity and eminence of African civilisation, we are indebted to one of the foremost scholars Africa has produced in this century. Unfortunately, he passed away a few months ago. I am referring to Cheikh Anta Diop, the Senegalese historian, physicist, linguist and Egyptologist who spent his career tracing the relations between African cultures and the Egypt of the Pharaohs.

When he first submitted his thesis in Paris, asserting that those who built the pyramids were not Europeans but Africans, were not white but black, his European professors got hot under the collar and refused to accept it. After all, it was a thesis which upset the white supremacist ideology of European colonialism. But Diop was a dogged man, and was determined to bring out the truth. He went back to work on his thesis, and eventually his professors had to concede that his thesis was correct, and give him his doctorate for demonstrating that Ancient Egypt, whose civilisation has all the renown in the world, was created by black people. Not content to demonstrate the African origin of Egyptian civilisation, Diop subsequently spent much of his life demonstrating the cultural unity of African societies. He maintained, from his studies of art forms, languages, customs and manners of all kinds, that the diverse peoples of Africa today have direct cultural links that go back to ancient Egypt.

We can take what Cheikh Anta Diop has done and elaborate it in the field of literature. If we had enough of the works of African literature, from the earliest days of Egypt till today, what patterns and similarities and cross influences might we discover? What themes, styles and world outlook connect Ancient Egyptian poetry to Zulu, Senegalese, Ethiopian or Nigerian traditional poetries? I am raising such questions so that African scholars and critics may recognise that they have plenty of work to do. They have five thousand years of documentation, and from all parts of the continent, to bring up to date. Which means that what Cheikh Anta Diop single-handedly initiated, and could not be expected to complete, needs to be taken up by, not one, not two, not ten, not twenty, but by whatever thousands of literary scholars there are in Africa today.

A renaissance of African traditions is vital for several reasons. First, it is our most effective weapon against the imperialisms and hegemonisms which have laid siege to our culture and its independence. Unless we effect a renaissance, it will remain easy for hegemonists, who want to alienate us from our traditions and hijack us for their own, to tell us that we must write like Shakespeare or Euripides or Molière or Brecht because they are the greatest in the whole world; or that we must imitate whatever happens to be the current fad in the West because we have no notable tradition of our own to turn to.

Secondly, when we have revived the African tradition in full scope, our pronouncements on contemporary African writings and writers will have a historical context that will clarify and make them sounder. To appreciate the damaging impact of false contexting on literary judgement, consider the following. Suppose the works of Shakespeare, Milton, Chaucer and the other heavyweights of England's literature were to vanish. It would then be quite easy for critics to elevate to high eminence some minor poets like Richard Aldington or Gerard Manley Hopkins, and to proclaim them the greatest literary forces to ever emerge from England.

If you have taken a close look at the Pyramid Texts of Ancient Egypt and felt their astonishing power; if you have read "The eloquent peasant" and felt its freshness and force; if you have read "The satire on the trades" and found yourself laughing at the fun poked by some scribe some 4,000 years ago, you would find it hard to accept certain bogus claims made by professional puffers for some contemporary

African writers. You would, for instance, be unimpressed by any claim that some present day satirist, who makes heavy weather of getting you to chuckle, is the greatest that Africa has produced. For if ancient Egyptians can still reach you across 4,000 years, and this contemporary of yours cannot, why should you be bamboozled into rating him the greatest thing that Africa has produced in literature?

Thirdly, let me emphasise that recapturing the great African tradition has a practical impact on whether we can read our writers or not. Here is an illustrative anecdote. I met a West Indian the other day. He lives in Canada. We were talking about poetry when he said he had decided to stop writing poetry and to write novels instead. Why, I asked? He said that the West Indian community in the part of Canada where he lives couldn't make head or tail out of a few poems he had written for them and read to them. Again I asked him why. He said he wrote from the tradition in which he had been trained, a tradition which was full of myths about Greek gods, and fantastic stories about Greek heroes. His poetry was full of echoes and allusions to figures and events in Greek mythology; but the community to whom he read them had no familiarity with such characters. All the subtle and teasing allusions he was making, and therefore most of what he was saying, was lost on them. Thereafter he decided to write novels instead.

For that West Indian writer, it was very useful to discover why his poems failed to get across. It was not that his audience was stupid; of that he was quite sure. It was due to the alien tradition from which he was writing. The value of his experience is that it demonstrates the need to have a living tradition within which writers and their readers can together operate. Clearly, a shared body of myths, heroes and values is necessary for accessibility. And if Africans must have a living tradition, why not our own? Why that of Europe or anywhere else?

Our scholars certainly need to recover our myths and

heroes and traditions and tell us about them so that they can become the foundation of our literary culture. When then a poet alludes to Mwindo, we will all know who he is talking about and what the relevant episode was. If he alludes to Da Monzon, we will all know who he is talking about and what happened to Da Monzon. So we won't have to stare at such allusions or scratch our heads in puzzlement.

The recovery, retelling and reinterpretation of the vast African tradition is very important for even the very simple matter of the accessibility of our writers. In its absence, communication will break down; alien traditions will have an open space to infiltrate and occupy; we would thus continue teaching our children Greek mythology so they can read African writers who presuppose Greek mythology! Worse still is the case where, lacking a living tradition which everybody shares, writers feel called upon to invent their own arbitrary tradition and private myths. That, incidentally, was one cause of havoc for the modernist poets in the West, and for some of their African imitators.

Because our repossession of our African tradition would bring us such far-reaching benefits, and especially help to restore our cultural confidence, Euro-hegemonists are strongly opposed to our reclaiming our illustrious African traditions. And they spare no trick or lies in their effort to keep the modern African intellectual enslaved to the Western tradition. Their basic strategy has been to deny, suppress or devalue the African tradition where they cannot steal it outright and declare it their own. They complement this by advertising their own parochial tradition as the universal tradition. And whenever their strategy is forcefully challenged, they mount a rearguard action, setting up roadblocks and diversionary signposts to impede our rout of their forces.

Some have put forward absurd arguments in their attempt to dissuade African scholars from following the path pioneered by Cheikh Anta Diop. Some urge Africans to reject the Pharaonic heritage because Egypt practised slavery. Some claim that if African scholars should succumb to African cultural nationalism and give centre stage to the African tradition, they would display a racist approach to intellectual history, one produced by inferiority complex. Some claim that an African renaissance which bases itself on the Pharaonic heritage would be a case of Gresham's Law in ideas, with bad ideas driving out the good. Some claim that our reclaiming our African intellectual tradition would be contrary to their doctrine of a free flow of ideas. Now, each of these claims is spurious, and those who make them are either ignorant or mischievous.

If slavery is an irredeemable cultural taint, and no tradition should be based on those of any slave society, then the West should reject and divest itself of the Greek and Roman heritages. After all, didn't Greece and Rome practice slavery? If the point is that black Africans should reject black Egypt because black Egypt enslaved white Jews, shouldn't the West reject itself on the grounds that the white West enslaved black Africans? When such scholars convince the West to scuttle its traditions, it would be time for them to preach such nonsense to Africans. Besides, those who have studied the matter tell us that every society that has passed the most rudimentary stage of organisation has practised slavery at some point in its career. In that case, and on that absurd argument, no contemporary society should learn from the heritage of any society whatever.

Let it be doubly emphasised that African cultural nationalism is racial, not racist! Perhaps some of these Western scholars don't appreciate the difference. Well, something can be racial without being racist. For something to be racist, it must not only be racial (i.e. concerned with the affairs of a race); it must also proclaim or imply the superiority of some race over others. For instance, apartheid and Nazism are racist. In contrast, African cultural nationalism, which focuses on the traditions of the African race, is not racist, only racial; its programme for the political equality of all races is non-racist, even anti-racist. It is a favourite trick of racists when on the defensive to confuse the distinction between racial and racist, so as to pretend that anti-racist opposition to their racism is also racist.

As for the talk of inferiority complex, it is enough to point out that inferiority complex drives people to belittle themselves, and to undervalue their achievements, and to cower before the exaggerated achievements of others. Which is quite a different behaviour from claiming what is legitimately yours and securing a correct valuation of it. Likewise, to reclaim and celebrate what is yours does not qualify as the sort of compensatory aggressive behaviour that an inferiority complex can lead to. For African cultural nationalism does not deny or devalue the legitimate achievements of others, nor does it steal them and parade them as its own—as the Greeks and their Western heirs have done with the heritage of black Egypt. In fact, Western racism began with the compensatory aggressive behaviour of the Greeks which led them to hide the Egyptian origins of what they proclaimed as the products of their own originality.

When some talk of a Gresham's Law in ideas, do they mean to imply that Ancient Egyptian ideas are bad or inferior, and should not drive out the good and superior ideas of Western civilisation? If so, why did the Greeks steal wholesale from the stock of 'bad' Egyptian ideas? And why has modern Europe not rejected the "Greek" heritage as "bad", because of its "bad" Egyptian foundations and components? Or are the same Egyptian ideas "good" when incorporated in the Greek heritage, but "bad" only when Africans want to directly reclaim them?

If those scholars who defensively raise the banner for a free flow of ideas are indeed committed to the free flow of ideas, why do they wish to block the free flow of Pharaonic ideas into modern Africa?

Some African "universalists" join their Western mentors

in decrying attempts to give the African tradition its central place in modern African intellectual life. They regard the effort as parochial, and claim that they do not wish to be parochial, but would rather redefine the entire world from an African standpoint. The marvel is how they expect to do that without first discovering the African tradition and making it their standpoint! If such "universalist" Africans are genuine about their aims, they have to start by grounding themselves on the African tradition, and so should eagerly follow in the footsteps of Cheikh Anta Diop.

After they have absorbed the African tradition in all its range and glory, they can take whatever they find useful in any other tradition (and not just that of Europe!); they can invent new things too; and they can bring everything together to fashion a modern and enriched extension of the African intellectual tradition. Which is precisely what the African cultural nationalist position advocates.

Africa's "universalists" should bear in mind this home truth: no matter what exotic ingredients you assemble, you cannot make soup without a pot and water. And, for Africans, their pot and water are the African heritage. They should also stop heeding alien hegemonists who want us to deny our mother, and to acknowledge as our only progenitor some wandering rapist who assaulted her and sprayed his seeds in her womb.

The fourth of these responsibilities is to judge works of African literature on the basis of their commitment to the Pan-African cause. Some may claim that this is a political requirement: I see it as a cultural requirement, a political requirement, a sensible requirement. African literature must be the only one in the world which is expected or even urged not to satisfy this requirement. The Chinese judge their works by how Chinese they are; by how they help the Chinese people; by how they help China fight off foreign invaders and hegemonists. Likewise, I doubt if, in an anthology of British literature, you would find a piece praising the Nazis. I am sure such works would be automatically excluded. And don't tell me that such exclusion wouldn't be for political reasons. Yet African works which glorify our European and Arab invaders provoke no objections, and works which rehabilitate the image of Africa are objected to.

To carry out this responsibility, our scholars need to have sound Pan-Africanist bearings. This requires that they understand the reasons for the cause and share its commitments. To help them do that, they would need to immerse themselves in the works of Pan-Africanist thinkers from Edward Blyden to Kwame Nkrumah, W.E.B. Du Bois to Julius Nyerere, Marcus Garvey to Walter Rodney, Aime Cesaire to Sedar Senghor, Amilcar Cabral to Malcolm X, Frantz Fanon to Chancellor Williams. Without such an intellectual foundation, they will remain disoriented, and prove easy prey to suicidal seductions from foreign cultural hegemonists.

The fifth of these responsibilities is to re-evaluate, from the Afrocentric position, all of the works of contemporary African literature. All that our writers have published since the century began needs such re-evaluation. If it is true that much of their reputations are based on literary and political criteria that were smuggled in from Europe, and so reflect their services to the interests of Europe, then skepticism toward their present reputations would be in order. It may turn out that some, when re-evaluated, will remain highly rated; but I won't be surprised if some should lose whatever positions they have held so far.

Re-evaluation is an enormous job; it calls not only for an acquaintance with all the African literary works that have been published in this century, but also for acquaintance with the long tradition into which we are going to insert them for re-evaluation. So, for instance, if you are going to re-evaluate a dirge or elegy written by one of our poets today, it might be necessary to ask: Where in this long

African tradition does it fit? Has the poet handled his theme as well as it has ever been within the African tradition? If you pick up a transcript of a similar poem by a 19th century Uganda women of the fields, or by an Ancient Egyptian, and compare it with what our modern writer has produced, which comes across better, fresher, and with greater impact? If the modern has not done as good a job, then, most sorry, sir, but his poem cannot rank as high as if that Ugandan woman or some Ancient Egyptian, had not spoken or written. And if we have to give any accolade for writing the best dirge or elegy, it would have to go to that 19th century woman, or to the Ancient Egyptian.

I can well imagine what opposition any call for a re-evaluation of reputations is going to provoke, not least from those who feel insecure about their reputations, and who dread that exposure to such comparative evaluation would reveal their mediocrity. However that may be, every tradition re-evaluates all its extant works from time to time. When a generation does not agree with its predecessors on what the best works are in the tradition, it goes ahead and re-evaluates them. Which helps to explain some of the critical revolutions which happen from time to time.

For instance, T.S. Eliot dug up the metaphysical poets of England, and argued for their accomplishments. From being an obscure and minor group, these poets thereafter became important in the 20th century literature and criticism of the English speaking world. Similarly, Eliot brought Milton out of 19th century eclipse and back into prominence. What had Eliot done? He effected a re-evaluation of the tradition of England's poetry, and shifted emphasis from some kinds of writing to others. Such re-evaluations are not only quite legitimate, but most necessary. They help to renew a tradition and keep it active, and they help each generation to make its own choices of what it finds valuable in the tradition it inherits. A man who inherits his father's estate will, in the normal course of things, rearrange its items to suit himself. So, even if a writer doesn't think he should be subjected to re-evaluation, he, luckily, like inherited property, has no say in the matter: it will be done for him.

Responsibilities to scholarship and criticism

Some time ago, I went around asking people whether they read African literary criticism. These were educated people who do quite a bit of general reading, but have no career need to read works of criticism. One of them put the predominant answer quite succinctly. He said that he had done so when he was studying literature in university, but hasn't ever since. But he reads book reviews in newspapers. I tried to find out why. Since he doesn't have to pass exams in criticism, he doesn't read our critics; but he wants to keep abreast of what books come on the market, and so has a need to read book reviews that tell him what a book is about, whether it is worth his bother to read it, and why. But the kinds of things professional literary critics choose to say about books, he said, have no relevance to his interests or to his life.

That, I think, is a challenge to our literary critics to make themselves relevant to the reading public. In other parts of the world, academics write reviews for the literary press and conduct public debates on significant books and new ideas. When a new edition of a classic work comes out, book reviews are written by experts in its field. If a book is on a musician, you will find university professors writing about it for the general reader who is interested in musical matters. What I am driving at ultimately is this: if our literary critics, especially those in academia, are going to prove relevant to the society in which they operate, the type of criticism they do should expand to emphasise what would interest the general reader who doesn't have to sit exams. They will have to endeavour to be popular and realistic and readable; they would have to anchor their reviews on the African tradition and relate them to contemporary interests.

In their intellectual procedures, there are certain things it would be proper for them to pay attention to:

1) Critics should remember that to pronounce on a work they have not actually read is foul play. Some of them feel accused when they are caught at it; and they think you are damaging their reputation if you point that out. But it is they themselves who are damaging themselves. They can avoid the embarrassment by making sure that, before they venture an opinion on a work, they have actually read it, from cover to cover, so they do not miss the heart of the matter wherever it might be buried in the work. Sometimes the most important part of a book will be tucked away inside it. If you read the first and last pages and think you can rush off to write your critical commentary, you do not know what there is on page 197, and that could be where the turning point of the whole story takes place.

2) Critics should remember that literary evaluation is an exercise in comparative scholarship. It is supposed to work on principles, not from whims or prejudices; and such principles ought to be clearly and correctly applied. Whether an evaluation is principled or whimsical may be sometimes discerned from the way it is formulated. For example, if you say "X is the best book or writer I have read", nobody in their right mind would disagree with you, for you have not made a statement that could be independently assessed. What you have done is make a personal, first hand report about yourself and your reading. If people think that your best book is awful, they may legitimately conclude that you have very bad taste, or that you haven't read enough to enable you make a sound judgement, and they may hope that you will read more so as to improve the context of your evaluation.

However, if you made a claim that "X is the best book or writer from Africa", you are going beyond personal reportage. You are making a statement that is open to independent assessment by others. It is then pertinent for people to wonder about the range of works against which you have compared the book in question, the principles and criteria you have applied, and your skill in applying them.

From the standpoint of scholarly and judicious criticism, the latter sort of statement is more valuable than the former. Even the general reader would be more interested in it. Unless he knew your taste and trusted your judgement, he would shrug his shoulders if you should recommend a book by saying it was the best book you have read.

Why am I stressing this distinction? Simply to spare ourselves pointless controversy. I find that much of the controversy over Nigerian writers and books consists of asserting and vitriolically reasserting such propositions as that "X is the best writer or book I know", or even that "I find some value in something X has written"—as if such personal reportage could decide the issue of whether or not "X is the best, or one of the best writers or books from Africa."

Our literary critics need to realise that for statements of comparative worth to carry weight, they must be supported by close and correct arguments based on relevant evidence; otherwise they deserve to be dismissed as puffery. It is most important for those who undertake to inform us about the value of literary works, and where they stand in our tradition, to take pains to understand that what we want from them are meticulously argued pieces of comparative analysis and evaluation, anchored on clear principles, and conducted with full respect for fact and logic. The reader can then, like a judge, evaluate the case made and come to his own decision.

3) Lastly, I don't think there is much value in interpreting a work of literature from one society or civilisation against the background of the myths, philosophy, history, ethics, politics, vested interests and world outlook of another society or civilisation. Yet this is routinely done by those who read works of African literature in the context of Greek mythology.

This goes back to the statement that literature is part of a dialogue that people conduct among themselves about their history and society. There are comparatists who are concerned with universal theories of literature and society, and whose job it is to investigate African myths and Greek myths to discover what universal traits they both demonstrate. That is legitimate in its own place. But when Greek mythology becomes a regular context for interpreting African literary works, there is something amiss.

It seems to me that most African readers would value more highly such critical evaluations as help us to place African works in our own African context—our history, our own philosophies, our own ethics, our own politics—so that when we begin to dissect and analyse these works, the process will be as engaging, as thrilling, and hopefully as fruitful as yesterday's when we discussed T.M. Aluko's book. Thank you.

INDEX

Achebe, Chinua
   history, views of on, 266
   and the Nobel Prize, 196
Africa
   Ancient Egypt in history of, 4, 82-9, 94-5, 119-20, 127, 274-5
   Arabisation of, 3, 102-3, 114-15, 116, 117-18, 121, 122-6, 163-4, 269-70
   armies in, as forces to be used against South Africa, 155-7
   colonial economic system of, 106-7
   European conquest and colonisation of, 3, 102-3, 114-115, 116, 121, 122-5; legacies of, 97-103
   history of, colonialist interpretations of, 75-81, 104-8, 111-112; need to decolonise, 71-96
   history of the arts in, in colonial period, 107
   industrial culture in, preconditions for, 6-8, 22-4
   literature in, need for autonomous development of, 270-85; Marxist criticisms of, 242-54; impact of structuralism and post-structuralism on, 238-41; role of in fostering cultural continuity and awareness, 211-30
   literary critics in, responsibilities of, 255-85
   nation-state in, difficulties of nurturing, 98-9; role of literature in fostering, 211-30
   pre-colonial links of with Americas 85, 93
   pre-Western links of with Asia, 93-4
   resistance to colonial conquest and rule in, 104-8, 115
   Unesco General History of, vols I, II, IV, VII, reviewed, 109-35; vol. VII, critique of review of by Roland Oliver, 104-8
   unification of, hindrances to, 98-99, 101, 102
Alhaji, Abubakar
   advocacy of IMF loan for Nigeria by, 53
Aluko, T.M.
   novel by (*Wrong One in the Dock*), 258
Amadi, Elechi, 265
   on colonialism, 268
   on foreign predominance in literature syllabuses in Africa, 270
   on the incongruities of Third World intellectuals' adherence to Marxism, 242
Amda Seyon
   resistance of to Islamisation in Ethiopia, 118
Americas
   pre-Columbian links of Africa with, 85, 93

INDEX

Ancient Egypt
  African history, role of in,
    Cheikh Anta Diop on, 69, 82-7,
    88-9, 113, 119, 127
  prefigurings of doctrines of Islam
    and Christianity in, Cheikh
    Anta Diop on, 71
  role of in civilising Greece and
    the West, 83-5
  scientific and cultural legacy of,
    G. Mokhtar on, 119-20
Arab-Israeli dispute
  irrelevance of to African affairs,
    140-8
Arab slave trade
  distortion of significance of by
    D.T. Niane (*UGHA*, vol. IV),
    129-30
  impact of on African societies,
    144-6
Arabisation, *see also* Islamisation
  in Africa, characteristics and
    strategies of, 117-18, 125-26,
    143-4, 269-70; shortcoming of
    interpretations of in *UGHA*,
    vol. IV, 128-35
  irrelevance of to creation of
    industrial culture in Africa, 8
  Muammar Gaddafi as an agent
    of, 149-53
  S. Anai Kelueljang, poem on,
    139-40, 149
  Pan-Africanism and, 102-3, 163-4
  and war in Sudan Republic, 157-8
Arabised Africans
  characteristics of, 3, 4-5
Ariel
  as a metaphor for collaboration
    with colonialism, 2-3, 5, 8-9
Armah, Ayi Kwei
  on the objectives of creators of
    African traditional literature,
    239-40

on the incongruity of Third World
    intellectuals' adherence to
    Marxism, 152-3, 242
armies
  in Africa, as a force to be used
    against South Africa, 155-7
Asia
  pre-Western links of with
    Africa, 93-4
Askiya Muhammad Toure, 118

Babangida, Ibrahim
  on Nobel Prize award to Wole
    Soyinka, 185
Behanzin, 116
Bennett, Lerone
  on image and reality, 211
Berbers
  impact of Islamisation among, 118
  impact of Roman conquest on,
    123-5
black identity, *see also* racial
  identity
  misapprehensions about, 170;
  Munyama Ngangura on, 1
Black World League of Nations
  proposed, 160-71
Brazil
  debt trap experienced by, 45-6
Busia, Kofi
  as a Europeanised African, 3
Bunche, Ralph
  underlying reasons for award of
    Nobel Prize to, 191

Cabral, Amilcar
  on colonial domination, 1
Caliban
  as a metaphor for opposition to
    colonialism, 2-3, 8
Cancún
  failure of North-South
    negotiations at, 13

Cargo Cults
  in Melanesia, 16-19
  response to industrial civilisation in Third World likened to, 16-18, 22-3, 24
Césaire, Aimé
  on colonisation and civilisation, 62
Cetshaweyo, 116
Chad
  OAU and conflict in, 166
Chaka
  role of artistic creativity in nation-building achievements of, 215-16
China
  development in, 24
Christianity
  and the Nigerian army, 5-6
  in Nubia, role in resisting Arab invasion, 121
  prefigurings of doctrines of in Ancient Egyptian culture, Cheikh Anta Diop on, 71
Ciroma, Adamu
  advocacy of increased Nigerian borrowing by, 53
COMECON, 5
Commonwealth, 5
Critical Theory, see structuralism and post-structuralism
cultural continuity and awareness
  role of literature in fostering, 211-30

Damas, Leon
  on theories, 62
debt trap peonage
  of Brazil, 45-6
  defined, 32-3
  Nigeria, prescriptions for avoidance of by, 40-56
  and OPEC, 38-9
  as a Western mechanism for controlling Third World development, 31-9
development
  debt trap peonage and, 33-5
  dependency theories concerning, 14
  false claims of Third World elites to be propagating, 25-6
  in Guinea, failure of under Sekou Toure, 58-60
  liberal theories concerning, 14
  Marxist theories concerning, 14
  in Nigeria, prerequisites for, 52-6
  self-reliance as a strategy for in Third World, 66-7
  suffering, inefficacy of as a motor of, 57-60
  Third World, prescriptions for, 29-30
  Western theories of, inadequacy for Third World conditions, 62-7
Diop, Cheikh Anta
  on role of Ancient Egypt in African history, 69, 255
  on religious doctrines of Ancient Egypt, 71
  role of in Africanising history of Ancient Egypt, 82-7, 127, 273-4, 276, 279
Dominican Republic
  US intervention in, 47
drama
  academic study of in Nigeria, 266-7
Du Bois, W.E.B.
  on cultural imperialism, 175
  on dangers of serfdom to international investment, 31, 40
  on the politics of race, 137
  Pan-Africanist ideas of, 102, 159

INDEX

Egypt, *see* Ancient Egypt
elites
   in the Third World, New
     International Economic Order
     as a strategy for survival of,
     26-27;
     pseudo-developmental policies
     of, 25-6
Ethiopia, 99
   Islamisation in, 118
Europe
   need to re-assess rise to world
     prominence of, 95-6
Europeanisation
   irrelevance of to creation of
     industrial culture in Africa, 8
Europeanised Africans
   characteristics of, 3, 4-5

Fagan, B.M.
   on Arab influences on origins of
     Great Zimbabwe, 128
Fage, J.D.
   on Hamitic Hypothesis, 77-8,
     78-9
Fanon, Frantz
   on ideology of race, 3
   on overthrow of colonial residues
     in independent states, 8-9, 13,
     62, 87
Fashanu, John, 183
Fatunde, Tunde
   Marxist analysis of Ouologuem's
     Bound to Violence by, 248-9
Finland
   ethnic literature as a focus of
     identity in, 212-13
French Community, 5

Gaddafi, Muammar, *see also* Libya
   Arab expansionist policies of in
     Africa, 149-53, 166
   misguided enthusiasm for of
     some African 'radicals' 152-3
García Márquez, Gabriel
   and the Nobel Prize, 177
Garvey, Marcus
   on defectors from Negro Race, 168
   Pan-Africanist ideas of, 102
   on strategies of white
     subjugation of blacks, 147,
     159, 173
Ghana
   adverse effects on of economic
     advice of Sir Arthur Lewis, 192
   under Nkrumah, causes of
     financial difficulties of, 31
Great Zimbabwe
   myth of Arab influences on the
     origins of, 128
Greece
   role of Ancient Egypt in
     spreading civilisation to, 83-5
   bogus notion of as originator of
     Western civilisation, 83
   imposition of culture of on
     northern Africa, 121
Gugelberger, Georg M.
   Marxist critique of African
     literature by, 244-54
Guinea
   under Sekou Touré, as an
     example of inefficacy of
     suffering as a development
     strategy, 58-60

Hamitic Hypothesis
   as a colonialist interpretation of
     African history, 76-80;
   C.G. Seligman on, 76;
   J.D. Fage on, 77-8, 78-9
Herodotus
   on civilising impact of Ancient
     Egypt, 83
history
   of Africa, colonialist

interpretations of, 75-81
of Africa and the Third World,
 need to decolonise, 71-96
liberating effects of an
 understanding of, Joseph
 Ki-Zerbo on, 71, 74
utility of, 109-10
Hitler, Adolf
 and the 1936 Olympic Games, 205

industrialisation, *see also*
 development
 in Africa, preconditions for, 6-8,
  22-3
 Cargo Cult-like response to in
  Third World, 16-18
 fundamental characteristics of
  and preconditions for, 4, 18-19,
  22-4
 in Japan, history of, 15
 in USA, history and character of
  15, 18-21
 in USSR, history and character
  of, 15, 18-19, 21
International Monetary fund
 impact of policies of on Third
  World, 26-7, 31, 45-6, 49
 proposed loan to Nigeria by, 53-4
Iran
 US economic warfare against,
  47-8
Islam
 and the Nigerian army, 5-6
 prefigurings of doctrines of in
  Ancient Egyptian culture,
  Cheikh Anta Diop quoted on, 71
Islamisation
 in Africa, between the 12th and
  16th centuries, 117-18; views
  of D.T. Niane on criticised,
  130-5
 among the Berbers, 118
 in Ethiopia, 118

 irrelevance of to creation of
  industrial culture in Africa, 8
 in Mali, 118, 131-2, 133
 threat of to objectives of
  Pan-Africanism, 102-3
 in Songhai, 118
Israeli-Arab dispute
 irrelevance of to African affairs,
  140-8

Jews
 role of Bible as a national
  anthology among, 217

Kabarega, 115
Kane, Cheikh Hamidou
 on intellectual colonialism, 268
Kanem
 Arabisation in, 118
Kelueljang, S. Anai
 poem by on Arabisation in
  Africa, 139-40
Kgositsile, Keorapetse
 on religious belief, 71
Ki-Zerbo, Joseph
 on the liberating effects of
  history, 71,74
King, Martin Luther
 underlying reasons for award of
  Nobel Prize to, 178
Kush, see *Nubia*

Latin America
 debt of, 48
Leavis, F.R., 262
Lewis, Sir Arthur
 adverse effects on Ghana of
  economic advice of, 192
 underlying reasons for award of
  Nobel Prize to, 180, 191-2
Libya, *see also* Gaddafi
 use of forces of
  against South Africa, 155-6

INDEX

literature
  in Africa, need for autonomous development of, 270-85; role of in fostering cultural awareness and nation-building, 211-30; hindrances to from external influences and criticism, 224-30
literary critics
  in Africa, responsibilities of, 255-85
Lugard, Lord, 99
Luthuli, Chief Albert
  underlying reasons for award of Nobel Prize to, 178, 191

Machemba, 116
Maillu, David
  on reasons why people read literature, 263
Maja-Pearce, Adewale
  on colonialism and literature, 267-8
Mali
  Islamisation in, 118, 131-2, 133
Mansa Musa, 118
Marley, Bob, 40
Marxism
  incongruity of Third World intellectuals' adherence to, 167-8; Elechi Amadi on, 242; Ayi Kwei Armah on, 152-3, 242
Marxist literary criticism
  approaches of to African literature, 242-54
  by Tunde Fatunde, 248-9;
  by Georg M. Gugelberger, 244-54
  by Emmanuel Ngara, 243-4
  by Omafume Onoge, 246-8
Mauretania
  Roman conquest of, 123-4
Menelik II, 99, 115, 116
Meroe, *see also* Nubia

exocentric interpretations of history of (*UGHA*, vol. IV), 128
Mesopotamia
  scientific legacy of, 4
Mohammed (The Prophet), 3
Mokhtar, G.
  on scientific and cultural legacy of Ancient Egypt, 119-20
Muslim Sisters' Organisation of Nigeria, 140
Mutwa, Vusamazulu Credo
  on impact of Arab slave trade in Central Africa, 145-6
  on Arab claims to be spokesmen of black people, 149
Mwanza, 116

Napata, *see* Nubia
nation-building
  role of literature in, 211-30
National Council of Women's Societies (Nigeria), 140
Neruda, Pablo
  and the Nobel Prize, 177
New International Economic Order
  as a strategy of survival by Third World elites, 26-7
Ngangura, Munyama
  on misapprehensions about racial identity, 1
Ngara, Emmanuel
  Marxist critique of African literature by, 243-4
Ngugi wa Thiong'o, 196
  on proletarian aesthetics, 250
Niane, D.T.
  distortion of significance of Arab slave trade by (*UGHA*, vol. IV), 129-30
  misinterpretations of spread of Islam in Africa by (*UGHA*, vol. IV), 130-5
Nigeria

army in, religious policy of, 5-6
debt trap peonage of, 40-56
development in, prerequisites of, 52-6
drama in, academic study of, 266-7
financial difficulties of, 31
IMF loan to, debate on advisability of, 53-54
import policies of, 54
injection of Arab-Israeli dispute into affairs of, 140
maldevelopment in, 24-5
inappropriate use of oil earnings in, 38
'underborrowed' status of, 53-5

Nkosi, Lewis
award of Nobel prize to Wole Soyinka, views of on, 185, 198

Nkrumah, Kwame
balkanisation of Africa, views of on, 98
Pan-Africanism of, 102, 160

Nobel Prize
as instrument of cultural and political emasculation of the Third World, 175-200, 229-30
underlying reasons for award of to Ralph Bunche, 191; Sir Arthur Lewis, 180, 191-2; Chief Albert Luthuli, 178, 191; Martin Luther King, 178; Bishop Desmond Tutu, 178-9, 191
Ntuli, Pitika on, 190-1
Sartre, Jean-Paul on, 177
award of to Wole Soyinka, applause for analysed, 175, 184-200; Ibrahim Babangida on, 185; Lewis Nkosi on, 185; J.J. Rawlings on, 184

Ntuli, Pikita
views of on Nobel Prize, 190-1

Nubia
role of in African resistance to foreign intervention, 120-1, 122, 132
slaving relations of with Arabs, 130
history of kingdoms of, 120-1

OAU
failures of in resolving disputes within Africa, 166
inadequacies of as Pan-Africanist organisation, 165-8
moral bankruptcy of in struggle against South Africa, 154-7

Ogaden dispute
OAU policy towards, 166

Ogot, B.A.
on role of pastoralists in African history, 128

Oil earnings
misuse of by Third World governments, 38

Okot p'Bitek, 197
Song of Lawino by, quoted, 201
on the social role of literature, 211

Oliver, Roland
critique of his review of *UGHA*, vol. VII, 104-8

Olympic Games
as forum for Third World sportsmen, 201-8

Onoge, Omafume
on fundamentals of the Marxist aesthetic, 246-7
Marxist analysis of the poetry of Senghor by, 247-8

Organisation of Black African States
proposals for creation of, 160

Organisation of the Islamic Conference, 5

OPEC
  and debt trap peonage, 38-9
Ouologuem, Yambo
  Marxist analysis of his *Bound to Violence* by Tunde Fatunde, 248-9
Ousmane, Sembene
  and the Nobel Prize, 157

Pan-Africanism
  ideas on, of W.E.B. Du Bois, 102, 159; of Marcus Garvey, 102; of Kwame Nkrumah, 102, 160
  proposals for practical implementation of, 160-71
  and Arabisation, 102-3, 163-4
pastoralists
  as conquerors and statebuilders, 128
Payer, Cheryl
  on debt trap, 32-3
Pound, Ezra, 262
Prempeh, 115-16
Prospero
  as a metaphor for colonizer and colonial control, 2, 3, 8

racial identity
  as a fundamental basis for human competition, 147-8, 160-2, 171
  misapprehensions about, 3, 170; Munyama Ngangura on, 1
Rawlings, J.J.
  on award of Nobel prize to Wole Soyinka, 184, 198
Rhodes, Cecil, 99
Richards, I.A., 262
Rodney, Walter
  on fundamental nature of racial identity, 147-8
Rome
  colonisation of northern Africa by, 121, 123-5

Samori Touré, 115
Sartre, Jean-Paul
  on Nobel Prize, 177
self-reliance
  as a Third World development strategy, 66-7
Seligman, C.G.
  formulation of Hamitic Hypothesis by, 76-7
Semitic racial group
  Arab and Israeli members of, 140-8
Senghor, Leopold Sedar
  on African humanities, 255
  on role of European socialist ideas in Africa, 242
  on ideological colonisation of Africans, 13
  Marxist analysis of the poetry of, 247-8
  on role of the state, 57
  on role of writers and artists in decolonisation, 209
Shakespeare, William, 2
slave trade
  Arab, distortion of significance of by D.T. Niane (*UGHA*, vol. IV), 129-30; impact of on Central Africa, 145-6
Sokoto Caliphate, 98, 99
Songhai
  Islamisation in, 118, 122
South Africa
  African armies and governments in struggle against, 154-7
  parallels between Arab colonisation and white minority rule in, 135
South-South cooperation
  preconditions for, 28-9

weaknesses of as strategy of
        development, 13-14, 17-18
Soyinka, Wole
    award of Nobel Prize to, critical
        assessment of, 193-8
    literary style of, 193-8
    contribution by to *UGHA*, vol.
        VII, 107
structuralism and post-structuralism
    fundamental tenets of, 231-8
        pernicious impact of on
            African literature, 238-41
Sudan Republic
    war in, 157-8
suffering
    inefficacy of as a motor of
        development, 57-60
    as development strategy in
        Guinea, 58-60
Sundiata
    violent role of in Islamisation of
        Mali, 131
Sunni Ali Ber, 118
Sunni Baare, 118

The Tempest
    as a parable of colonialism, 2-3
Third World
    history of, need to decolonise,
        71-96
    historical links between
        components of, 91-4
Tolson, Melvin
    poem ('Harlem Gallery') by
        discussed, 214
Touré, Sekou
    inefficacy of development
        policies of, 58-60
Tutu, Bishop Desmond
    underlying reasons for award of
        Nobel Prize to, 178-9, 191

Unesco General History of Africa
    vols I, II, IV, VII,
        reviewed, 109-35
    vol. VII, review of by Roland
        Oliver, critique of, 104-8
    shortcomings of in
        interpretation of Arab slave
        trade (Vol. IV), 129-30
    shortcomings of in correcting
        colonialist and Arabist
        interpretations of African
        history, 128-35
USA
    Dominican Republic,
        intervention of in, 47
    economic warfare of against
        Iran, 47-8
    industrialisation in, history and
        character of, 15, 18-21
    unification of, reasons for
        success of, 99
USSR
    industrialisation in, history and
        character of, 15, 18-19, 21
Uthman Biri ibn Idris
    as example of Arabised African, 3
    complaints of against capture
        of African Muslims by Arabs,
        145, 149
Uthman, dan Fodio, 99

Wiredu, Kwasi
    on African philosophy, 271

Zimbabwe, *see* Great Zimbabwe
Zionism
    irrelevance of to African
        problems, 140-1